Dismantling Utopia

Dismantling Utopia

HOW INFORMATION ENDED THE SOVIET UNION

SCOTT SHANE

Ivan R. Dee   *Chicago*

1994

Library of Congress Cataloging-in-Publication Data:
Shane, Scott, 1954–
    Dismantling Utopia : how information ended the Soviet Union /
Scott Shane.
        p.   cm.
    Includes bibliographical references and index.
    ISBN 1-56663-048-7 (alk. paper)
    1. Communication policy—Soviet Union.   2. Soviet Union—Politics and
government—1985–1991.   I. Title.
P95.82.S65S5   1994
363.3'1'094709048—dc20   93-48710

To Francie

Contents

Information in the Soviet Union: A Prophecy

"Ah, my dear comrades," Madyarov said suddenly, "can you imagine what it's like to have freedom of the press? One quiet morning after the war you open your newspaper, and instead of exultant editorials, instead of a letter addressed by some workers to the great Stalin, instead of articles about a brigade of steelworkers who have done an extra day's work in honor of the elections to the Supreme Soviet, instead of stories about workers in the United States who are beginning the New Year in a state of despondency, poverty, and growing unemployment, guess what you find in the newspaper! Information! Can you imagine a newspaper like that? A newspaper that provides information!

"And so, you start to read: crop failure in Kursk region, an inspection report on conditions in Butyrsky Prison, a debate on whether the White Sea–Baltic Canal is really necessary; you read about how the worker Golopyzov opposes the issuance of new bonds.

"In general, you know everything that's happening in the country: good harvests, and crop failures; enthusiasm, and breaking-and-entering; the opening of new mines, and mine disasters; the disputes between Molotov and Malenkov. You read reports on the course of a strike set off when a factory director fired a 70-year-old chemist; you read the speeches of Churchill and Bloom, and not that they 'stated that allegedly...'; you read reports of the debates in the House of Commons; you know how many people committed suicide yesterday in Moscow, and how many people were taken to Sklifosovsky emergency room to be stitched up. You know why there's no buckwheat groats in the stores, and not just that the year's first strawberries have just been delivered from Tashkent to Moscow by air. You know how many grams of bread a collective farm worker gets per working day—from the newspaper, and not from the cleaning woman whose niece from the village has come to Moscow to buy bread. Yes, yes, and on top of that you remain fully and completely a Soviet citizen.

"You go into a bookstore and buy a book, remaining a Soviet citizen, you read American, English, French philosophers, historians, economists, political observers. You figure out for yourself where they're wrong; you yourself, without a nanny, walk the streets. . . ."

All at once Sokolov brought his fist down on the table and said: "Enough! I emphatically and insistently demand that you stop such talk."

—from Vasily Grossman, *Life and Fate*. This epic novel of Stalinism and Nazism was submitted for publication in a Soviet journal in 1961, rejected, and turned over to the authorities. The KGB destroyed all known manuscripts, but one copy was hidden by a friend, smuggled abroad on microfiche, and first published in Russian in Switzerland in 1980, sixteen years after Grossman's death. *Life and Fate* was first published in the Soviet Union in 1988 and immediately became a bestseller.

Dismantling Utopia

Introduction

Until 1989 the Moscow maps sold for kopecks in street kiosks were all but useless. The main one, called "Tourist Plan," omitted smaller streets, listed no institutions, and was so distorted as to be inadequate for a stroll across town, let alone a nighttime search for an apartment in one of the high-rise ghettos on the outskirts of the city.

Typical Soviet *brak,* junk, a Russian visitor to Moscow might grumble, trying to blunder his way to a friend's flat with his Tourist Plan. But the maps were useless not because Soviet mapmakers were incompetent. Oil geologists had access to excellent maps—which they were permitted to examine only in certain guarded rooms, no note-taking allowed. Ordinary people's maps were useless because they were designed to be useless. Stalin's NKVD had decreed in the late 1930s that no accurate maps should be given to the public for fear that they would fall into the hands of potential military adversaries.

Of course, those adversaries didn't bother with the Tourist Plan. For twenty years diplomats and correspondents relied on a paperback-sized, spiral-bound street map of Moscow whose authors modestly preferred not to be named on or inside its covers. It was a CIA map, wonderfully detailed since it was drawn from satellite photos. An Armenian doctor offered me a big wad of rubles for mine, but I could not part with it. The map paradox demonstrated vividly how Soviet information control had lasted into a new era, an era in which technology that respected neither borders nor ideologies was making censorship both more difficult and less functional.

Finally, in the autumn of 1988 the country's chief cartographer fessed up in *Izvestiya,* acknowledging that maps had been deliberately distorted and promising an end to this outmoded practice. Accurate city maps went on sale in kiosks a few months later. It seemed just another quirky tale, a small victory of *glasnost*—openness—over absurdity.

It was more than that. It was a symbol for the information revolution, held off for so long by the KGB's banning and jamming, that between 1987 and 1991 swept across Soviet existence, touching every nook of daily life, battering hoary myths and lies, and ultimately eroding the foundations of Soviet power. Information, the long-forbidden fruit, was around every corner, on everyone's mind— the young woman on the Metro with her copy of the journal *Novy Mir* bent open to the latest installment of Solzhenitsyn's *Gulag Archipelago;* scores of Muscovites elbowing one another to get a glimpse of the latest copy of *Moscow News,* pinned behind glass each Wednesday night at Pushkin Square; friends hustling you into their apartment direct to the TV to catch the latest sensation. Ordinary people lined up at dawn at newspaper stands to devour facts about the Stalinist terror, the privileges of party bosses, the devastation of the environment, the living standards of American workers.

The question Americans asked most often in 1988 or 1989 or 1990 when they found out I worked in Moscow went something like this: What do you think, can Gorby make it? I was tempted to reply, He can make it, what with the Swiss bank account and everything, but I'm not so sure about the other 287 million people. Americans naturally were grateful to Gorbachev because he had lifted the threat of annihilation under which they had spent their lives. Russians felt instinctively that Gorbachev was not the idealist Americans saw but a pragmatist responding to realities he couldn't control. As regards the last ten years of the Soviet Union, I subscribe strongly to the history-without-heroes of Paul Kennedy's 1987 book, *The Rise and Fall of the Great Powers:* "There exists a dynamic for change, driven chiefly by economic and technological developments, which then impact upon social structures, political systems, military power, and the position of individual states and empires." Kennedy was particularly prescient on the dilemma faced by the Soviet Union under Gorbachev.

The Russian historian Leonid Batkin once compared Gorbachev with an apocryphal old man who was said to have pulled the chain to flush his toilet at the precise moment of the Tashkent earthquake. "If I'd known all *that* was going to happen," the man is supposed to have said, emerging from the rubble and surveying the devastation, "I never would have pulled the chain in the first place."

The analogy is as unfair as any mean-spirited political joke, but any citizen of the former Soviet Union instantly recognizes the deep truth behind it: what happened was very different from what Gorbachev wanted to happen. He set out to renew socialism, not to destroy it, to make the empire stronger, not to break it apart. As events repeatedly took a course he had not charted, he sometimes showed the flexibility and courage of the democratic reformer beloved in the West, sometimes the stubbornness and cruelty of the Komsomol and Communist party apparatchik despised by most of his fellow citizens. But however brave a face he put on the state of the post–Soviet Union when he made his exit speech on Christmas Day 1991, Gorbachev succeeded by Western criteria, not by his own.

Paradoxically, the party conservatives who warned that glasnost would lead to disaster turned out to be right. Gorbachev had designed glasnost, this old Russian notion of the public airing of problems, as a blowtorch that could strip the layers of old and peeling paint from Soviet society. But the Communist system proved dry tinder. From the first touch of flame the conservatives began to warn that glasnost was in danger of igniting the entire edifice of Soviet communism. Gorbachev meanwhile was insisting, "No, no, don't worry, comrades, we're just going to renovate the place, everything's fine." Later, as the conflagration began—Lithuania declaring its independence in March 1990, anti-Communist demonstrators marching raucously across Red Square in May 1990—Gorbachev himself seemed to be losing heart. Increasingly, between the spring of 1990 and the spring of 1991, Gorbachev seemed unwilling to accept the consequences of the reforms he had initiated. He seemed to cross over to the camp of his old, conservative opponents—

who ultimately would turn on him in the short-lived coup of August 1991. In his vacillation he confirmed that his original intentions were more modest than his Western admirers sometimes imputed to him. He had come to save the system, not to bury it.

Mikhail Gorbachev, a giant and fascinating figure, has had numerous chroniclers and will justifiably have many more. But by focusing on the dynamism and boldness of Gorbachev and the unprecedented drama of Kremlin politics in the late 1980s, Western writers have underplayed certain bigger, impersonal forces that drove a superpower into reform, then revolution, and finally collapse.

The most important of these forces was information. Information is the most revealing prism through which to view the essence and the end of the Soviet Union. Information slew the totalitarian giant.

On Lenin's birthday, April 22, 1988, my wife, Francie Weeks, and I, along with our daughters, Martha, then four, and Laura, two, arrived at Sheremetevo Airport to take over the *Baltimore Sun*'s Moscow bureau. The enduring irony of Russian life made itself felt immediately: as Laura, exhausted, began to howl in the long line for passport control, a uniformed KGB officer waved us out of line to an unmanned booth, where he ordered a baby-faced border guard to process our papers. The KGB man's sympathy for babies was only one of many paradoxes awaiting us in the tumultuous years ahead. "All those who have lived long in Russia," wrote George Kennan, one of those who had, "have had occasion to observe that when the question is placed as to which of two contrary and seemingly irreconcilable phenomena in Russian life is the true one, the answer is invariably: both."

We arrived just as the political change was beginning to accelerate, convincing the doubters that whatever this *perestroika*—restructuring—was, it was for real. We left thirty-nine months later as the Soviet Communist party, and then the Soviet Union itself, disintegrated and slipped into history. It was an astonishing revolution to live through and watch close-up: coming to treat the spectacular architecture of the parliament buildings inside the Kremlin as a daily workplace; sticking a tape recorder in the faces of political leaders locked in mortal political combat over the future of the empire; hearing the rattle of machine-gun fire interrupt a late-night tea party in Yerevan, Armenia; feeling the adrenalin as the deafening chant of "Down with the KGB" echoed from the stone walls of the Lubyanka, security police headquarters, back to an angry crowd of thousands of people who had lost their fear.

A few months after we arrived in Moscow my mother, Emily Shane, sent me something she had stumbled across forgotten in a desk drawer. It was the business card of a certain Mr. Mezhlauk, a Soviet trade official, which she had found in her father's house after his death. She recalled Mr. Mezhlauk's visits to her family's house in Cleveland in the early 1930s, when her father's engineering construction firm was helping build the huge steel plant at Magnitogorsk in the Urals. She and her sisters had liked the kind Russian visitor, and she was puzzled and sad when she was told a few years later by her parents that Mr. Mezhlauk had "disappeared."

Consulting a few reference books, I learned that V. I. Mezhlauk, after a period as a trade official in New York, had gone on to become chairman of powerful Gosplan, the State Planning Committee, and thus overseer of the economy. In 1938 he met the eventual fate of virtually every top official during the great purges: he was arrested on trumped-up charges. In jail he seems to have maintained the illusion of so many of those who were arrested that it was all a big mistake, and that once the snafu was discovered and corrected, he would be freed with apologies. Just before he was shot, the historian Roy Medvedev wrote, Mezhlauk wrote an essay entitled, with poignant irony, "On Planning and Ways to Improve It."

In life Mezhlauk represented the Stalinist economy, exporting grain while peasants starved to pay for American technology like my grandfather's to build industrial megaprojects. In death Mezhlauk was swallowed by the Stalinist terror, the insatiable machine that consumed millions of the most talented and promising lives. It was this world Stalin had built that began to be dismantled during our time in Moscow, and is still being dismantled today.

Particularly in light of the disquieting chaos, deprivation, and violence that have followed the breakup of the Soviet Union, it is worth remembering the violence and the lies that came before. Once in 1991, under fire because of Moscow's rising crime rate, then-Mayor Gavriil Popov stiffly reminded a television audience that the highest murder rate in the city's history had been seen in an earlier era, lionized in the neo-Stalinist imagination as a time of great public "order"—the late 1930s, when a thousand Muscovites a day were being shot by NKVD executioners. One can only hope the fierce courage with which most people in the Soviet republics faced their history will not give way to a false nostalgia for the "iron fist" of Stalinism.

The exponential advance of information technology in this century surely is among its most important developments. We have gone from a relative handful of telegraph operators, slowly tapping out messages in Morse code, to an incomprehensibly complex network incorporating satellite television, computers linked by modems, wealth that flashes around the globe at the speed of light. Increasingly we tie into this network from home, work, or car. We live in a sloshing sea of information and grow accustomed every year to new machines designed to move it, store it, display it, and play with it. It is my conviction that these developments doomed the seventy-four-year Bolshevik experiment, and that the end of the USSR demonstrates the power of information both to liberate and to destroy. In any case, information is now a force that we must struggle to understand, even as once cave dwellers gazed awestruck at fire, Phoenician traders studied the winds, Renaissance thinkers pondered the printed book, or pioneers of nineteenth-century industry pored over the interaction of railroad, coal mine, and steam engine.

1

Before:
Information Criminal

To liquidate *samizdat* [loosely, underground publishing] is possible only having understood that it's not the result of a few evil-minded people but a social phenomenon, responding to a ripened demand.... The sole resolution of the problem of *samizdat* is the introduction of an authentically free press. There is no other way.
> —Kronid Lyubarsky, Soviet astrophysicist and dissident, at his 1972 trial

For a man whose mother tongue is Russian, to speak about political evil is as natural as digestion.
> —Joseph Brodsky, Nobel lecture, 1987

A few minutes after 6 a.m. on August 7, 1985, five months after Mikhail Gorbachev came to power, a KGB major and two lieutenants rang the doorbell of apartment 37 at 222 Kommunarov Street in the provincial Russian city of Ustinov. The ring was long and insistent. Yevgeniya Semyonovna Mironova opened the door. It was already light.

Yevgeniya Semyonovna, a small, no-nonsense woman of fifty-eight, stepped back into the entrance where boots and slippers were lined up beneath a coat rack. Her husband, Nikolai Alexeyevich

Mironov, a lanky, energetic man of sixty-three, heard the commotion and came to her side. Major Felix Korolyov began to read some kind of legal mumbo jumbo, but there was no need. They knew the KGB had come to take their son.

When Andrei Mironov had been in second grade in a village school, he recounted to me much later when we had become friends, the teacher solemnly informed the children that March had thirty days. All except Andrei obediently recorded this piece of news about the world in their notebooks. Andrei raised his hand to object. There is a March 31, he said. He knew there was, he told the teacher, because his birthday was March 31. She scolded him for his impudence and told him he did not know what he was talking about. He responded in kind. There was a scandal, but Andrei refused to abandon his position. Thus, brandishing his fact like a weapon, was a dissident born.

Years later, what struck him most strongly about his memory of the incident was that the other kids had believed the teacher. "She was a higher authority," he said.

When the KGB came for him, Andrei Nikolayevich Mironov was thirty-one, working as a museum restorationist, an open-faced, bearded man with an intense curiosity about the world. As a child he had traveled widely in Siberia with his geologist parents, living in a variety of Soviet settings and gaining unusual perspective. Later he had taught himself Italian and English, read widely, and listened incessantly to "the voices," as the Western shortwave stations were known in Russian. In Moscow he had befriended foreign students at the Pushkin Institute, trading language lessons and worldviews. His self-effacing friendliness and soft-spoken, slightly absentminded manner masked an independence and fearlessness that took casual acquaintances by surprise. He had formed his own political views, which he did not hide. Eventually he had become part of a small ring of dissidents who were secretly photocopying and distributing banned books. Andrei Mironov's hobbies were a modest enough assault on a superpower. But by the special rules of Russian and Soviet political culture, they were more than enough to bring him into collision with the state.

There are moments that seem to capture the end of an epoch, events that make no headlines but that happen where history seems to swivel, that are found exactly at the junction between two worlds. Such was the case of Andrei Mironov.

It was a classic—an unadulterated political crime without even an allegation of messy adjuncts such as contact with foreign spies or sneaking over the Soviet border. The case was one of the last to be prosecuted under the infamous Article 70 of the criminal code of the Russian Soviet Federative Socialist Republic, which prohibited "anti-Soviet agitation and propaganda with the goal of undermining and weakening the Soviet state and social system."

In a dismal Russian tradition that dated at least to the time of Ivan the Terrible, the state on that August morning in Ustinov was enforcing its monopoly on truth, reminding the people that it, not they, would decide what they could read and write and say. Andrei Mironov, an "especially dangerous state criminal" (as the legal papers put it), had committed the most fearful of offenses against the Soviet order—he was "worse than a murderer," as the secretary who transcribed his trial put it. His crime was *information.*

Nobody suspected it then—neither Andrei nor his parents; certainly not Korolyov, the KGB major, nor Viktor Pokhodin, the prosecutor who signed the arrest warrant, nor the KGB brass back in Moscow who ordered the arrest; not even the enigmatic leader who would do the most to make it happen, Mikhail Gorbachev—but the last act of a great historical drama was beginning. The views that in 1985 so appalled the defenders of Marxist-Leninist propriety, the facts they found it so important to keep from the public, the behavior they punished with imprisonment, would all within a few years become the norm. That morning in Ustinov it was still unimaginable, but behavior like Mironov's would soon be commonplace. His views would be mainstream. His facts would fill the pages of official newspapers and the airtime of radio and TV. It would happen in a nonviolent, slow-motion revolution the likes of which world history had never seen. That revolution would not only vanquish seven decades of Soviet totalitarianism but break with a thousand years of Russian authoritarianism as well.

For the Mironovs it had begun a couple of years earlier with discreet messages delivered to them by their supervisors at their jobs as geologists in the Soviet oil-prospecting bureaucracy. They were told that their middle son, Andrei, who lived in Moscow, was reading anti-Soviet literature, socializing with foreign students, and exhibiting unsound views. Such warnings were part of what the KGB liked to call *prophylaktika*—the security organs' compassionate attempt to save a wayward citizen from himself. "In Soviet society," KGB chief Yuri Andropov had declared a few years earlier, celebrating the hundredth birthday of the founder of the Soviet secret police, "Iron Felix" Dzerzhinsky, "deluded individuals are helped through persuasion to correct their mistakes." But Andropov, who after ascending to the post of party leader would anoint his young protégé Gorbachev as his successor, emphasized the limits to this socialist benevolence. "Different measures are required when some of the so-called 'dissidents' commit acts infringing Soviet laws.... All talk about humanism in such instances is irrelevant. We consider it humane to stop in good time the activity of those who are interfering with the normal life and work of Soviet citizens."

Andrei's parents, far from orthodox in their private political opinions, nonetheless were children of the Stalin era. They telephoned Andrei and told him he should tone down his behavior. The point, they told him, was not whether he was right but whether he would accomplish anything by sacrificing himself. He demurred.

Then, in November 1984, the KGB had ordered Andrei to leave Moscow. His parents gladly had taken him in, hoping that away from the superheated dissident circles of the capital he would put aside politics. He didn't. The friendly chats with his parents became frank warnings. His parents pleaded, but Andrei would not respond to the prophylaktika. In early 1985 the case had moved into its final phase. Nikolai Alexeyevich was in the habit of kicking off his slippers when he dressed in the morning; one evening he came home to find his slippers placed neatly, side by side, next to the bed. On other occasions there were other subtle signs left by the visitors; it was their way of letting the Mironovs know they had been there.

In June a KGB squad came with a warrant, searched the

apartment, and took Andrei to headquarters. Andrei remembered that though it was quite warm on the streets, it was chilly in the high-ceilinged corridors they led him down. The interrogator appealed to him as a Soviet patriot to assist the KGB in its investigation of an acquaintance named Goldovich, who had been arrested trying to flee the Soviet Union across the Black Sea in a little rubber boat. The man was opening the last exit door for Andrei, offering him a deal, but Andrei curtly declined to become an informer. The interrogation ended badly. Andrei flew to Moscow a few days later to warn his friends to destroy any compromising material. There could be little doubt then that it all would end with the ring of the doorbell at dawn.

Like springtime love in English poetry, the political arrest is a classic theme in Russian literature. Mikhail Lermontov, who died in a duel in 1841 without suspecting that the Bolsheviks would seize power in the next century, wrote a bitter little poem when the tsarist secret police came to ship him into exile in the Caucasus:

> Farewell, unwashed Russia,
> Nation of slaves, nation of masters,
> And you, blue uniforms,
> And you, a people betrayed.
>
> Perhaps beyond the Caucasus wall
> I can hide out from your agents,
> From their all-seeing eyes,
> From their all-hearing ears.

The last lines in particular carry the little jolt that always comes when one stumbles across in pre–Soviet Russia the unmistakable ancestry of Soviet totalitarianism. In an age before electronics, Lermontov's all-seeing eyes and all-hearing ears were mere metaphor. The KGB, successor to the "blue uniforms," used technology and a huge agent force to make it literal. Alexander Solzhenitsyn, whose own odyssey through the Stalinist camps began with remarks about "the man with the mustache" in letters to a friend, devoted the sizzling first chapter of *Gulag Archipelago* to the nuances of the political arrest. "Arrest is an instantaneous, shattering thrust, expulsion, somersault from one state into another," he wrote. As if he had been there in Ustinov in 1985, he described "trembling hands packing for the victim—a change of underwear, a piece of soap, something to eat; and no one knows what is needed, what is permitted, what clothes are best to wear; and the agents keep interrupting and hurrying you: 'You don't need anything. They'll feed you there. It's warm there.' (They are lying.)"

It was 146 years after Lermontov's arrest, forty-one years after Solzhenitsyn's. But like those in Lermontov's poems and Solzhenitsyn's letters, words—information—could still constitute a crime against the state.

The KGB agents went briskly to work in the Kommunarov Street apartment, summoning the obligatory citizen-witnesses, bustling back and forth to the two Volgas parked outside, searching the cozy, two-room apartment with its floor-to-ceiling bookshelves and piles of clutter. They looked inside the homemade, insulated box where Mrs. Mironov in the old days had left the dinner she cooked early in the morning for her three sons to eat when they got home from school. They opened the boxes of slides taken with the stereoscopic camera invented by Mr. Mironov, an inveterate tinkerer. The agents gathered up all the papers they could find—scribbled phone messages, addresses, postcards, newspapers—and pedantically recorded each in a search protocol, like bloodstained carpet or bullet fragments at a murder scene: "magazine, *L'Expresso*, 3 May 1981, in Italian, 114 pages... book, *The New Testament of Our Lord Jesus Christ*, 1977, 490 pages... piece of paper, yellow in color, size 7.5 by 10 cm. with the notation: 'Jan Jostma Sophia 3743CT Baard Holland 4520198.'" At one point an agent asked Andrei: "Maybe you have some other anti-Soviet books?" Andrei handed him Nikolai Berdyaev's 1916 book of Christian philosophy, *The Meaning of Creation*, saying sarcastically, "How about this?" He regretted his insolence when they confiscated the book.

Some six hours later the Mironovs looked on as the agents hustled Andrei to the waiting Volga. For them it was an incalculable blow. "I know now, they can do anything they want. Anything," Yevgeniya

Semyonovna would say later, using the anonymous third-person plural that in Russia has always expressed the alienation of the people from the power.

By contrast, Andrei, as they drove him downtown to the marble-columned KGB headquarters, felt almost relieved. After months of glimpsing the shadows behind him on the sidewalk, of hearing the clicks during telephone conversations, of worrying that his politics would rebound against his friends and family, the waiting was finally over. Now there would be clarity.

After another interrogation, this time more brusque and without the appeals for patriotic cooperation, Andrei was delivered to the Ustinov Detention Center, a peeling jumble of buildings a couple of miles away. He was pushed into a hot, stinking holding cell with about thirty defendants, most of them charged with serious non-political crimes. Thuggish-looking characters gathered around him. *"Skazhi za zhizn!"* one said, using prison slang: Tell us about yourself. Andrei sat down on a steel cot and began his story. Later he would remember watching a rat crawl out of the cell's foul single toilet and scurry around the cots, sniffing for crumbs of food.

Andrei Mironov was unknown in the West, and his arrest would send not the slightest tremor through the offices where human rights cases were tracked in London or New York. Ustinov, where nearly everyone worked in the defense industry, was closed to foreigners and a good five hundred miles from Moscow's nosy corps of foreign correspondents. In any case, they would have had little reason to visit this nondescript town of 650,000, capital of the autonomous republic of Udmurtia within the Russian federation; Russians outnumbered Udmurts, an agrarian people whose language resembles Finnish, and the Udmurts were mostly quite assimilated anyway. The town had been established as Izhevsk in the mid-eighteenth century as an iron foundry, was sacked by the peasant rebel Pugachev in 1774, and was a White stronghold for a time in the civil war that followed the Bolshevik Revolution. After Soviet power was established it became a stable industrial center, a reliable cog in the Soviet defense machine. Even on the brink of the collapse of communism in 1991, a red and white Lenin billboard towered above the road into the city from the airport, inscribed: "The Ideas of Lenin Live and Will Be Victorious."

About the biggest thing to happen in Izhevsk in all the years of Soviet rule was the time it suddenly ceased to be Izhevsk: at the beginning of 1985 it was renamed Ustinov, for the late, longtime defense chief, Dmitri Ustinov. The change was simply announced one morning on the radio, with no pretense of consulting public opinion, and many residents resented it. But the new Gorbachevian modesty frowned on such Brezhnev-style aggrandizement; Andrei Mironov was arrested and tried in Ustinov, but in late 1987 Moscow quietly ordered the original name restored.

There was a local joke about the CIA's attempt to penetrate the city's missile plants that captured both the cold war atmosphere and the dreary privations of the Soviet provinces. The first American spy sent to probe the secrets of Izhevsk, the joke went, was soon crushed to death on one of the brutally crowded city buses. The CIA, assuming he had been unmasked and killed, dispatched a second man. He died of food poisoning after eating in one of the factory cafeterias. Not to be deterred, the CIA sent its most skilled and cunning spy. He was walking down Lenin Street on the day of his arrival when he was spotted by two drunks, searching for someone to share the price of a bottle of vodka. "There's a third man!" one drunk called to the other, pointing at the undercover American. The spy, figuring he had somehow been exposed, bit into a cyanide capsule and dropped dead on the spot.

The truth, according to an Izhevsk KGB man I interviewed in 1991, was that no spy had ever been caught in Soviet history in Izhevsk or anywhere else in Udmurtia. The disproportion between this inglorious fact and the massive edifice which the agency occupied underscored the fact that the KGB had plenty of functions beyond counterespionage. In fact, as in the USSR as a whole, the big white-columned building stood more for the state's fear of its own citizens than its fear of other states. Stalin and his henchmen had hit upon the efficient idea of using the latter to disguise the former: the great purge trials of the 1930s saw Stalin's rivals and opponents falsely accused of plotting sabotage and assassination on behalf of Germany, Japan, and England. The enemy without and the enemy within were inextricably entangled in Soviet propaganda, particularly in KGB tracts. Opponents of any Soviet policy, whether collectivization of agriculture or "international assistance" to Afghanistan, were responsible for weakening Soviet socialism. Thus they were aiding the Soviet Union's imperialist adversaries. By the same logic that Americans tasted during the McCarthy era, a Soviet citizen who criticized a specific government policy was virtually indistinguishable from a Soviet citizen recruited by a foreign intelligence agency. The same basic formula survived long after Stalin was gone; in 1988, when *Washington Post* and *Newsweek* editors asked Gorbachev about the arrest of dissident Sergei Grigoryants, he replied icily: "People know that Grigoryants's 'organization' is tied not only organizationally but also financially to the West, that his constant visitors and guests are Western correspondents. Therefore people think of him as some kind of alien phenomenon in our society." The resulting miasma of fear, suspicion, and denunciation waxed and waned over the years, but it was as surely a part of the world a Soviet child was born into as red Pioneer scarves and Lenin portraits.

In such an atmosphere some join heartily in and thrive, most silently conform or silently resent, and a few resist. Andrei Mironov's parents seem to have been silent resenters, though his father occasionally showed a flash of open resistance. His moments of political recklessness became a part of family lore. In 1953, when Nikolai Alexeyevich heard that Lavrenty Beria, Stalin's ghoulish secret police chief, had been arrested, he came bursting into a room filled with his colleagues and cheerfully exclaimed, "Heard the good news?" Yevgeniya Semyonovna, who was in the room, bit her tongue at the time but later, at home, gave her husband an angry scolding. Yet she had her own scorn for the system. A few weeks after Beria's arrest and execution, a state publishing house mailed to the Mironovs and all other subscribers to the 1950 edition of the Great Soviet Encyclopedia instructions to razor out pages 21–24 of volume 5, destroy them, and replace them with the enclosed insert. In this way the long, laudatory article on Beria would be replaced with the supplied innocuous *ber-* entries, from Bering Strait to George Berkeley. In the new material, Beria was not so much as mentioned. Yevgeniya Semyonovna as well as her husband were outraged by the absurdity and condescension of this attempt by the state to persuade the citizens to protect themselves from the information they already had. They put the insert into volume 5 but left the offensive Beria entry in place; Andrei dug it out and read it over repeatedly as a teenager, savoring the forbidden fruit.

Yevgeniya Semyonovna's parents had been farmers in a village about a hundred miles from Moscow. When she was four years old the neighbors came and warned that they had been identified as *kulaks*—literally, "fists"—the successful farmers whom Stalin had vowed to annihilate because of their resistance to the new collective farms. The family fled to Moscow to escape exile, arrest, or worse. She remembers that they abandoned a spacious farmhouse where each person had his own room and jammed into a single room in the capital. Her parents, she said, "never openly criticized Soviet power, but they never praised it either. They were never in ecstasy about it."

Nikolai Alexeyevich was born into a peasant family near the ancient Russian capital of Novgorod in 1922, toward the end of a terrible famine. Shortly after his birth the family fled south to Baku, the capital of Azerbaijan, where he lived until completing an oil institute and beginning his career.

The two of them met in Siberia in 1951 on a summer oil-prospecting expedition. They married despite the fact that Yevgeniya had not completed her studies in Moscow; they naturally assumed that the Ministry of Geology would assign her to work in Irkutsk, the Siberian city where Nikolai was stationed. Instead she was informed just before graduation that she was being sent to another region, thousands of miles away. Nikolai heard this shattering news in a 5 a.m. phone call he placed from the post office in Irkutsk. He was so angry that he sent a telegram on the spot to Stalin, whose text he remembers verbatim: "The Board of Leading Cadres of the Ministry of Geology is wrecking families and treating people like animals. Example: job assignments of the Mironovs." The risks of an angry telegram to Stalin in 1951 were enormous; its author could get dispatched to the Gulag or even to an NKVD execution squad. At 6 a.m. Nikolai ran into the telegraph operator's husband, an acquaintance. "What have you done?" the man asked incredulously. He said his wife had already been chewed out for merely accepting the telegram. "It was dangerous," Nikolai Mironov acknowledges today, but as a geologist working in the wastes of Siberia, he didn't fear exile. "Where would they send me, Kolyma?"—the infamous arctic death camp. As it turned out, his gamble paid off. The telegram reached Moscow after midnight. Late on the same day a chastened clerk from the Ministry of Geology found Yevgeniya and told her she would be assigned to Irkutsk.

That kind of courage and directness influenced Andrei. He was born in 1954 in Irkutsk and remembers climbing on a roof to see the sensational Sputnik in 1957, only to be deeply disappointed that it looked like a dim star. He recalls the frontier-style excitement of his parents' prospecting expeditions, which gave him his first helicopter ride at the age of three. As an older child he saw his father's dismay as his various inventions and innovations were rejected or ignored by the conservative state bureaucracy. He heard his parents' scorn for the ideological blather and pervasive corruption they encountered at work. Unguarded remarks stuck with him. Once when his younger brother, Alexei, complained that his mother was giving too much candy to some other children, Yevgeniya Semyonovna snapped at him: "Keep on like that and you'll grow up to join the [Communist] party." As is common in Russian families, he stayed for months at a time in Krasnogorsk, outside Moscow, with his grandmother, a power-plant engineer who had been well educated in a *gymnasium* before the Revolution. At home she referred scathingly to Stalin as *"ryaboy"*—the pockmarked one—and showed a memorable fearlessness.

Nonetheless Andrei said he experienced the same wide-eyed enthusiasm for his country shared by most Soviet youngsters, who were told from nursery school how fortunate they were to have been born in the world's first socialist country. He was active in Pioneers, the nine-to-fourteen-year-old Boy Scouts of communism, as a "Red Pathfinder," interviewing elderly veterans of the Revolution. At fourteen he entered the Komsomol, the Young Communist League,

with everyone else. "I thought the idea of communism was good—
that exploitation was bad and that there should be universal happiness for everybody. But Khrushchev seemed so stupid, and Brezhnev
seemed so stupid," he said.

After graduating from school in Izhevsk, Andrei studied chemistry on his own, hoping to get into a prestigious Moscow institute. He
did well on the chemistry exams, but math was his nemesis, and he
did not survive the brutal entrance competition. Without a student
deferment, he was drafted into the army. There he found the same
mindlessness and devotion to hierarchy that are part of any mass
military force. But his experience persuaded him that the Soviet
army's ideological indoctrination, in a country with universal con-
scription, played an important part in shaping *homo sovieticus,* Soviet
Man.

"It trained people in the psychology of the slave," Andrei said. "A
soldier was an object, like a carbine or an automatic." Young men
learned in the army that labor was a form of punishment and that
authority was not to be challenged, and those lessons carried over to
civilian life, he said. The first words of his commanding officer, he
recalled, had been: *"Nu, duraki..."*—Well, you idiots....He served
in a radio communications unit in the Ural Mountains, a few miles
from the site of a 1957 explosion of nuclear waste that had
contaminated a large area. At the time, in the early 1970s, the
accident was secret; though the exiled Russian biologist Zhores
Medvedev would soon publish a speculative book on it in the West,
the Soviet press would only begin to write about it mid-1989. But
Andrei spoke with witnesses of the blast, saw the trees whose limbs
had been blown off on the side of the impact, and came across
snakes and fish with strange mutations. He remembers deep, crystal-
clear lakes so clean that the bottom was visible thirty feet down—
but where signs warned "No drinking, no swimming, no fishing."
Alexander Solzhenitsyn was at that time defying the regime by
publishing *The Gulag Archipelago* in the West, and Andrei learned
that the KGB was checking the views of every army officer on
Solzhenitsyn and his writings.

When he was discharged after two years of service, he took and
passed the entrance exams for Moscow's world-class Mendeleyev

Institute and began his studies there. But he had trouble adjusting to a student's regimen, he said. At the same time, while he was entranced by the beauty and complexity of chemistry, he found himself less and less interested in science and more and more interested in history and politics. "In normal times, I could have worked in theoretical chemistry with great pleasure," he told me. "I still remember the formulas; ten or fifteen years later I would suddenly think of the answer to some chemistry problem I had been working on then. But I decided chemistry couldn't solve the problems I saw around me. I felt like a man who sits reading poetry while his house is burning down around him." Andrei quit the institute before the first year was up and moved in with his grandmother in Krasnogorsk. He held a number of jobs—as a jack-of-all-trades for the Soviet state firm responsible for the export of gemstones; as a laborer for a bakery; and, after he moved to Ustinov, as a restorationist for the local history museum. But that work was never more than a meal ticket and a way of fending off the "parasite" charges often leveled against political activists who held no regular job. With each year he devoted more of his time to searching out and reading newspapers, magazines, and books that had only one thing in common: the Soviet state had concluded that they were not fit reading for Soviet citizens.

What first drew the KGB's serious attention to Andrei was not the underground publishing he ultimately became involved in but something far more innocuous: his socializing with foreign students of Russian language at Moscow's Pushkin Institute, whom he met in 1982 through an American working as a proofreader for the English-language edition of *Moscow News*. He was far from alone in hanging around at this institution to make the acquaintance of the students whose loud voices and loud clothing advertised their Western origins. But most of the young Russians who approached Americans and Europeans on their way to the Metro were *fartsovsh-chiki,* slang for the small-time black marketeers whose first questions after "Do you speak English?" were "Want to sell blue jeans?

Rock records? Chewing gum? Want to change money?" After the police began to pick up Andrei on the way to or from meetings with Pushkin Institute friends, they were puzzled not to find the give-away evidence of the fartsovshchik—foreign banknotes, pop-music cassettes, T-shirts bearing the names of foreign universities.

For a long time they found nothing politically compromising either. "I had no overt political goals when I started going to the Pushkin Institute. I never got foreign books from my friends at first. I just wanted to know something about the outside world," Andrei explained.

In an expenditure quite typical for middle-class Russians, Andrei's parents had found the rubles to pay for forty private English lessons beginning when he was eight years old. He had tried to keep up the language on his own, and it was for linguistic as well as political reasons that he had become in the late 1970s a devotee of shortwave radio: the Russian-language broadcasts beamed from the West were jammed by the Soviet authorities, but the English broadcasts could be heard clearly. By chance he fell in at first with a group of Italian students from the Pushkin Institute, and in return for his gentle correction of their Russian grammar, he got lessons in beginning Italian instead of the intermediate English he had in mind. If the police were befuddled by Andrei's motives, the foreign students, who soon tired of "friendships" with Russians whose interests seemed to be crassly commercial, were enthralled. Soon he was a Russian leader of a multinational group of Pushkin students that jocularly called itself "Razgulyai International," *razgulyai* meaning in Russian something like "have a good time." They would meet for meals, sharing national dishes and practicing their various languages—Italian, English, German, and Russian. The culinary emphasis was such that Andrei's Italian vocabulary is even today heavily weighted toward kitchen terms; the radio "voices" tilted his English vocabulary toward politics. As any Westerner who studied in Moscow or Leningrad under Soviet rule can attest, friendships that crossed the formidable linguistic and political barriers of the Iron Curtain often had an unforgettable joy and intensity, and that seems to have been the case with Razgulyai International.

The KGB saw things differently. The first trouble Andrei ever had with the authorities that he can recall came in 1977, before his Pushkin Institute friendships, when KGB plainclothesmen stopped him on the way out of a foreign book show at Moscow's grandiose theme park of socialism, the Exhibit of Economic Achievement. As a lark he had picked up a few free books from North Korea, mostly leaden works by and about Kim Il Sung, the North Korean dictator, which Andrei said "read like a parody of the USSR." The KGB man confiscated the Communist propaganda and turned him over to a cop. The cop listened to Andrei's uninhibited defense of his right to read what he pleased and offered him a word to the wise. "You have to change your character," the policeman told him. Unbeknownst to the cop, it was a revelatory moment for Andrei. "I thought, how can a person change his character? So I concluded that eventually I was going to be arrested."

A far more serious brush with the law came on December 10, 1980, Human Rights Day. Andrei was sufficiently involved in the Moscow political scene to be among a few dozen activists who showed up at Pushkin Square for the annual would-be demonstration and roundup of dissidents. In a fifteen-year-old tradition, protesters would gather around the Pushkin statue, whose base was inscribed with a famous passage from the poem, "Unto myself I reared a monument":

Long shall I be loved by the people
For awakening kind feelings with my lyre,
For praising freedom in this cruel age
And asking mercy for the fallen.

As a symbolic gesture of respect for freedom, they would remove their hats. Then they would be arrested. On that particular day, Andrei said, about thirty police trucks were waiting. "I didn't even get my hat off before they swept me off my feet and forced me into one of them," Andrei remembered. "An arm appeared through the window and someone demanded, 'Passport.' And I answered, 'And your passport?'" After questioning at a nearby police station, he was released with a warning.

In 1983, about a year after he began visiting his friends at the Pushkin Institute, he began to be picked up frequently for questioning, usually by the police but under the evident direction of the KGB. Twice psychiatrists were summoned to evaluate his mental status; the diagnosis of "sluggish schizophrenia," an illness found only in the Soviet Union, was effectively substituted by the Brezhnev-era KGB for the less subtle terror of earlier days. Neither psychiatrist, however, found any symptoms of mental illness, and one doctor's clear contempt for the KGB's mockery of medicine made a strong impression on Andrei, though undoubtedly it did little to advance the doctor's career.

"Why were you at the Pushkin Institute?" the doctor asked.

"To attend the birthday party of my friend who is a student there," Andrei replied.

"Why do you go there so often?"

"Because I'm interested in Italian language and culture."

And so on. The doctor pronounced Andrei completely sane. One of the KGB plainclothesmen pushed harder: Didn't the doctor find Mironov's behavior somewhat strange? The doctor replied: "I find nothing strange in his behavior. I find something strange in the behavior of the police who detained him." The Soviet system forced stark moral choices on people in positions of responsibility, daily challenges to conscience that were not painted in the more ambiguous and muted hues of Western life. Years later Andrei recalled that doctor with grateful surprise.

By Latin etymology, a dissident is "one who sits apart." It is thus an appropriate linguistic irony that in Russian, "to sit" means to serve time in a prison or labor camp. Under Stalin, anyone so reckless as to dissent openly from official policy literally sat apart, usually far apart in the arctic camps of Siberia—if he survived at all. But under Stalin there was no need to dissent to be arrested. The dissident movement of recent decades really began after the ouster of Nikita Khrushchev in 1964, which frosted the buds of liberalism and tolerance that had blossomed in Khrushchev's thaw. The year 1965 saw the trial of the writers Yuli Daniel and Andrei Sinyavsky, who had published controversial essays and stories abroad under pseudonyms. On the one hand it marked the start of a crackdown; on the other hand, as the writer Anatoly Yakobson put it, it was the beginning "of people's self-liberation from the humiliation of fear, from connivance in evil." The trial ended, naturally, with convictions (seven years for Sinyavsky, five for Daniel), but it stirred a street demonstration and a flurry of written protests from the intelligentsia. A class of people was emerging who would not parrot the state's line or denounce those whom the state denounced. They would "sit apart." They were few, but the significance of their constant challenge to the regime, forcing it to make a choice between bad publicity and total control, was immeasurable.

Such giants as Solzhenitsyn and the physicist Andrei Sakharov, both of whom were officially honored by the state in earlier times, lent the dissident movement a moral weight that swayed at least some of the general public. Andrei Mironov remembered hearing his parents say, "Sakharov is right"; Yevgeniya Semyonovna confirms this recollection, saying she thought "such a brilliant man could not be wrong." Solzhenitsyn's quintessentially Russian opinion that a great writer could be a "second government" was not much of an exaggeration. Writing in the early 1980s, Amnesty International activist Joshua Rubenstein found the importance of the Soviet human rights movement in its ability to breach the information barriers the regime had built. "The human rights movement reflects and reinforces a breakdown in the cultural and political isolation of the Soviet Union," Rubenstein wrote. "As unsanctioned poetry circulated, then novels, and finally detailed information about political trials and conditions in labor camps, the regime's control of information grew less effective."

Rubenstein added a more debatable assertion: "The dissidents did not think differently from everyone else, as the word dissent implies. Rather, they decided to say what everyone else knows." In the absence of relevant public opinion polls from the pre-Gorbachev era, it is hard to say with much certainty what everyone else knew. Robert Kaiser of the *Washington Post,* one of the most perceptive American observers of the Soviet Union, concluded just the opposite in his 1976 book, *Russia: The People and the Power:* "The fact that only a few speak out is important. The dissidents represent a small fraction of the educated population, a tiny fraction of the Soviet citizenry. Throughout Russian history they have failed to attract a mass following, and it is hard to imagine that they ever will win over their countrymen." As a student in Leningrad in 1976, I found that most of my Soviet contemporaries, with whom I had very open conversations on many topics, were simply struck dumb by a question such as, "What do you think of Brezhnev?" It was not that they were afraid to answer; it simply did not seem to be a relevant question for them. It was as if I had asked whether they thought the Rocky Mountains were beautiful. Because it was useless or dangerous to become involved in politics, most people avoided forming serious opinions and muddled through with a superficial cynicism about leaders combined with a general belief in the system. Andrei Mironov recalls thinking as a child that there were no political events in the Soviet Union, which was too bad, because it made life boring.

But two historical trends were preparing the ground for political change, eroding the foundation that ignorance and isolation provides for received dogma. Between Stalin's death in 1953 and Gorbachev's accession to power in 1985 occurred a remarkable transformation of both educational levels and urbanization. In his 1988 book *The Gorbachev Phenomenon,* the Sovietologist Moshe Lewin argued cogently that the West was paying too much attention to Gorbachev and too little to the social changes that were making reform inevitable. Events in the ensuing years certainly bear him out. Just 600,000 people finished secondary school in the year 1950; by 1988 the figure had increased sixfold to 3.8 million. The number of students in higher educational institutions quadrupled, from 1.2 million to 5 million. Lewin noted that the urban population in the USSR became more than half the total only in the 1960s; the 50 percent mark had been exceeded in the United States, France, and Germany, by contrast, in the 1920s. By the mid-1980s almost two-thirds of Soviet citizens lived in cities.

This urbanized, educated population was ready for information, but in the pre-Gorbachev era the state was not about to give it to them. Thus it is no accident that the word *samizdat*—from *sam,* self, and *izdat,* publish—appeared in the early 1960s, a new name for the thousands of fuzzy carbon copies on onionskin paper that were circulating illegally from friend to friend. *Magnitizdat,* from *magnitofon,* or tape recorder, appeared later and reached a far larger audience, as cassettes of the sardonic ballads of Alexander Galich, Bulat Okudzhava, and especially Vladimir Vysotsky, as well as the satirical monologues of comedian Mikhail Zhvanetsky, were copied and passed around.

> There is no orchestra, no loge or tier,
> No claque with its hullabaloo
> A "Yauza" tape recorder's here,
> That is all, but it will do.

So sang Galich, asserting the power of a Soviet-made portable tape recorder. Samizdat and magnitizdat reached a small fraction of the total population, but they reached a significant number of well-educated big-city dwellers whose influence on the cultural and political milieu was disproportionately large. By the late 1970s some of the same subversive messages of the "bards" and the underground comedians were beginning to reach a huge audience of young people in the form of rock music, in later years the subject of a bitter political debate. Talented lyricists such as Yuri Shevchuk of the rock group DDT raised such serious issues in their lyrics as the death-grip of the bureaucracy and the decline of the Russian village. Andrei Mironov remembered one haunting pair of lines from a DDT song that seemed to be addressed to the entire Soviet state:

> I read what I should read, because you need it.
> But when you're drowning, I won't save you,
> I'll push you down.

Certainly in the 1970s and 1980s the dissidents, those who "sat apart," had a lot of passive sympathizers huddled around tape recorders or poring over blurry carbon copies in the night kitchens of the cities. They were not as far "apart" from society as appeared on the almost unruffled surface of Leonid Brezhnev's rule.

Into the midst of the young Moscow intelligentsia who hungered for real news fell Andrei Mironov after dropping out of Mendeleyev Institute in 1975. His parents' honest upbringing, his reading, his eye for the gap between Pioneer rhetoric and Russian reality, and the contradictions of his army stint all had combined to undermine the official Soviet view of the world. He was in search of his own view, which took shape under the combined influence of samizdat and the great Russian art of talk.

"I found people in Moscow with similar views and interests literally everywhere," he recalled. "I would estimate there were no fewer than 100,000 copies of banned books circulating in Moscow. Lots of young people were curious. There was a desire to know what was happening in the world." The changes in society, he said, were reflected in the black-market prices of pre-Revolutionary classics such as Nikolai Karamzin's massive, early nineteenth-century *History of the Russian State.* Such books could be purchased for less than a ruble a volume in the early 1970s, but by the end of the decade the price was ten times higher. "The situation changed quickly," Andrei said. "People started reading philosophy. They read Solzhenitsyn, and Shalamov [Varlam Shalamov, author of stories about the Stalinist camps, published abroad], and Orwell. Externally, everything remained as it had been—it was the 'era of stagnation.' But it was the beginning of the public consciousness you saw under Gorbachev on the streets in rallies and demonstrations."

Andrei had stumbled onto a vocation to take the place of chemistry. "I saw only one way out of the predicament—to distribute accurate information to people. Not only information I considered accurate, but access to all information, so that people could decide things for themselves," he said. "I gradually went from exchange of books to reproduction." He and a few like-thinkers discovered that it was not too difficult to arrange for prohibited books to be secretly photocopied at night at state institutions, some of them, ironically, military plants. It was strictly illegal; the machines were under lock and key, and the amount of paper used was supposed to be carefully tracked. But, said Andrei, "the KGB watchers were lazy, and for money people would copy anything."

The target audience was the political intelligentsia and the booklist correspondingly sober. One of the first books Andrei reproduced was *The Meaning of Creation,* by Berdyaev, a philosopher whom Lenin had expelled from the Soviet Union in 1922—the original of which would be confiscated upon Andrei's arrest in 1985. "It was 360 pages long and cost twenty-one rubles to get it copied. I had no money, so I had to find someone who could put the money up in advance," Andrei said. He never saw the people who actually did the photocopying; his contacts were people who knew people who worked at factories or institutes that had photocopiers. To avoid detection, everything was handled with a nod and a wink, with excruciating delays and great discretion. "I never said the word 'book' on the telephone," Andrei said. Once, however, when he was walking down a main street with a knapsack full of photocopies, he happened upon an overexcited colleague in the underground publishing venture, who called out, "What do you have there, *kseroksi* [Xeroxes]?" Andrei's heart skipped a beat as he waited for plain-clothesmen to pounce. But no one was watching. Still, the hazardous nature of the operation kept its pace slow and its scale minuscule: the largest number of copies of a single work produced by his circle of night-owl publishers was twenty-one, and Andrei estimates they copied about ten titles before he was arrested, including Erich Fromm's *Escape from Freedom,* George Orwell's *Animal Farm* and *1984,* Varlam Shalamov's *Kolyma Tales,* and works by the dissident mathematician Igor Shafarevich and the emigré historian Abdurakh-man Avtorkhanov. Given the samizdat multiplier effect, which anyone understands who saw in those days a photocopy of some coveted work thumbed almost to the point of illegibility, the books he and his friends distributed probably were read by several thousand people. In Andrei's opinion then and now, it was the most important work he could do to undermine the Communist regime, attacking the state's soft underbelly of myth and legend with banned facts and dissenting interpretations of reality.

Beginning in 1982, Soviet dissidents and Western human rights advocates began to notice a new KGB strategy: "Intimidation and frequent arrests of people who were not identified publicly as active dissidents, but who read and circulated samizdat," Joshua Ruben-stein writes. Somewhere along the line in this new campaign of ideological vigilance, a case officer must have tagged Andrei's file. Someone must have put some diverse pieces of paper together— from the Pushkin Institute detainments, from the 1980 Human

Rights Day arrest, perhaps some phone-tap transcriptions or reports from the numerous "dissidents"-for-hire who had infiltrated politically active circles in the capital. Some go-getter in the KGB's Fifth Directorate, which was assigned the task of suppressing domestic dissent, must have had a lightbulb go off in his head: This Mironov guy is for real. He is dangerous. He must be stopped.

In 1984 KGB watchers began to follow Andrei openly on the streets of Moscow. It was an amazing operation that Andrei observed with his habitual combination of engagement and detachment. On the one hand he hated these sleazy, self-important servants of power. "You could tell them on the street, even when they were trying to be unnoticed," Andrei said. "They stood very confidently, with a feeling of secret power. If you stared at them, they didn't change their expression." On the other hand he made them an object of study—counting the number of different faces in his tail, figuring which shifts they worked and how many man-hours the whole business was taking. "Sometimes there would be three or four guys beside me and another three or four trailing us. They usually didn't try to be subtle; it was all aimed at intimidating me. They'd say, 'Don't walk so fast, we're tired.'" Sometimes he would turn on the speed to evade them; once after he succeeded briefly in doing so, one caught up and muttered in his ear, "Try to get away again and we'll tear your legs off." If someone stopped and chatted with him on the street—even if it happened to be a stranger asking the time—an agent would peel off and follow that person. When he stayed with friends they would await him in the street all night long, if necessary, replacing one another on four-hour shifts. Eight on a shift, say; six four-hour shifts: that would make forty-eight people in street observation alone. Later Andrei taunted his interrogators by saying that with the money spent on the investigation they could have built the "Mironov Kindergarten" and done Ustinov a great deal more good. But at the time the scale of the probe was a clear signal to Andrei that he was doomed: after such expenditure there would have to be an arrest.

Andrei was sometimes puzzled, sometimes complimented, by the scale of the KGB's drive against him. True, Razgulyai International was growing in size and reputation. "They were afraid of what it might become," Andrei said. "From one side it looked harmless—childish, almost stupid. But from another side, open, continuing contact between Russians and foreigners was not without dangers for them." At some point Andrei began to suspect what details of his own interrogations and those of his friends eventually proved: KGB counterespionage people got involved in the case, trying mightily to prove that he was spying for a Western country, most likely Germany. Andrei had been friendly with a German student at the Pushkin Institute named Volkmar Schmidt, with whom he had long conversations about Hitler and Stalin, and who was eventually expelled from the country. But the attempt went nowhere. In the end it was necessary to attribute Andrei Mironov's slanders not to a wallet fattened by the Western enemy but to his own Soviet mind. This was not an espionage case. This would have to be Article 70.

The most remarkable irony of the Mironov case was that while the state recognized Andrei as its enemy, it never understood just how subversive he was. Despite the energy of its shadows, its interrogations, and its searches, the KGB conducted such an incompetent investigation that it never cracked the samizdat ring. Andrei's friends lay low for a while after his arrest, but they soon resumed their photocopying and kept it up the whole time he was locked up. *"Tufta"*—bungling, Andrei fumed later about the KGB's workmanship, sounding for all the world like a taxpayer who felt he wasn't getting his money's worth. The old maxim of Soviet socialism—we pretend to work, and they pretend to pay us—at times extended to the secret police too.

The boys from the KGB did scrape together five fat volumes of evidence, enough for a respectable case against a thirty-one-year-old unknown. The files recorded Mironov's actions and contacts for months before his arrest. They diligently catalogued the incriminating material found during numerous searches—of the Mironovs' apartment, friends' and relatives' apartments, and even their little cottage a half-hour outside the city. Presumably the files included transcribed phone calls and chats at home; the family's phone had cut off inexplicably on occasion for months before and after the arrest, and Nikolai Alexeyevich once surprised a man in the stairwell as he climbed down from the vent to the duct leading to their kitchen.

The KGB interrogated dozens of Andrei's friends, relatives, co-workers, even grade-school teachers. They searched the Krasnogorsk home of Andrei's ailing eighty-four-year-old grandmother, who was distraught about his arrest and believed Andrei would not survive incarceration. They brought in Alexei Sukharev, a childhood friend who worked at a defense plant, for two long interrogations. "They started from far, far away. They wanted to know what, when, where about Andrei almost from infancy. They kept asking me questions about second grade," Sukharev told me in 1991. They scoured remembered conversations for hints of subversion.

Most important, while missing the forest they found some incriminating trees. They documented the fact that Andrei Mironov had himself read, and given to friends to read, two Russian-language books published abroad and banned in the USSR. One was Shalamov's *Kolyma Tales,* hard little gems of short stories documenting the Stalinist arctic camps. Andrei's Russian-language edition, published in Paris by the YMCA Press, was prefaced by a bitterly anti-Soviet essay by the exiled dissident Andrei Sinyavsky. The other book was *Socialism as a Phenomenon of World History* by Igor Shafarevich, which offered a slant on socialism somewhat different from one they had given at Pioneer camp. Shafarevich, a Moscow mathematician and one-time political associate of Alexander Solzhenitsyn, later discredited himself with a viciously anti-Semitic essay pinning all of Russia's woes on the Jews. But the socialism book bore no trace of such sentiments and offered a historical case that socialism was not the wave of the future but rather a kind of prefeudal collectivism.

Unlike Solzhenitsyn, Andrei Mironov could be fairly certain at the time of his arrest that he was not going to get a bullet in the back of his skull. But the incomplete de-Stalinization of the Khrushchev thaw, refrozen for the next two decades, had never freed the KGB and the criminal justice system of their grisly legacy. As a result, the spirit and many of the details of the Mironov case could have come from the Stalin era. The case showed that though the scale of terror was incomparably smaller, its essence survived into the mid-1980s: Gulag rubbed shoulders with glasnost. For Andrei's parents, his two brothers, and friends, the taint of association with a dissident affected their lives and their work. Long after her son had been released, Yevgeniya Semyonovna would weep, telling about the whole experience, and say, not altogether in the past tense: "It destroyed our lives."

One of Andrei's close friends, a Moscow chemist and amateur historian named Nikita Petrov, himself became the target of a criminal investigation after a search of his apartment turned up his files on the Stalin-era secret police. The books, documents, and notes he had accumulated in years of private research were confiscated, and he later learned that he escaped arrest by a hair's breadth.

Another friend, a Sverdlovsk filmmaker named Alexander Nagovitsyn, considered suicide as he weighed the betrayal of cooperation with the KGB against the cost to himself and his family of remaining silent. During four grueling interrogations at the Ustinov KGB—the first one lasting from 6 p.m. to 1 a.m.—KGB officers threatened Nagovitsyn with jail if he did not cooperate, describing in lurid detail how he would be raped and beaten behind bars by common criminals. He was terrified, he told me, so he tried to sound "loyal" while avoiding any admission that would seriously compromise Andrei. It was an agonizing balancing act. "I had this growing feeling of treachery that was almost unendurable," he said. Waiting alone in the third-floor interrogation room—and hearing from nearby the sound of real or staged beatings—he fought despair. "I thought constantly about jumping onto the balcony and screaming the truth down to the people on the street: 'This will happen to all of you, too!' I felt like throwing myself off the balcony, anything, to stop the interrogation," he said. He ended up enduring a so-called "comrade court" at the Sverdlovsk film studio, hearing his colleagues take turns denouncing him for his recklessness in associating with Citizen Mironov. Although he believed he would never be permitted to make another film, he felt only joy, he said—because the attacks showed he had not really betrayed his friend.

The conditions of Andrei's confinement also echoed the Stalin era. During his thirteen months in the Ustinov jail, Andrei was punished for his unrepentant attitude by being confined for a total of thirty-five days in the *kartser*, a tiny isolation cell so cold that winter that frost formed on the stone walls. "It was about the size of a grave, only deeper," Andrei said wryly. "A grave is only two meters deep; this was three meters." During the day there was no furniture. At night, for exactly eight hours, a guard brought in a steel-and-wood bench to sleep on. Reading and writing were not permitted. There was no toilet paper, and the toilet was a stinking hole in the floor. Every day Andrei received a piece of bread, often moldy, a pinch of salt, and three cupfuls of water; every other day this was supplemented with a bowl of watery soup with a few pieces of potato floating in it. His clothes were taken from him, and he was dressed in a jail outfit that offered little protection against the cold—a loose, papery nightshirt without buttons, and rubber shoes. He found it possible to sleep only about fifteen minutes before the chill awakened him; then he rose and ran in place to warm up. His hands shook violently. Once he lost consciousness and had to be taken to the jail physician to be revived. He was hungry, he said later, but it was the cold that he would never forget.

Beyond the horrors of the kartser, there was actual physical torture. In keeping with post-Stalinist decorum, however, it was carried out not by guards but by convicts, permitting the KGB and jail bosses officially to know nothing. Most of the ordinary criminals were respectful toward dissidents, because they too, for different reasons, considered themselves opponents of the system. "Kill Cops and Communists" was a common graffito on Soviet prison walls. But during Andrei's twenty-four-day trial, the KGB had him placed in what was known in jailhouse jargon as a "pressure cell" with two recidivists who, it became clear, had been ordered to keep him awake at night. For their trouble both were rewarded with extra food and, unlike their fellow prisoners, were permitted to sleep during the day. One, named Khlirullin, took the lead and seemed to take pleasure in his work; the other, Maltsev, was more timid and seemed to be strictly following orders. Khlirullin whiled away the hours lighting handfuls of mattress stuffing and throwing the flaming cotton at Andrei, yelling "Chemical warfare!" On other nights the convicts would beat him—but never on the face, where the bruises would be visible in court—or strangle him with a towel until he lost consciousness. Whenever Andrei dozed off, they would attack again.

The object was to leave him incapacitated by fatigue during long days of testimony and cross-examination. It worked. "The fire in the face, the strangling, all of that, I could stand. But sleep deprivation was intolerable," Andrei said. "The slightest noise was agonizing to my ears. The slightest light hurt my eyes. It was impossible to concentrate. I couldn't answer as I wished to; the words just would not come out right." Naturally, Andrei's eloquence could not influence the trial's outcome; the KGB never lost a case. But for the sake of Soviet and potentially Western public opinion, the authorities apparently wanted to prevent him from mounting a coherent and dignified defense. Andrei fought to maintain his composure and to get his points across, doing so with sufficient success to have the judge berate him repeatedly.

Whatever he wanted said in his own defense, explanation or justification, he had to say himself. After his arrest his parents had approached dozens of lawyers, asking them to take on Andrei's defense, but the attorneys invariably refused when they heard it was a KGB political case. "If it were murder, I'd take it, but not this," one man told them. "It wouldn't do him any good anyway." Another distinguished member of the bar asked them if they were Jewish. "Only Jews read this stuff," he said, referring to the banned books Andrei was accused of reading. Eventually they were forced to accept a court-appointed attorney, Irina Borzenkova, who spoke candidly of her admiration for Stalin and the need for a "tougher regime" and made no attempt to disguise her contempt for her client.

Some of Andrei's acquaintances who were called to testify held up bravely under cross-examination; others disappointed him by meekly allowing the prosecutor to lead them. The KGB had even tracked down a timorous grade-school teacher to attest to early signs of subversiveness in her former pupil. Showing off his Marxism, the judge interrupted her testimony with a question from Scientific

Communism class. "Do you believe that matter precedes consciousness?" the judge asked. The elderly teacher, baffled and scared,
leaned forward and asked him to repeat the question, which he did.
She paused to think but couldn't fathom what answer was required
of her. So she replied nervously: "Well, of course, I believe what all
normal Soviet people believe."

To bolster the case against him, the KGB arranged for some of
Andrei's cellmates to testify about what he allegedly had told them.
One was a character named Vodakshanov, nicknamed "Siberian,"
who had spent twenty-nine of his forty-three years locked up; he
had been used as a witness-to-order so many times that he could not
be sent to a labor camp or he would be killed. From time to time
during others' testimony, Vodakshanov would appear to be overcome
with patriotic indignation and declare, "I may be a criminal, but I'm
not like this traitor!" When his turn came, Vodakshanov was asked:
"What did Mironov say about Afghanistan?" He replied: "He said
he wanted to go to Afghanistan and kill our soldiers." It was a
laughable fabrication about Andrei, a gentle person who became a
favorite visitor for our two little daughters.

On April 2, 1986, more than a year after Gorbachev had come to
power, Andrei Mironov was sentenced by the Supreme Court of the
Udmurt Autonomous Soviet Socialist Republic to four years in a
strict-regime labor camp, to be followed by three years of exile. But
the penal system was in no hurry to move him from the jail in
Ustinov. Only in September was he transported to a camp called
Dubrovlag in a locked train car that followed a circuitous, eleven-
day route hitched to a series of freight, postal, and passenger trains.
Dubrovlag was actually a chain of a dozen camps off a rail line built
by prisoners beginning shortly after the Revolution in the autonomous republic of Mordovia, another region in the Russian heartland.
One acquaintance questioned by the KGB remembered an agent
remarking long before Andrei's trial, "We're sending him to Du-
brovka," the nickname for Dubrovlag; evidently his case had been
scripted well in advance. In his memoirs Andrei Sakharov gives a
striking account of the trip to Dubrovlag, which he visited in 1977
in an unsuccessful attempt to see an imprisoned dissident. "The
world seems to alter mysteriously as you leave Potma [on the last leg

of the train journey]. Colors fade; bright hues give way to greys and browns. People's voices seem—or perhaps they are—vicious and grating. The camps...along both sides of the right-of-way bear a close resemblance to the German concentration camps familiar from war photos and films....Each camp zone comprises a rectangle surrounded by a high grey fence topped with barbed wire. Watchtowers at the corners are manned by guards with submachine guns. Just inside the fence is a 'forbidden zone' of plowed earth followed by another fence of barbed wire, and then, at the center, are rows of long, low barracks, single-story grey-plank buildings with darkened windows. The whole scene is illuminated by the lifeless glare of spotlights attached to tall posts."

Andrei Mironov's specific camp was called, in Gulag code, ZhKh-385/3-5: the Russian letters Zh and Kh stood for the words "railroad enterprise," a euphemistic name designating, along with the number 385, the rail line along which the camps were located; 3 stood for "third zone," or camp; 5 meant "fifth sector," or camp section. ZhKh-385/3-5 held about sixty prisoners, half of them sentenced, like Andrei, under Article 70; the other half had been convicted of treason, either for alleged collaboration during World War II or for attempting to leave the USSR illegally. Because the camp was for political prisoners, not ordinary criminals, there was no violence, less tension, and better relations among inmates than in the Ustinov jail. Still, camp officials did not like Andrei's defiant attitude, and he was often sent to the camp's solitary punishment cell, known as the *shizo,* where conditions were tough but not nearly as brutal as in the kartser in Ustinov. "I didn't repent," he said. "They wanted me to repent, and I didn't repent. That was the main thing."

For Andrei's parents, the months of his incarceration were a time of frantic despair. They were not allowed to visit. Jail officials turned away their food packets. Even in the 1980s, they knew, prisoners occasionally died in custody, of untreated medical problems exacerbated by the rigors of incarceration, in attacks by other inmates, or in "accidents" staged by guards. At the time of Andrei's transfer to Dubrovlag, Colonel Zakirov, the jail director, complained to Andrei's parents about his provocative manner. "If he doesn't change his behavior, he'll never leave the camp alive," he told them.

Meanwhile, the Ministry of Geology organized meetings to inform the Mironovs' fellow employees that their son's anti-Soviet activity had been exposed. Ritual denunciations followed. But Yevgeniya Semyonovna was surprised that a number of her co-workers, including a few she hadn't known, approached her quietly to express their sympathy and support. In three interrogations she kept her promise to herself that she would not cry in front of the KGB officers. She was more concerned about her husband, who suffered from high blood pressure, had had one stroke, and found it difficult to sit for long. But Nikolai Alexeyevich weathered a dozen interrogations and kept his spirit: in a small gesture of contempt he refused to sign the official protocols of his interrogations. Between visits to the KGB Nikolai Alexeyevich spent many hours in official waiting rooms, making the rounds of party bosses, prosecutors, parliamentary deputies—anyone who might be in a position to intervene in his son's case. At best he got a polite brush-off; at worst he was treated like a criminal himself. Once, at local party headquarters, an earnest police officer assigned to watch over him had actually followed him into the men's room. If the crime was political—if it concerned not theft or assault but books and ideas—no official would touch it.

Yet even as the Mironovs were rebuffed in Ustinov, unfamiliar winds were blowing from Moscow. Given the timing of Andrei's arrest and trial, the Mironovs had not been inclined to place much hope in Mikhail Gorbachev, the party apparatchik who had become Soviet leader the previous year at the astonishingly early age of fifty-four. But now Gorbachev was cautiously easing up on control of the media. Exposés of social problems and mild criticism of official policies were beginning to turn up in the official press. With every month the borders of the printable were pushed back a little further. The advent of glasnost, which millions watched with growing excitement, evoked a mixture of hope and fury in the Mironovs. The critical opinions appearing in print promised that cases like Andrei's might be reviewed. But the changes also made his imprisonment seem all the more unjust.

In the Russian tradition of centralized rule and the ultimate authority of the top leader, people with grievances often had appealed directly to the tsar. Under Soviet rule, justice-seekers, or *pravdaiskateli,* came from the provinces and languished in Moscow train and bus stations for months on end, hoping for an audience with high officials. Now Yevgeniya Semyonovna directed one of her many handwritten appeals to the very top, to the man whose new policy of glasnost seemed so at odds with the punishment of her son:

To the General Secretary, CC-CPSU,
Gorbachev, Mikhail Sergeyevich

From Mironova, Yevgeniya Semyonovna,
Residing at: City of Ustinov, Kommunarov Street, House 222, Apartment 37

10 October 1986

Statement

7 August 1985 my son Mironov, Andrei Nikolayevich, year of birth 1954, was arrested. He was charged under Article 70, Part 1, of the Criminal Code of the RSFSR....

He is accused in connection with things that all our newspapers have written about during the last two years....

In twenty-eight pages of cramped handwriting, Yevgeniya Semyonovna detailed violations of legal procedure she had documented in Andrei's case. Then she put together a sort of anthology of early glasnost, pairing phrases from the accusations against Andrei with the latest news clippings. She quoted, for instance, Andrei's supposedly seditious opinion that "Corruption is flourishing" and replied: "There have been many newspaper articles about corruption and the reasons for its emergence and spread. (*Literaturnaya Gazeta:* 7 May 1986, 'Ability to live?' by Y. Andryushenko, department chief, Institute of Sociological Research, USSR Academy of Sciences. *Literaturnaya Gazeta:* 16 July 1986, Yuri Shchekochikhin, 'Commentary on a Request for Pardon')."

Or another of Andrei's slanders, "Party influence on the development of art and the censorship of the press," Yevgeniya Semyonovna
answered, "On this question as well in all the papers have been
published many articles of writers and journalists. *Sovietskaya Rossiya,* 23 February 1986...."

But all her trips to the library, all her culling of daring moments
from the papers, all her letters and appeals, seemed to count for
nothing. The appeal to Gorbachev was answered like all the others,
with reflex denials from a low rung on the bureaucratic ladder.
"Your appeal of [date] on the case of Mironov A. N. has been
reviewed," read a typical reply. "No basis has been found for further
action at this time."

Doubtless the clerks who read her letters in various offices had
merely to notice that she was referring to an Article 70 case before
they could punch out the requisite reply. But if they had read over
Andrei Mironov's twenty-three-page official sentence, it would likely
only have strengthened their conviction that justice had been done.
True enough, the press, under the guidance of the party, was
growing more critical, less slavishly accepting of every claim and act
of the bureaucracy. But this Mironov was charged with expressing
and spreading news far more slanderous than anything that could be
tolerated in a newspaper. Indeed, the official sentence is a remarkable document—if anything, more striking today than it was then,
though for different reasons. It should speak for itself.

"Mironov A. N.," the sentence began, "systematically listened to
broadcasts of foreign radio stations, including subversive ones, became acquainted with literature published abroad, and entered into
contact with foreigners and people with negative views of Soviet
reality....Mironov A. N. conducted anti-Soviet agitation and propaganda with the aim of undermining and weakening Soviet power,
spreading slanderous fabrications, discrediting the Soviet state and
social system."

The "slanderous fabrications," according to the sentence, covered
the whole landscape of Soviet policy, from Stalinism to Afghanistan,
from elections to the economy.

Mironov, the sentence said, spread the views expressed in the
Shalamov book, "in which the difficult period in the life of the

country in the 1930s and 40s is treated as slavery and equated with fascism." Mironov "declared that the Soviet economy is on the verge of collapse." Speaking of Afghanistan, "he called our aid an intervention." He "talked about how our elections are not free, because one candidate is nominated for one seat." He denounced "the absence in our country of democracy, personal rights and freedoms." He spoke of "the superiority of the West, including in the area of health care."

What made him most dangerous, the sentence made clear, was that he had insisted on expressing such opinions publicly. "The views of Mironov," the sentence declared, "could change the convictions of another person."

On January 17, 1987, eighteen months after his arrest, Andrei Mironov and several dozen of his fellow political prisoners were driven from the Dubrovlag camp to a jail in Saransk, the nearest city. No one would tell them why, but their new diet was a tip-off. "They fed us better than the residents of Saransk," Andrei said. "They bought us meat, milk, butter—with our money, it's true—but they'd buy whatever we asked for. These KGB guys were running everywhere for us."

Two weeks later the prosecutor's office in Ustinov suddenly dispatched a car to pick up Andrei's father and chauffeur him to the same office building where earlier he had made his fruitless appeals. The same officials who had previously walked by him without speaking or peremptorily refused to take his calls greeted him like a long-lost friend. Their obsequiousness, Nikolai Alexeyevich said later, was at once exhilarating, since it promised a break in the case, and revolting. One official remarked that Andrei was "a real intellectual," a son of whom Nikolai Alexeyevich must be proud.

In the Saransk jail a different message was conveyed. A representative of the prosecutor general's office in Moscow visited to urge the political prisoners not to blab to the press, especially the foreign press, about their cases or conditions in the camps. They could be rearrested for slander, he told them, and locked up with

common criminals. "You could get your throats cut," the prosecutor
said.

On February 4, 1987, Mr. Mironov was driven to the Ustinov
airport in a black Volga and flown to Saransk to meet Andrei, who
was released with a large cohort of Article 70 prisoners. Together
Andrei and his father took the overnight train to Moscow. They
spotted KGB plainclothesmen lurking aboard the train but concluded that the agents were there mainly to protect the political
ex-convicts from the vagaries of Soviet train travel. At this point,
after all, a drunk hitting an ex-prisoner with a bottle could create an
international scandal. They made it without incident.

Nikolai Alexeyevich left his son in the capital and flew home to
Ustinov on an air ticket thoughtfully provided gratis by the prosecutor who had overseen his son's prosecution in 1985.

Transported from the silence of the camp to the cacophony of
Moscow, where he was suddenly news for sensation-hungry foreign
correspondents, Andrei found himself disoriented. His freedom was
prima facie evidence that real political change was underway. Yet he
had plenty of reason to be skeptical. "My mood was good, but there
were a lot of mysteries," he recalled. "We didn't know what they'd
do with us—maybe rearrest us, maybe send us to the West." He got
to know other former political prisoners and dissidents, talked
strategy for the human rights movement, established contacts with
the foreign press. With the barbed wire of the camp just a few
weeks behind him, he found himself one day in a dissident's Moscow
apartment facing a small army of journalists from around the world,
jostling for space between the television cameras. No one interfered
with the ex-prisoners' press conference. But when Andrei left a few
hours later, his practiced eye noticed a contradictory fact: KGB tails
were following him again.

The especially dangerous state criminal, author of slanderous
fabrications, was free. The Soviet Union seemed to be teetering on
the precipice of momentous change. What were the rules in this
strange, new world?

2

Information Control and the Soviet Crisis

AUTHOR: I have here, my dear sir, a book which I wish to print.
CENSOR: It must be scrutinized before it can be printed. And what is the title, may I ask?
AUTHOR: It is called Truth, good sir.
CENSOR: Truth! Oh! We shall have to scrutinize it very thoroughly.
—from a satirical piece by Russian journalist Ivan Petrovich Pnin, circa 1810

If they don't understand that we are bringing them mathematically flawless happiness, it is our duty to force them to be happy. But before we use our weapons, we will try words.
—*We,* by Yevgeny Zamyatin, an anti-utopian vision of a future world state, written in 1920 and banned in the Soviet Union

In 1983 Mikhail Gorbachev and two other top officials who were analyzing the country's deepening economic quagmire went to Soviet leader Yuri Andropov to ask for hard data on the national budget—in particular, about defense spending. Gorbachev was the

Politburo's wunderkind, chairing meetings of the powerful Central Committee secretariat in Andropov's absence and already being touted by perceptive Sovietologists as heir to the throne. On top of this he enjoyed a twenty-year personal friendship with Andropov. Gorbachev was accompanied by Nikolai Ryzhkov, the future prime minister. A successful industrial manager promoted by Andropov for economic troubleshooting, Ryzhkov was chief of the Central Committee's economic department. Vladimir Dolgikh, the third official, was the Politburo's man in charge of heavy industry. In short, all three were in the Kremlin's innermost circle, at the center of power in a land where power was hypercentralized.

Yet Andropov, according to Gorbachev, flatly refused to give them the information. "He said we younger ones were poking around where we shouldn't be. That it was none of our business," Gorbachev recounted to a meeting of industrial bosses in December 1990.

How could three officials at the very pinnacle of state economic management—in a *planned* economy, after all—operate without fundamental information on the budget? If it was none of their business, whose business was it? Only Andropov's? Did his successor at the KGB have the information? The minister of defense? Or is it possible that reliable information on defense spending did not exist at all?

The story captures the fatal predicament of the Soviet leadership: their tight grip on information was a key source of their power, but by the 1980s it had become a crippling handicap for themselves and their country. The entire Soviet Union, this sprawling empire of twelve time zones, 110 official ethnic groups, and 287 million people, was operated on a need-to-know basis, and the assumption was that few people needed to know very much. The strictures on information that sent Andrei Mironov and thousands like him to labor camps in the post-Stalin era were, in certain circumstances, manacles even for the most powerful.

The secrecy and censorship, banning and jamming that fenced the Soviet citizenry off from the truth about their own history and the outside world had long been viewed in the Kremlin as a necessary bulwark against subversion. And it was true that on occasion, in this oft-invaded country, secrecy had paid off. In 1941 the maps of the

German invaders proved disastrously unreliable once they penetrated beyond the air reconnaissance zone a hundred miles or so inside the Soviet border. But technology had remade the world since then. The trappings of information control were so pervasive and seemed so archaic that for many Westerners they had come to define the regime. Banned books, bugged telephones, travel prohibitions, political prisoners, the Gulag—all held a morbid fascination for outsiders.

Gorbachev, inheriting from Andropov a mandate for change but no coherent program, understood that information control had become a blindfold for the regime. As a loyal apparatchik through the long twilight of self-delusion that was the latter half of Leonid Brezhnev's eighteen-year rule, Gorbachev knew the Communist party had been holding up a gaudy and fantastic oil painting to the country and pretending it was a mirror.

He knew, too, that even as the Soviet Union had matched or outpaced the United States by certain older indicators of industrial production, the rules of economic competition had been transformed. Prosperity would be determined less by mega-industry on the Stalinist model than by information technology. Success would be measured not in steel beams but in silicon chips.

Encouraged by a few of his own advisers and certain Western contacts, Gorbachev seized upon information as reality therapy, a lever to pry loose an encrusted and immobile bureaucracy, and as a new commodity as crucial to the global economy as oil. He gradually eased the myriad controls on access to information and the technology that moves it.

In 1988, 1989, and 1990 Moscow factory drudges and Harvard Kremlinologists alike contrasted the thriving vitality of the liberated media to the steady shrinkage of the economy and declared that Gorbachev's only achievement at home was glasnost. "To read is very interesting, to live is not so interesting," grumbled a Moscow film critic in the summer of 1988. Such comments were meant to be dismissive. In fact, curtailing information control would turn out to be Gorbachev's greatest domestic achievement, as his unilateral steps toward disarmament and the end of cold war would be his greatest achievement in foreign policy. The protean power of information loosed by Gorbachev would quickly take on independent life, reproducing and spreading at a pace and on a scale and with consequences that he neither anticipated nor desired.

Coming to power in 1985, Gorbachev faced "the dilemma of the reforming despot"—the resonant phrase of the historian James H. Billington for the predicament of the Romanov tsars: "How can one retain absolute power and a hierarchical social system while at the same time introducing reforms and encouraging education? How can an absolute ruler hold out hope for improvement without confronting a 'revolution of rising expectations'?" This time the answer was: He couldn't. Gorbachev's experiment with information produced just such a revolution, thus proving fatal to his party, his country, and his own political career.

In September 1826 the Russian poet Alexander Pushkin was summoned to Moscow and rushed under escort to the Kremlin to meet with Tsar Nicholas I. The ruler of Russia was in a magnanimous mood. He informed the astonished poet that from now on he would not have to submit his work to the official government censor. The emperor himself would censor all of Pushkin's poems.

In the ensuing days Pushkin happened to read the manuscript of his new verse drama, *Boris Godunov,* aloud to groups of friends in private homes. Count Alexander Beckendorff, chief of the Third Department of His Majesty's Own Chancery, the tsarist secret police, got wind of the readings and reprimanded Pushkin for reading the play in public before the emperor had censored it. A chastened Pushkin duly sent along his only copy of the manuscript for imperial blue-penciling, accompanied by a note saying he had read the unexpurgated work "not out of disobedience, of course, but only because I had not clearly understood the Emperor's exalted wishes." An article Pushkin wrote on government orders came back via Beckendorff with Nicholas I's telling annotation: "Answer him, thanking him for this paper, but point out to him that the principle he advances to the effect that education and genius are everything is a dangerous one for all governments; one which has actually led him to the edge of the abyss."

To understand the roots of pervasive Soviet controls on information and the consequences of their removal at the end of the 1980s, it is necessary to reach back a century or two into pre-Soviet history. When printed literature was the sole form of mass information, Russian rulers paid it close and nervous attention. The extraordinary tale of Pushkin and the tsar is only a celebrated instance of a long-lived phenomenon: the fear, and respect, shown by rulers toward writers.

Thirty-six years before the Pushkin incident, in 1790, Alexander Radishchev, a courtier and customs official, had published a long social and political critique under the title *A Journey from Petersburg to Moscow.* Catherine the Great reportedly grew furious after reading only the first thirty pages, summoned an aide, and ordered Radishchev arrested immediately. She wrote detailed notes on the book's contents, concluding that "the purpose of this book is clear on every page: the author...is trying in every possible way to break down respect for authority and for the authorities, to stir up in the people indignation against their superiors and against the government." Radishchev was condemned by a court to decapitation; the sovereign commuted the sentence to perpetual banishment to Siberia. He was released after Catherine's death but committed suicide about a year after achieving full rehabilitation. His martyrdom was promoted by later generations of Russian intelligentsia, and dissidents in the Communist era would occasionally cite Radishchev's *Journey* as a precursor of samizdat.

As censorship eroded or was abolished in the West, the Russian monarchy clung to it, codified it, and relied on it as a bulwark against the spread of foreign freethinking and revolution. Words in Russian culture came to be invested with a special force, regarded by rulers as a kind of moral and political dynamite that could be kept under safe control only by powerful police bureaucracies. In the index to Prince D. S. Mirsky's classic history of Russian literature through 1900 are some thirty references under the entry for "censorship."

The Marquis de Custine, a shrewd French diplomat whose reports on his 1839 travels still make fascinating reading, was astonished by the Russians' restrictions on information. "Let but the liberty of the press be accorded to Russia for twenty four hours," he wrote, "and we should learn things that would make us recoil with horror. Silence is indispensable to oppression. Under an absolute government every indiscretion of speech is equivalent to a crime of high treason." Custine quoted a Russian nobleman whom he protected, in a practice often used by the Moscow correspondents of the next century, by identifying him only by initial as Prince K. "Russian despotism," the anonymous prince told Custine, "not only pays little respect to ideas and sentiments, it will also deny facts; it will struggle against evidence, and triumph in the struggle! For evidence, when it is inconvenient to power, has no more voice among us than has justice."

The tsars did not have to worry about shortwave radio, photocopiers, or computers. But it is interesting to note that the communications technology of earlier times made reactionaries uneasy. In 1835 the Russian minister of finance opposed building a comprehensive rail network, saying it was unnecessary, costly, and might undermine public morals. Railways encouraged "frequent purposeless travel, thus fostering the restless spirit of our age," he said. The economic pressure to adopt this threatening new technology nonetheless grew so strong as to overwhelm the government's political qualms. In a pattern of technological borrowing familiar throughout Russian history, Russia's first major rail line, linking St. Petersburg and Moscow, was built between 1842 and 1851 to the design of American engineers and with the financial backing of American capital.

The influence of nonmilitary technology on history is often subtle and debatable. Yet it is beyond dispute that the railroads played a significant role in the political ferment that culminated with the end of Romanov rule in the February Revolution of 1917. Revolutionaries in different cities and regions, who once might have lived and died ignorant of one another, were linked by the ease of travel and correspondence into national movements. Subversive tracts reached the literate population rapidly, and illegally, by train.

When Lenin was sent into Siberian exile in 1897, he traveled nearly the whole way on the newly constructed Trans-Siberian Railroad, which cut mail transit time between Moscow or St. Petersburg and the village of his exile to about fifteen days. His sister, Anna, kept him supplied via the railroad with the latest newspapers, journals, and books; by return train came a steady flow of Marxist tracts and articles which were published in St. Petersburg under the pseudonyms "Tulin" and "Ilin." Meanwhile the Russian railroad kept expanding, its mileage across the empire doubling between 1895 and 1905, the year of the first abortive revolution. It is an apt symbol that when Lenin returned from Europe in 1917 to take charge of the Bolsheviks, he came by train, disembarking at St. Petersburg's Finland Station. Perhaps the doomsaying bureaucrats of the 1830s, so reminiscent of the reactionary Communists ranting against glasnost in the 1980s, were right about the fatal consequences of technological change for the old order?

In the old debate over the watershed of 1917, the Bolsheviks themselves and their bitterest enemies, ironically enough, agreed on one thing: the Soviet Union was a new creation that had nothing in common with tsarist Russia. The above brief excursion into Russian history suggests just the opposite—that the "world's first socialist country" carried a great deal of baggage into the new age. Among the heaviest was the regime's sensitivity to the threat posed by literature, information, and technology.

But tsarist repression was to Stalinist repression as the blunderbusses of Nicholas I were to Stalin's nuclear weapons: they had the same goal, but their scale and consequences were hardly comparable. Vladimir Nabokov was not just speaking out of emigré nostalgia when he remarked in the late 1950s that while in the nineteenth century "books and writers might be banned and banished, censors might be rogues and fools, bewhiskered Tsars might stamp and storm; but that wonderful discovery of Soviet times, the method of making the entire literary corporation write what the state deems fit—this method was unknown in old Russia." Nineteenth-century Russian writers, Nabokov wrote, were "quite certain that they lived in a country of oppression and slavery, but they had something one can appreciate only now, namely, the immense advantage over their grandsons in modern Russia of not being compelled to say that there was no oppression and no slavery."

Nabokov was onto something important in identifying what he called the "happy agreement between the poet and the policeman" in the USSR. A number of critical factors distinguished Soviet from tsarist censorship practices. First was the Bolsheviks' stunning success in expanding literacy. The tsars might be upset by the Radishchevs and Pushkins of their day, but there was no danger that the empire's illiterate masses would ever be able to read their books. At the time of the Revolution less than half the population could read. By the census of 1939, 81.1 percent were recorded as literate. By the 1970s all but a tiny percentage of the population were able to read. Because it could reach directly a far larger audience than in the last century, subversive literature posed a far more serious political threat.

Second, the Communists had seized power in a coup d'état. They accordingly never ceased to look over their shoulders for hints of the sort of underground activity with which they or their predecessors had ousted the Romanovs. Much of that activity, celebrated in countless Soviet agitprop books and movies, consisted of the secret printing of incendiary literature. In his famous 1902 tract *What Is to Be Done?*, Lenin spoke of the role he had in mind for a revolutionary newspaper: "This newspaper would become a part of an enormous bellows that would blow every spark of class struggle and popular indignation into a general conflagration." After his newspaper, *Iskra* (The Spark), had indeed helped touch off the conflagration that brought him to power, Lenin's approach accordingly shifted: "Why should freedom of speech and freedom of the press be allowed? Why should a government which is doing what it believes is right allow itself to be criticized? It would not allow opposition by lethal weapons. Ideas are much more fatal things than guns."

Third, the Soviets had a messianic ideology, a supreme goal of world revolution, the end of exploitation, the shriveling of the state, and general abundance and eternal happiness for all. The tsars, for the most part, cared only about preserving and expanding their wealth, their power, and their empire. The Bolsheviks, with their more ambitious plans, could afford far greater sacrifices along the way. Solzhenitsyn puts it starkly: "The imagination and spiritual strength of Shakespeare's evildoers stopped short at a dozen corpses. Because they had no *ideology*.... Thanks to *ideology,* the twentieth century was fated to experience evildoing on a scale calculated in the millions." Nicholas I and his Third Department were a nasty piece of work, but it is hard to imagine the earnest editor of Pushkin declaring, as Stalin did, that writers must be "the engineers of human souls."

All this added up to a feeling of vulnerability to information on the part of the Soviet rulers even greater than that of the tsars, and a willingness to use unprecedented expenditure and violence to suppress it. Stalin's personal telephone calls to such Russian writers as Mikhail Bulgakov and Boris Pasternak were legendary, and the analogy with Pushkin and Nicholas I is irresistible. But Pushkin could not have said, as did the great Soviet-era poet Osip Mandelstam, "Only in our country is poetry respected—they'll kill you for it. Only in our country, and no other." Mandelstam's own death, of starvation and exhaustion at a Gulag transit-point in 1938, served tragically to prove his point.

"Truth is good," says an old Russian proverb, "but happiness is better." Embellishing dreary reality is an old Russian tradition, the most notorious instance being the façades of prosperous villages erected in 1787 in advance of a riverboat tour by Catherine the Great at the instructions of her lover and courtier, Prince Gregory Potemkin. But the Potemkin villages were a temporary job.

From the Revolution on, the Bolshevik regime built its prestige and power on myth. Legend plays a role in the imagined past of every country; Americans have (or had) their storybook savage Indians and happy slaves to help ease the national conscience. But in Soviet Russia the myths were peculiarly pervasive and central, and censorship backed by terror protected them from public challenge.

The real Russian Revolution, after all, was the popular rising in February 1917 which ended the Romanov monarchy; the Bolsheviks simply took advantage of the ensuing chaos to seize power in

October 1917 in a nearly bloodless coup. Yet it was the Great *October* Socialist Revolution that was celebrated every November 7 (by the new calendar), as tanks rolled through Red Square followed by workers clutching paper carnations, shouting "Oorah!" on cue, and waving to their beloved Politburo atop Lenin's mausoleum.

Indeed, "Lenin" was in fact Vladimir Ulyanov, son of a tsarist school inspector, who took his pseudonym from the Siberian river Lena. "Stalin" was Josef Dzhugashvili, a one-time Georgian theology student who took his name from the Russian word for steel, *stal,* the root meaning of Dzhugashvili in Georgian. The Bolsheviks preserved their pseudonyms, which had been functional when they were conspiring against the tsar, for leadership and history. The choice seems to foreshadow the regime's continuing penchant for using language to disguise human imperfection and failure. Under Soviet power most cities and streets were renamed, and scarcely a Bolshevik was too minor to have his name attached to a place. By the 1980s cities listed in the Soviet atlas included thirteen Leninskoyes, ten Leninskys, six Leninos, five Leninsks, two Lenins, two Leninabads, two Leningrads, two Leninogorsks, and one each Leninism, Leninka, Leninkent, and Leninpol. One could find the center of the capital city of any Soviet republic by following Lenin Prospekt to Lenin Square.

In the 1930s, when the Great Depression seemed to betray a fundamental flaw in capitalism, many Western intellectuals were captivated by the spectacular promise of the Bolsheviks' mythmaking. One was the French writer André Gide. In 1936, when Gide visited the country he had been praising from afar, it was the regime's use of language that set him on a course to disillusion. Touring the southern resorts of Stalin's native Georgia in a luxury train car, he did not know much about the government-created famine that had taken as many as seven million lives a few years earlier, or of the beginnings of the Great Terror that would take several million more. His doubts grew from a more modest seed. When Gide tried to send a telegram of thanks to Stalin, his translator objected to his reference to the leader as "you" ("in the course of our wonderful journey, I feel the need to send you my most cordial…"). Gide watched, amazed, as his squad of official

Soviet companions argued what phrase should be appended: "You, leader of the workers," "You, father of the peoples," or something still more grandiloquent. On another occasion he was informed that he would have to add the word "glorious" to a speech text referring to "the destiny of the Soviet Union." The country's destiny could only be glorious—in language, whether or not in fact.

Something strange happened to language under Soviet-style socialism. Vaclav Havel, Czechoslovakia's playwright-turned-dissident-turned-president, described it in a thoughtful essay in 1965. The heel of the Soviet boot on Havel's country was so heavy that what he says can be applied without adjustment to the Soviet Union. He decried the "conventionalized, pseudo-ideological thinking" that "without our noticing it, separated thought from its immediate contact with reality." Havel attributed this break with reality to what he called "a ritualization of language. From being a means of signifying reality, and of enabling us to come to an understanding of it, language seems to have become an end in itself.... Notice, for example, how often the words we use these days are more important than what we are talking about. The word—as such—has ceased to be a sign for a category, and has gained a kind of occult power to transform one reality into another."

Havel here is analyzing what Gide experienced: that what came to matter was not the nation's destiny but the phrase "glorious destiny." If before, reality preceded language, now language preceded reality, and reality was burdened with the impossible task of always catching up. This is a phenomenon familiar to the student of bureaucracy in any country, and Americans have in recent years a missile named Peacemaker and taxes called "revenue enhancements." But as in other areas, the Soviet Union took the natural traits of any bureaucracy and elevated them to the level of ersatz national culture. In the absence of the competition (except for the dissidents' collective whisper) provided elsewhere by free media and political opposition, bureaucratic language had free rein in cloaking and distorting reality.

It took any foreigner a while to realize that the words *propaganda* and *propagandist* in official Soviet Russian were not pejorative, as they are in English. People would not say, dismissively, "That's just a bunch of propaganda." On the contrary, you could find in a Soviet political dictionary a long, admiring entry on *propagandisti* devoid of any hint of embarrassment. "The February (1988) Plenum of the Central Committee of the Communist Party gave a high assessment of the results of the activity carried out by propagandists, lecturers, and ideological workers. 'By means of their words, the ideas of the Party, the ideas of the renewal of society are conquering the hearts and minds of people,' emphasized M. S. Gorbachev." Indeed, the dictionary said, in 1987 no fewer than 2.5 million propagandists, volunteer and professional, were at work in the Soviet Union—about the number of all the teachers in U.S. public schools.

In the Soviet lexicon that this army of propagandists was paid to elaborate, Marxism-Leninism was a science—one so powerful that it could not only analyze the past but predict the future. As the natural sciences had taken the terror out of sunrise and thunderstorms, so Marxism brought rationality to the far more mysterious laws of human social and economic behavior. "The Marxist science of the laws of social development," said an authoritative Soviet text in the usual cinderblock prose of such works, "enables us not only to chart a correct path through the labyrinth of social contradictions, but to predict the course events will take, the direction of historical progress and the next stage of social advance." Every university student took a course called "Scientific Communism." The revolution had vanquished superstition, they learned, and religion would die out within a few generations.

But as Freud taught—though not in the Soviet Union, where his works were banned until 1989—what is repressed has a tendency to exact revenge. The vehement assertion of scientific method itself betrayed the Soviet ideologists' worry that they had merely created another faith; Harvard Business School never offered mandatory courses on "Scientific Capitalism." Evidence to justify their fears was all around them. The antireligious Soviet state kept the body of its saint-founder, Ulyanov-Lenin, miraculously preserved in a granite temple in a holy place guarded by the most trusted soldiers. Pilgrims came in their millions to gaze and pay homage. The founder's sacred writings were quoted to settle all arguments and chart the nation's future, even six decades after his death. Heretics were warned and counseled, and if they failed to change their false teachings they were severely persecuted. Heathens from other nations were admitted only with escorts, watched and followed to mitigate their subversive influence. Only devout believers were permitted to travel abroad, for others might succumb to the allure of the rival faith of capitalism.

From the beginning the Soviet regime was built on a system of belief, a mythology that citizens learned from earliest childhood and that suffused every aspect of life. Soviet nine-year-olds were given a book about Lenin called *Our Very Best Friend,* marking their entry into the Pioneers. Its 1978 edition told them: "We see how day by day, hour by hour, with enthusiasm, joy and pride the Soviet people are building the radiant edifice of Communism. You, kids, also will build Communist society, and not only build but work under Communism."

Early in the Gorbachev era Robert Kaiser wrote a perceptive essay labeling this flaunted faith as "the Soviet pretense," which he defined as "official confidence in the superiority of the Soviet system and in the certain victory of socialism over capitalism." He accurately identified the explosive nature of glasnost by saying it was threatening to undermine precisely this legend. I would adjust Kaiser's thesis in one respect: I would call the phenomenon "the Soviet illusion" rather than "the Soviet pretense." To the West it may have looked like pretense. To most of those living inside the pretense, to a greater or lesser degree, it was an illusion.

At least from the early 1960s on this mythology, this Soviet illusion, was increasingly vulnerable to puncture: many builders of the radiant edifice of communism, after all, were spending their lives on waiting lists for the dark, crumbling buildings of socialism. If under Stalin there was terror to back up belief, and therefore belief did not matter so much, now the fear was subsiding and belief was consequently more important. The more vulnerable the regime felt, the greater the urgency of its efforts at information control.

The regime's reaction to certain major literary works dramatized its feeling of vulnerability. Boris Pasternak's novel *Doctor Zhivago* was by no means an anti-Communist tract, but it was banned from publication. In 1958 Pasternak handed the manuscript over to a visiting Italian publisher with a remark that captured the predicament of the writer seeking readers under Soviet totalitarianism: "You have invited me to take part in my own execution." Indeed, the runaway success of the novel in the West and the award of the Nobel Prize to its author provoked such a storm of invective from on high aimed at Pasternak that he rejected the prize. Yet on the day he turned it down, Vladimir Semichastny, then leader of the Komsomol and future chief of the KGB, made a public speech declaring: "If we compare Pasternak with a pig...then we have to say that a pig will never do what he has done. Pasternak has fouled the spot where he ate and messed on those by whose labor he lives and breathes." This vulgar attack met with enthusiastic applause from Khrushchev and the rest of the top leadership.

Or consider one of the greatest Soviet novels, one too little known in the West, Vasily Grossman's *Life and Fate.* Born in 1905, Vasily Semyonovich Grossman for many years was a proficient but unremarkable practitioner of socialist realism whose works did not challenge the system in any way. He won a national reputation for his war reporting for the army newspaper *Krasnaya Zvezda* (Red Star); he wrote searing eyewitness accounts of the battle of Stalingrad and the Nazi death camp at Treblinka. At the height of Khrushchev's thaw in 1961, he finished *Life and Fate,* an epic of *War and Peace* scale that deliberately asserts the moral equivalence of Nazism and Stalinism. With naive hope, Grossman gave it to the literary monthly *Znamya* (Banner), whose editors not only rejected it but turned it over to the KGB. In July 1962 Grossman appealed the ban to the party's chief ideologist, the éminence grise Mikhail Suslov, in the Kremlin. According to Grossman's notes, Suslov told him that though he had not read *Life and Fate* himself, he knew it could not be published because he had been informed of its comparisons of Stalinism and Hitlerism, its positive comments about religion, its neutral mention of Trotsky, and so on. Suslov said the novel could not be published "for at least two hundred years" because it was so dangerous to the Soviet state. "For all who have read your book, for all who are familiar with the responses to it, it is completely beyond question that the harm from the book *Life and Fate* would be incomparably more dangerous for us than *Doctor Zhivago,*" Suslov told him. The orders accordingly went out to destroy every copy of the novel, and the KGB apparently thought it had succeeded. It was saved from annihilation by a single microfiche copy preserved by Grossman's friends, smuggled to the West by an Austrian diplomat, and eventually published abroad in Russian, French, and English. Anyone who reads *Life and Fate* today will find passages of remarkable relevance to the Gorbachev era, beginning with the discussion of the press printed as a frontispiece to this book.

Or consider Alexander Solzhenitsyn's majestic *Gulag Archipelago,* which documents with excruciating precision the Leninist and Stalinist terror. Having failed to prevent its composition and publication abroad at the end of 1973, despite the energetic efforts of an army of KGB informants, harassers, and thieves, the regime threw its resources into a grand-scale campaign of denunciation and slander, culminating in Solzhenitsyn's deportation in February 1974. Five years earlier, after being expelled from the Writers' Union, Solzhenitsyn had used an interesting word in his furious written reply to the union's secretariat: "*Glasnost,* honest and complete *glasnost*—that is the first condition of health in all societies, including our own." Years later, in late 1988, when the word had entered the international vocabulary, Gorbachev's ideology chief, Vadim Medvedev, told a Moscow press conference that neither *Gulag* nor certain other anti-Leninist works of Solzhenitsyn could be published in the Soviet Union. His explanation, like Suslov's to Grossman, was at once a tribute to the work under ban and another reminder of the power which the regime attributed to books. Publication of Solzhenitsyn's works, Medvedev said, in a resonant phrase, "would undermine the very foundations on which our life is built."

Great books got the personal attention of top Communist leaders. But to keep watch over the huge volume of ordinary publications there was a big, semisecret censorship bureaucracy known by its old shorthand name as Glavlit, though its actual name had been changed to Chief Administration for Safeguarding State Secrets in Print. Every newspaper editor had a fat Glavlit volume, usually kept in his office safe, listing prohibited topics in pedantic detail. From time to time the editor would receive a secret update for this secret list: floods are okay if casualty figures are omitted, say, but space program accidents are still off limits. The existence of the Glavlit guide, of course, was itself a secret. Various government agencies lobbied to have materials associated with their work declared classified, and with no counterpressure from the media or the public, the agencies usually got their way. The Ministry of Fisheries, to offer one little example of the resulting absurd web of prohibitions, was able to make a secret of "instances of sea fish and nonfish objects being jettisoned overboard," presumably to cover up the prodigious waste in the state fisheries.

A parallel system kept track of the books that were banned. I have a 1981 brochure put out for librarians and booksellers by the state publishing bureaucracy, listing books and magazines published in Russian *by official Soviet publishers inside the Soviet Union* since 1940—and subsequently banned. There are no foreign publications, no pre-Revolutionary books, and no samizdat here; this is just the stuff that Glavlit once had approved and later, due to shifting political winds, prohibited. The list is 119 pages of fine print.

It would be a great challenge to an expert in Soviet literary trivia to try to figure out just why these particular books fell from favor. Of course, the eleven Solzhenitsyn listings, consisting of his official publications during the Khrushchev thaw, are no mystery. Titles like *Stalin: Great Continuer of the Work of Lenin* understandably lost their imprimatur after Khrushchev's 1956 secret speech denouncing Stalin's crimes.

But what could possibly be wrong with *A. S. Pushkin and Azerbaijani Literature?* Whom did *American Imperialism: The Worst Enemy of Peace, Democracy and Socialism* offend? Or how about *Growing Tea: A Textbook for Technical Schools?* Maybe their authors had sneaked anti-Soviet double entendres into their texts? Or perhaps the works were innocent but the authors had later veered into dissent and had to be punished by the withdrawal of their earlier works?

Whatever the reason, nothing could be published without a Glavlit index number, showing the censors had given their approval. And publishing had the broadest of definitions. Even stand-up comedians, a hardy breed in Russia, were required to submit to the censor advance texts of their monologues, with every one-liner, every digression, every punch line just as it would be heard on stage.

Though you might not suspect it from the censors' hypersensitivity to the exposure of Soviet weaknesses, the Soviet regime could honestly point to unmistakable economic and social achievements. Khrushchev's boast in the late 1950s that the Soviet Union would overtake the United States by the 1980s was not mere bravado. When Gorbachev came to power the USSR indeed led the world in the production of many commodities—steel, cement, lumber, oil, tractors, wheat, potatoes, milk. On the base of a gross national product far smaller than that of the United States, the Soviet Union had managed approximately to match American achievements in military power and space exploration. It had achieved not only near-universal literacy but a very high level of general education; ask a random Russian to quote Pushkin's poetry or explain trigonometry and you'll almost certainly be impressed. By focusing investment on training in sports and music, the Soviet Union easily outclassed the United States and virtually every other country in the number of top Olympic athletes and world-class musicians. It had dramatically improved public health, a fact sometimes obscured by Western reporting; life expectancy was low and infant mortality high only by Western standards. For instance, the infant mortality rate in the Soviet Union in 1987 was 25.4 per thousand live births, compared with 10.1 in the United States and just 6 per thousand in Sweden. But as recently as 1960 the U.S. rate had been 26.0, and no one thought of the U.S. at the time as a catastrophically backward country.

Despite this record, when Yuri Andropov succeeded Leonid

Brezhnev at the end of 1982 he seems to have concluded that
economically the country's back was to the wall. "He understood
that the country was on the threshold of a crisis," said Eduard
Shevardnadze, who had been a tough police general and party boss
in Georgia before becoming Soviet foreign minister under Gorbachev. "When he spoke to the leadership circle he said the country
was faced with a question of survival. Many people were shocked at
that time by that phrase, 'survival.' It wasn't published, but he did
say that to a group of party leaders." In his brief rule Andropov
groped for a solution, clutching at the notion of "discipline"—a
crackdown on drunkenness, absenteeism, corruption, and dissent.
After the brief interregnum of Konstantin Chernenko, Brezhnev's
toady, Gorbachev picked up where Andropov had left off in the
search for a way out of the country's economic morass.

That morass was defined by a series of paradoxes, for there was a
flip side to all the big production statistics. The biggest tractor
producer in the world was also the biggest grain importer. The
biggest steel manufacturer was also a country where an ordinary
person had to wait a decade to buy a car. Though the Soviet Union
was the world's leading oil producer, there were in many regions
mile-long lines for gasoline. Despite its leadership position in cement
and lumber, the country suffered from a perennial housing shortage
that kept millions of people in shared flats or crowded dormitories.

While the economy that Stalin had built continued to run up
production figures and reward managers according to gross output,
other developed countries had evolved. "The rest of the world went
off in a different direction, emphasizing finished products and the
standard of living, not individual industrial commodities," economist Marshall I. Goldman wrote in 1983. The Soviet Union had
indeed won Khrushchev's industrial race, Goldman said, but it had
"won the wrong race." The Stalinist economic model, emphasizing
central planning and gross production, was completely mismatched
with the new tasks of raising living standards and meeting consumer
demand.

Something else was happening, too. Computers and the semiconductors from which they were built were transforming economies,
even as the railroad had a century or so before. And just as the

conservative tsarist bureaucrats had fretted about the political and moral consequences of rapid rail transport, so Communist bureaucrats feared the subversive effects of the new information technology. As the new machines for duplicating, storing, manipulating, and transmitting information took the West by storm, in the Soviet Union they ran into the brick wall of information control.

So it was that while the CIA was drawing its Soviet maps from 1980s satellite photos, the Soviet Union was publishing for public use maps simplified and distorted in accordance with 1930s regulations— regulations whose existence was itself a secret. So it was that a considerable share of the state broadcasting network's electronic might went to the production of powerful signals of static to cover up programs beamed east from the Voice of America, the BBC, Deutsche Welle, and Radio Liberty—the use of information technology to block information. (The scale of the operation could be glimpsed from the fact that in Byelorussia alone, on the western Soviet border, jamming involved eighty-nine transmitters manned by one hundred technicians.) So it was that photocopiers were illegal in private hands; even in 1988 visitors would gawk at the primitive copier I had in my office, regarding as a miracle the same kind of machine I had been using as a teenager at a public library twenty years before.

On this side of the Looking Glass there were no residential phone books, no Yellow Pages, no retail catalogs. There were no usable bank checks and no credit cards; paying a bill required hand-carrying three (carbon) copies of the bill to the bank. Telephoning Moscow from a Moscow suburb was often impossible—even for those fortunate souls who had a telephone. Scientists used slide rules. Cashiers used abacuses. I often thought, as some activist handed me a fuzzy carbon copy of a manifesto that looked like it had been ten layers of paper away from the typewriter keys, that this country seemed to have missed out on fifty years of technology.

As with the maps, however, the backwardness often was a question of policy, not poverty. The state-of-the-art eavesdropping equipment imbedded in the concrete of the new U.S. embassy tower in Moscow impressed and stumped the CIA. Throughout the 1980s, day and night, CIA experts and their high-priced consultants banged and buzzed away inside the unoccupied building trying to figure out what the KGB had done. They were still at work in December 1991 when Vadim Bakatin, who was overseeing the post-Communist dismantling of the KGB, handed to a nonplussed U.S. Ambassador Robert Strauss the detailed bugging plans for the embassy. High technology was within the capability of the Soviet regime—albeit technology often stolen or copied from the West— but it remained exclusively in the hands of the leadership. It was neither to be wasted on the trivial desires of Soviet consumers nor used to arm potential internal or external enemies of the regime.

In 1987 the Soviet Union produced about twice as much steel as the United States. But in that year there were approximately 200,000 microcomputers in use in the USSR compared with roughly 25 million in the United States. The numbers were a telling symptom of the economic crisis Gorbachev inherited.

A few prophets had seen what was coming. When the M.I.T. scientist Norbert Wiener, in the late 1940s, coined the word *cybernetics* for the science of control and communications, the feedback that operates in both biological organisms and machines, Stalin swiftly labeled the new field a false science. His antipathy may have been mere reflex in his last years of anti-Semitic paranoia; Wiener was an American Jew. But he just may have sensed that cybernetics— the word has the same Greek root as the word *govern*—held some profoundly bad news for the Soviet information-control tradition.

Denouncing spy-paranoia on both sides of the cold war in 1950, Wiener declared: "This demand for secrecy is scarcely more than the wish of a sick civilization not to learn the progress of its own disease." Such hypersecrecy would be far more disabling in the future, Wiener presciently suggested, because "a second industrial revolution is coming" which would be characterized by "mass production of computing machines" and in which information would be a critical economic resource. "Information is more a matter of process than of storage," Wiener wrote. "That country will have the greatest security whose informational and scientific situation is adequate to meet the demands that may be put upon it—the country in which it is fully realized that information is important as a stage in the continuous process by which we observe the outer world and act effectively upon it."

One Soviet scientist who clearly had read Wiener was the dissident astrophysicist Kronid Lyubarsky, who was sent to a labor camp in 1972 under Article 70, the anti-Soviet propaganda statute. A top figure in the Mars probe program and a loyal Soviet citizen who came to break with the regime only gradually and reluctantly, Lyubarsky used his own trial to denounce the increasing harm done to Soviet society by information control.

Replying to the prosecutor's assertion that the scientific intelligentsia do not produce goods of value, Lyubarsky declared: "Citizen prosecutor, you are behind by twenty years! You have missed such a thing as the science-and-technology revolution, which has changed the face of the world! I could cite, but won't, dozens of books by sociologists and economists who show what the science-and-technology revolution has brought, in which it is said that in the developed industrial countries [i.e., the West] at the current time 75 percent of the increase in national income is based not on the expansion of production but on the expansion of the use of knowledge, the level of knowledge—on the basis of the labor of the intelligentsia."

Lyubarsky went on to defend his use of samizdat literature to study Stalin's rise to power, to follow Soviet political trials, and to keep up with events in the West. "As the peasant works with the soil, a worker with metal, so an intellectual works with information. It is possible to form an independent opinion only having at your disposal information," he said.

"The sole resolution of the problem of samizdat," Lyubarsky told the court, "is the introduction of an authentically free press. There is no other way."

Lyubarsky was offering the Soviet regime a valuable warning—for which he was rewarded with a five-year sentence. But if the regime could stop Lyubarsky, it could not stop the world. What Wiener predicted as a "second industrial revolution" in 1950, and Lyubarsky described as a "science-and-technology revolution" in

1972, surged ahead, a complicated, inexorable transformation of social and economic life that no one sought or planned. As the firearm or the steam engine had in earlier times changed living standards and power balances, so now the microprocessor touched everything. The capitalist countries were gradually being linked into a global economy, in which what moved over copper cables or fiber optics could be as important as what moved on oil tankers or rail lines.

In 1987 the Yale University historian Paul Kennedy brilliantly sketched the ironies of the dilemma the Soviet leadership faced as its political system clashed with history. "[Marxist] philosophy asserts that the ongoing, dialectical process of change in world affairs is driven by technology and new means of production, and inevitably causes all sorts of political and social transformations, yet its own autocratic and bureaucratic habits, the privileges that cushion the party elites, the restrictions upon the free interchange of knowledge, and the lack of personal incentive make it horribly ill-equipped to handle the explosive but subtle 'high-tech' future that is already emerging in Japan and the United States." For instance, Kennedy wrote, large-scale introduction of computers into energy production and distribution could produce huge savings—but such technology "challenges the intensely secretive, bureaucratic, and centralized Soviet system."

"Computers, word-processors, and telecommunications equipment, tools of a knowledge-intensive industry, can best be exploited by a society with a technologically trained population that is encouraged to experiment freely and to exchange new ideas and hypotheses," Kennedy wrote. "However, what works well in the United States and Japan threatens to loosen the Soviet state's monopoly on information. If even today senior scientists and scholars are reluctant to use copying machines (the copying departments are staffed by the KGB), then it is hard to see how the country could move toward the widespread use of word-processors, interactive computers, electronic mail, and so forth without a substantial relaxation of police controls and censorship."

Early official portraits of General Secretary Gorbachev look strange today. It takes a moment to realize why: the birthmark is missing. The forehead of the leader of a country with a "glorious destiny" could not, even in 1985, be flawed. The experienced retouchers of the state printing houses saw to that.

But Gorbachev quickly demonstrated an impatience with the Soviet reflexes of embellishment and cover-up and a dramatically different approach to information. Twenty-five years younger than Leonid Brezhnev, seventeen years younger than Yuri Andropov, twenty years younger than Konstantin Chernenko, he had a dynamic presence that made a stunning contrast with his ailing immediate predecessors. More important, he was of a different political generation. Having graduated from law school in 1955, two years after Stalin's death, he was the first Soviet leader whose early career was shaped not by Stalinism, not by service in World War II—but by Khrushchev's anti-Stalinist thaw. He was far better educated than his predecessors, and his book-learning was supplemented by the highly unusual experience of travel to both France and Italy as a young man.

On March 11, 1985, the day he was elected party leader, he declared that the leadership was "obliged to continue to expand glasnost in the work of Party, administrative, state, and public organizations.... The better informed people are, the more intelligently they act and the more actively they support the Party and its plans and programmatic goals." Soon the press was stretching the limits of Marxist-Leninist "criticism and self-criticism," then giddily experimenting with something like Western-style investigative journalism. Gradually, over the ensuing five years, the bans fell: shortwave jamming stations were shut down or converted for local broadcasting; detailed maps were printed for the public; photocopiers were legalized; banned books appeared—*Doctor Zhivago* and *Life and Fate* in 1988, *Gulag Archipelago* in 1989, three landmarks among hundreds of works officially published for the first time.

In loosing the information bonds, Gorbachev wanted to shake up the stagnant bureaucracy he had inherited, to light a fire under toocomfortable functionaries, to shine a light—a feisty new Gorbachev-era TV show was Spotlight of Perestroika—on stubborn problems.

In effect Gorbachev wanted to restore some measure of feedback to Soviet society. It was a highly utilitarian conception of information and of the media. Shortcomings, he told people gathered to meet him in 1988 in a village outside the Siberian city of Krasnoyarsk, "have to be written about, so that our defects may be known about and seen, and so that they may be treated and got rid of"—the press as x-ray machine guiding the political surgeons. "Comrades, we must resolutely get rid of window dressing in what is the main issue—information," Gorbachev said at the beginning of 1989. "Window dressing is dangerous when reporting or supplying data on construction, on the commissioning of various installations, or on the work of various spheres and branches. But if we receive political information which, on the whole, fails to reflect the real processes and does not contain the objective impulses provided by life itself, such distortions could form the basis for major miscalculations."

Many times Gorbachev made it quite clear that glasnost was not the same thing as unbridled freedom of the press. "Glasnost," he said on his Siberian tour in the autumn of 1988, "is necessary. But it must be based on our values. It must be everything that serves socialism and serves the people." Again, a couple of weeks later, addressing top editors and broadcast executives, he seemed to be speaking in oxymorons: "Publish everything. There must be plurality of opinions. But plurality aimed at defending and strengthening the line of perestroika and the cause of socialism.... We are not talking about any kind of limits on glasnost or democracy. What limits? Glasnost in the interest of the people and of socialism should be without limits. I repeat—in the interests of the people and of socialism."

Whatever the contradictions in this unlimited, limited license, the history of this old Russian word backed up Gorbachev's utilitarian interpretation. The emigré Lithuanian literary critic Thomas Venclova pointed out in 1987 that a century before Gorbachev the Russian radical writer Nikolai Chernyshevsky "gave a famous and probably right definition of glasnost. He said something of the kind: glasnost is an invention of bureaucrats for abrogating the ideal freedom of speech." Even in the Soviet lexicon, Solzhenitsyn and the dissidents of the 1970s had been far from the only voices urging more glasnost. The eager-to-please apparatchiki of Politizdat, the state political publishing house, managed in 1989 to compile and publish an entire 351-page book entitled *V. I. Lenin on Glasnost.* Right there on page 334 was a telling quote from Ulyanov-Lenin setting the limits of glasnost: "Daily propaganda and agitation should have a really Communist character. All press organs in the hands of the Party should be edited by reliable Communists who have proven their devotion to the cause of proletarian revolution. . . . It is unacceptable for a publisher, abusing his autonomy, to pursue a politics not completely Party in character."

Gorbachev had a second, economic goal in reducing information control that was more fuzzily defined and long term. Gorbachev's speeches reflect a growing awareness that the Stalinist orientation to heavy industry was folly as the Soviet Union's international competitors moved into high-technology, information-based economic development. "Acceleration of scientific and technological progress," or simply "Acceleration," was the Gorbachev era's first slogan, as if tramping a little harder on the gas pedal was all the leadership needed to do. In his May 1985 speech in Leningrad, which set a new tone for tough, candid criticism, the phrase "science and technology" recurs a dozen times. In June 1985 he convened a Central Committee conference on science and technology—a meeting that had been planned, and then canceled, under Brezhnev more than a decade earlier. "Microelectronics, computer technology, instrument-making, and the entire information-science industry are the catalysts of progress," he told the conference. "They require accelerated development." At the February 1986 27th Communist Party Congress he spoke of how "the capitalism of the age of electronics and informatics, computers and robots" was throwing people out of work, but his words had the sound of sour grapes. He acknowledged that "the scientific and technological revolution . . . pose[s] problems for socialist society as well" and that participation in that revolution would determine whether or not a country "remains on the periphery of world development."

Many voices were whispering in Gorbachev's ear on the topic of the information revolution. One was that of Fyodor Burlatsky, a

moderate reformer who had served as aide to both Khrushchev and
Andropov and who informally advised Gorbachev and traveled
abroad with him four times in his first three years in office. Even
under Andropov and Chernenko, Burlatsky had been sounding the
alarm about the postindustrial turn in capitalist development, which
he compared in its significance to the original industrial revolution.
Though he was writing explicitly of the information-technology race
between the United States and Japan, Burlatsky's implicit message
was a barely muffled scream to Soviet leaders to join the race or
perish. The new technology "is destined, in a rather brief historical
period, to alter and replace the industrial base throughout the
world," Burlatsky wrote in *Literaturnaya Gazeta* five months before
Gorbachev took office. "Need anyone be reminded of the great
impact that the first industrial revolution, in the eighteenth century,
had on the world?" Because "by no means will everyone wind up in
technological paradise right away," the resulting inequalities between
countries will be "one of the most crucial problems of the coming
era."

Certain foreigners were still blunter with Gorbachev. Alvin Toffler, the popular American futurist, told Gorbachev at a 1986 forum
in Kirghizia that reform in all countries depends on "change in
information policy. The necessity of free transmission of information
is an immediate economic demand, because the new economics is
based to a significant degree on the use of information technology."
U.S. Secretary of State George Shultz, an economics professor, made
it his personal project to brief Gorbachev about the cost of Soviet
isolation from the information revolution. In one meeting, described
by *Washington Post* reporter Don Oberdorfer, "Shultz pulled out
four-color graphs and pie charts of global trends [showing that] the
Soviet Union accounted for 15 percent of world production of goods
and services (compared with 28 percent for the United States) but
only 2 percent of world trade. The charts showed that the shares of
both the U.S. and Soviet economies in world manufactured exports
were slipping, while Japan and East Asia were coming up fast,
having mastered the Third Industrial Revolution of high technology,
which had scarcely a toehold in the Soviet economy outside the
military sector. There was a single global economy to a greater

degree than ever before, but the Soviet Union was hardly a part of it."

It was evidently an effective tutorial, though perhaps not one Gorbachev needed. Accustomed to lagging behind the United States, Soviet officials were shaken and sobered in the 1980s to watch certain Asian countries, toward which they had always felt a patronizing superiority, pass the USSR in levels of technology and development. Gorbachev spoke in increasingly frank terms of the Soviet lag in information technology and its dire consequences. "Over the last few years," he told a student conference in November 1989, "the gap between the USSR and the developed countries in the assimilation of new, high, and in the first place information technologies, based upon the broad use of the latest achievements in science, has steadily increased. The world is on the threshold of a new information-technology society. We have to recognize that, to recognize that any delay in that direction of the development of society is tantamount to a strategic defeat."

The urgency of the task Gorbachev saw ahead was underscored by the shift of the American military threat, symbolized by Reagan's Strategic Defense Initiative, toward high technology. Marshal Nikolai Ogarkov, chief of the general staff under Andropov, warned repeatedly in the early 1980s that the Soviet military could not keep pace. "The rapid development of science and technology in recent years is creating realistic prerequisites for the appearance in the near future of even more destructive and heretofore unknown types of weapons," Ogarkov told an interviewer in May 1984, warning that military security depended on economic progress. Four months later Chernenko fired him. But Gorbachev and his scientific advisers took the threat of Star Wars extremely seriously, as the volume and vehemence of their denunciations showed. While domestic concerns were the engine for glasnost, General William E. Odom, a Sovietologist and former director of the National Security Agency, is probably right in saying that the Carter-Reagan defense buildup and its high-tech orientation "intensified the sense of crisis and the need for sweeping change in the Soviet Union."

A second foreign policy influence on information policy was Gorbachev's drive for East-West détente and disarmament. Because

Soviet information control loomed so large in the Western picture of Soviet repression, it could be bargained profitably away as proof of Soviet sincerity in improving relations. It was not by chance that announcements of certain key changes in information policy were made not by domestic officials addressing Soviet citizens but by Foreign Ministry officials speaking, via the foreign press corps, to Western governments. Still, these decisions to ease information controls were only incidentally foreign policy "concessions." Gorbachev had concluded that glasnost was necessary for Soviet progress. If it aided East-West relations, so much the better.

ꙮ

Launching this experiment in expanding freedom of information, Gorbachev had no idea where it would lead. Neither, of course, did anyone else—though the party conservatives who protested that glasnost was "undermining socialism" were closer to the truth than the party reformers who believed they were "renewing socialism."

Gorbachev operated—this is a crucial point—inside the Soviet illusion. He had the self-confidence of a man who believed in the bedrock rightness of 1917, who was certain that the problems facing the Soviet Union were a consequence of deviation from the Leninist path, not of adherence to it. Despite his refreshing realism about many Soviet problems, he had an unassailable faith in the Marxist-Leninist framework. This faith was not a political tactic, as some Western admirers of Gorbachev suspected. It was a conviction, a habit of belief, as anyone who listened to his off-the-cuff speeches over the years can attest. He fell easily and often into the language of official Soviet religion: the Communist party was for him *svyatoye delo*—a sacred cause, and attacks on the party or its founder were *koshchunstvo*—blasphemy.

In his Leningrad speech two months after taking office, Gorbachev drew a revealing parallel between the 1930s and the 1980s, between crash industrialization *(industrializatsia)* under Stalin and crash informatization *(informatizatsia,* a Soviet coinage) today. "You remember that, before the war, the older generation was resolving the problem of having to cover in a decade what other countries had covered in a hundred years, so that the country would not find itself in a critical situation—and even then it was sensed that the threat to the socialist country, above all, was growing," Gorbachev said. Rapid industrialization "was the basis of the victory in 1945"—in other words, it had saved "the socialist country." Now, he said, "we also have to traverse a long road, but in a short space of time. That is the point." Why? Implicitly, to save socialism.

In his first years in power Gorbachev clung to the "acceleration" fallacy, a sort of Stakhanovite approach to economic advance (for the legendary Stalin-era coal miner Stakhanov who supposedly—glasnost subsequently revealed the episode to have been a fraud—produced fourteen times his quota in one shift on the strength of teamwork and enthusiasm). In a 1987 speech to a Komsomol congress, Gorbachev singled out for praise a team of young engineers working to develop a Soviet supercomputer. "For these people, the questions of pay and working hours did not arise. They were all absorbed by their idea. And just this unlimited devotion to the cause and high qualifications permitted these young people to make a breakthrough in this vitally important direction of our development. Yes, we believe in the success of this huge work!" (Note again the religious diction: "unlimited devotion," "we believe.") Gorbachev described the giant steps planned by the supercomputer team in the 12th Five Year Plan, and the 13th Five Year Plan, and named the members of the team: "Sergei Tarasov, Fyodor Gruzdov..." As the ovation died down, he added in a challenging tone: "Certain people in the West have tied a great many of their calculations to the backwardness of the Soviet Union in science and technology, including in the problem of creating a supercomputer. Let those who have ears hear this information today from the rostrum!"

The plan was clear: a big, Stakhanovite push would introduce computers and other modern information technologies into the economy and society on a rush basis, and thus would socialism and the Soviet Union be saved. Gorbachev's worldwide bestseller of 1987, *Perestroika: New Thinking for Our Country and the World,* makes instructive reading in retrospect.

"If our plans are carried out successfully," Gorbachev asked in his book, "how then will it be possible to pull the wool over people's eyes, claiming that socialism is a failure, unable to feed and clothe people? It will shatter the whole conception with the help of which they [Western anti-Communists] labeled our country an 'evil empire' and portrayed the October Revolution as an historic mistake and our postrevolutionary path as a 'zigzag of history.'" More than that, Gorbachev said: "The success of perestroika will be a deciding argument in the historical debate: what system [capitalism or socialism] to a greater degree meets the interests of the people? The face of the Soviet Union, cleansed of layers deposited in extreme circumstances [presumably meaning the Revolution, the Civil War, the Stalinist terror, and World War II] will achieve a new magnetism, becoming a living embodiment of the advantages inherent by principle in the socialist system. The ideals of socialism will receive a new impulse.... Those who hope we will turn from the socialist path are destined for a bitter disappointment."

Gorbachev did not foresee the central contradiction that would lead to the destruction of the Soviet Union: that the Soviet system and freedom of information were mutually exclusive. Ultimately there would have to be a choice between control and information. But in 1987 glasnost may still have seemed a mere matter of ridding the system of certain anachronisms and absurdities. Valentin Turchin, an exiled dissident physicist, said in 1987: "I believe Gorbachev himself probably thinks what he is doing is eliminating absurdities. Of course, it's absurd to keep Sakharov in Gorky. It's absurd to put people in jail for writing letters to the Presidium of the Supreme Soviet, and so on. It is absurd to cut informational channels and to prevent people from exchanging ideas in our society. That's true. And they now realize it's absurd."

In the event, absurdities turned out not to be, as Gorbachev believed at the outset—and as most people in the West believed too—mere baroque embellishments of the Soviet order. They were its structural beams, its bricks and mortar. Myth—the Soviet illusion—was its core. Therefore ordinary information, mere facts, exploded like grenades, ripping the system and its legitimacy. How many skeletons, each with an NKVD bullet hole in the skull, were buried in Kuropaty Woods outside Minsk? Who were those classy apartments on Moscow's Sivtsev Vrazhek Street being built for? What can you buy on an average day on an average salary in an average American supermarket? The answers to such questions appeared in the pages of official newspapers, resounded from millions of radios and televisions, began to bounce around the country on photocopied leaflets and telefax news services.

The paradox of Gorbachev—his maddening combination of brilliance and obtuseness, vision and blindness—was never better captured than in a speech he gave to writers and other cultural figures in November 1990. For the first time he disclosed that not just one but both of his grandfathers had been arrested under Stalin: one for failing to fulfill the plan to sow grain in 1933, when half his family had starved to death; the other after confessing, under torture, to crimes he had not committed. As a result, Gorbachev said, "I lived in this plague house, where he [the second grandfather] was called an enemy of the people."

One might think young Misha Gorbachev, enduring such a childhood, would grow up a bitter enemy of the Communist system. But in his speech, as in his life, he somehow turned his family's suffering into a reason for his enduring faith in the system. "Well, should we renounce things?" he asked. "What shall I do, renounce my grandfather, who was dedicated to everything right to the end and, having come back [from a labor camp], spent a further seventeen years as collective farm chairman? Never did I hear him have doubts about...what was taking place in this land where he was born....That is why I cannot go against my grandfather."

In spirit the passage is a striking non sequitur: the Communist regime arrested my grandfathers in a gross injustice, therefore I am a Communist. No one clung to the Soviet illusion harder and longer than the man whose policies brought it to a crashing collapse.

In the same speech Gorbachev told of his walk with Eduard Shevardnadze on a beach at Pitsunda, a resort on the Black Sea in Georgia, on the eve of his becoming Soviet leader. As he told it, Shevardnadze declared that "Everything's rotten," and the two of them agreed that "We can't live like this." Such was the inchoate dissatisfaction in which perestroika was born.

But in 1990, after nearly six accelerating years of Gorbachev's glasnost, the instincts for information control were still powerful. On television Gorbachev was shown saying he vacationed regularly at Pitsunda, considered a posh resort. Apparently someone in the bureaucracy decided it was unwise to let the people know their leader had nice vacations—or perhaps discovered that the leader's vacation spots were on Glavlit's long list of secrets. When the speech appeared in the newspapers, the reference to Pitsunda was gone. Now Gorbachev only went "on vacation." The people did not need to know where.

3

What Price Socialism? An Economy Without Information

CUSTOMER IN MEAT STORE: Miss, can you slice 100 grams of ham for me?
SALESWOMAN: Certainly, citizen, if you bring me the ham.
—Soviet joke, 1988

Glasnost is when the mouth is already open, but there's nothing to put in it.
—Soviet joke, 1989

The line snaked out the door of the little store, wound around the base of the scaffolding that seemed to be holding up the building's façade, and trailed off down Prospekt Mira, Peace Avenue, toward an ice cream stand.

"*Shto dayoot?*"—What're they giving out? asked a young woman in a denim jacket, pausing on the sidewalk in deference to the first law of Soviet shopping: the longer the line, the greater the reward for those who stand in it.

"*Tufli. Khoroshiye*"—Shoes. Good ones, replied a stout babushka halfway back.

The woman in denim pushed through the crowd near the door to get a look at the window display: grey pumps with a sort of bird's-egg speckle. Price: twenty–three rubles, two days' pay for an average person in the summer of 1989, but quite reasonable for good-looking shoes. Any price was reasonable for good-looking shoes.

The young woman hurried down the road to join the end of the line, about an hour and a half from the counter where sullen saleswomen handed shoes across to a seething mass of shoppers shouting sizes. These single-minded people would no doubt have had no patience that day for a theoretical point elegantly demonstrated by their shoe queue: they too were suffering the consequences of information control.

To make the connection, one must first understand the central position of the waiting line in the Soviet economy. No institution of Soviet life was more ubiquitous. An elaborate subculture had grown up around the line, with its own habits and rules: when it was legitimate to ask the person behind you to hold your place, and for how long; which lines might justifiably be jumped by a woman with small children or a veteran of the Great Patriotic War; what time, for what products, in what stores, promised the shortest waits; and whether it was permissible to send babushka, the pensioner, to do the family's waiting. A person with a number inked on his hand was not necessarily a Gulag survivor but merely needed to remember that he was 617th in some crucial queue.

For a correspondent the line often provided interesting tidbits of insight. One line I stopped to check turned out to be the panicked elite, trying to beat the rumored deadline to cash in their "certificate rubles"—coupons purchased with hard currency earned abroad that could be used in special stores to buy coveted items. Another line led to Danish canned hams, landed like manna on an icy sidewalk on the Garden Ring: ours not to wonder why, ours just to elbow our way to that white-coated babushka before she empties her miraculous carton and disappears. One day it was Boris Yeltsin's autobiography, hot off the presses with titillating details about how Politburo members live (they didn't stand in lines). Another day the queue stopped at the door of the nondescript building near Byelorussky train station where the burgeoning number of people allowed to go abroad were permitted to change a limited number of rubles into hard currency. (To retain their places, people had to turn up at a preestablished hour once a month to check in and continue their slow advance toward the dollars or deutsche marks they wanted.)

The line was the enemy, lurking out there in below-zero weather, that you could try to outsmart but threatened always to defeat you. But the line also represented hope, promising a material reward for the very Russian virtue of waiting.

My informal survey suggested that some of the longest lines in Moscow were for shoes. At first I assumed that the inefficient Soviet economy simply did not produce enough shoes, and for that reason, even in the capital, people were forced to line up for hours to buy them. *Defitsit*, shortage, was a workhorse of colloquial Soviet speech. The adjectival form, *defitsitny*, had become a term of praise, since everything desirable was in short supply: Look at this pottery I found—it's very *defitsitny*. So they needed to make more shoes, I figured. Then I looked up the statistics.

I was wrong. *The Soviet Union was the largest producer of shoes in the world.* It was turning out 800 million pairs of shoes a year—twice as many as Italy, three times as many as the United States, four times as many as China. Production amounted to more than three pairs of shoes per year for every Soviet man, woman, and child.

The problem with shoes, it turned out, was not an absolute shortage. It was a far more subtle malfunction. The comfort, the fit, the design, and the size mix of Soviet shoes were so out of sync with what people needed and wanted that they were willing to stand in line for hours to buy the occasional pair, usually imported, that they liked.

At the root of the dysfunction was the state's control of information. Prices are information—the information producers need in order to know what and how much to produce. In a market for a product as varied in material and design as footwear, shifting prices are like sensors taped to the skin of a patient in a medical experiment; they provide a constant flow of information about consumer needs and preferences. When the state controlled prices, it deprived producers of information about demand.

The shoe factory boss churned out shoes to meet the Plan, a production quota set by bureaucrats who reported to Moscow's hulking Gosplan, the State Planning Committee. The shoes were priced according to arcane formulae by another *gos*-institution (for *gosudarstvo*, state), Goskomtsen, the State Price Committee. The shoes were distributed by another beefy bureaucracy, Gossnab, the State Supply Committee. If the shoe factory boss was smart, he might produce 10 percent over plan, win himself a bonus, and be named a Hero of Socialist Labor. But as far as the consumer was concerned, the factory manager operated in the dark, without any information from the market, without feedback.

Indeed, the factory's real customer was the state, not the consumer. The state purchased all the shoe factory's production, good, bad, or indifferent. The consumer's choices were not allowed to enter into the matter. So, driven by the tireless efforts of the shoe factory hero and those like him, gross national product might rise and the Politburo might express satisfaction at the obvious economic progress. But on the street the picture looked less triumphant: many stores had bins of clunky shoes sitting around unbought, while down the street hundreds of people sacrificed their mornings waiting for imports.

The vague impression in the West that the Soviet economy was merely an enfeebled version of a Western economy was inaccurate. It was a different beast altogether. It was dreadfully inefficient, stubbornly resistant to change, but capable of huge feats of production. The statistical yearbooks, with their selective but impressive tables of "Comparison with Leading Capitalist Countries," proved as much.

The shoes Soviet industry produced might end up in a landfill, but comrade, it could produce shoes.

As much as the censorship of literature or the jamming of shortwave broadcasts, information control in economics was driven by politics—by the imperative of state power. The totalitarian state could not leave to the citizens' whims a power so important as control over prices. But it was not merely a question of who had power over the economy. Especially in the case of food and housing, prices carried a crucial political message. Prices functioned as propaganda and therefore malfunctioned as economic indicators.

Every Soviet schoolchild knew that workers in capitalist countries were vulnerable to the ravages of inflation, which could tear the heart out of a paycheck before it was spent. But Soviet workers, in the world's first socialist country, could count on cheap food and cheap housing. The state was looking out for them. The subsidized prices were the economic equivalent of the bombastic language of Soviet politics—Gide's "glorious destiny"—and showed the same avoidance of reality. Controlled prices were an indispensable prop for the Soviet illusion.

Far more than most tenets of official ideology, the notion of stable, official prices really was a fixture of Soviet popular culture. Many people who scoffed at the Communist party nonetheless took stable prices as an article of faith. People tended to see a price not as a number applied by an individual seller to an item but as an intrinsic, permanent trait of the item. Viktor Karasyov, the "driver" who did the *Baltimore Sun* Moscow bureau's innumerable bureaucratic errands, griped in 1988 that some guy had been selling candy near a Metro stop for thirty-five kopecks per piece instead of the state price of fifteen kopecks. These were individually wrapped chocolates from the Red October chocolate factory, which blessed a whole central Moscow neighborhood with its delicious smell. Well, I said to Viktor, people don't have to buy it from him, do they? Maybe they're tired after work and they're willing to pay more to avoid a trip to the store. No, Viktor said, *Eto grabyozh!*—It's robbery! The price should be fifteen kopecks. Well, I persisted, if his price is too high, people won't buy it, and the price will come down. No, Viktor insisted, it is illegal. He should be locked up.

Preserving such attitudes cost the state dearly. By the mid-1980s the state was selling for an average of 1.77 rubles a kilogram of beef that cost it 4.75 rubles to raise and transport. In some regions where climatic conditions drove up costs, the production cost was as high as 16 rubles. But everywhere, in every meat store across one-sixth of the earth's land surface, the retail price remained under 2 rubles.

The state made up the difference in the form of enormous and growing subsidies.

The same was true of most other food products. The notorious instance was bread, where the subsidy was sufficient to bring the price of a loaf of hearty, tasty dark Russian bread well below the price of an equivalent amount of livestock feed. Peasants, no dummies, fed bread instead of feed to the pigs and chickens they grew to sell on the private market, thus boosting their profit margins but driving up the subsidy cost to the state. Local officials and scandalized newspaper writers complained of this practice for years, but private pigs continued to dine on subsidized bread. The behavior of the state may have been irrational, but the peasants were simply acting on the information contained in the prices.

Who was paying the food subsidies? Soviet workers, of course, but they generally didn't know it. One Soviet economist, Alexander Zaichenko, calculated that in the United States in 1985, 65 percent of manufacturing income was paid out in the form of wages to workers. In the Soviet Union the figure was 36.6 percent. The state used the unpaid wages to subsidize retail food prices, to pay for education and health care, and to keep apartment rents low. Other money went to pay novelists and poets to do their creative work; to build the finest Olympic team in the world; and to train some of the greatest virtuosos in ballet and classical music. But the forgone wages also went to make tanks and missiles, to eavesdrop on people to detect subversives, to buy privileges for bureaucrats to insulate them from the privations suffered by ordinary people, to stave off economic disaster in Cuba and military collapse in Afghanistan. Soviet workers were the only source of the state's wealth, but the state, not the workers, decided how the lion's share of the wealth was spent.

In a sense, the subsidized prices were disinformation. They were distortions of the true state of affairs no less than the claim that Czechoslovakia had urgently requested the "fraternal assistance" of the Soviet army in 1968 or that 99 percent of the electorate had backed their deputies in Supreme Soviet elections. All three claims were accurate in a literal sense: You *could* buy a kilogram of meat for two rubles. There *was* a document from Czechoslovakia requesting intervention. The voters really *had* trooped to the polls and dropped their ballots, bearing the name of the single candidate for each seat, into the urn.

But the truth behind these claims was more complicated. Most Czechs bitterly opposed the invasion. Soviet voters had no choice. And the meat was not as cheap as it looked. Roughly speaking, the meat actually cost the worker five rubles—the two he paid in the store and the three taken from his potential wages to pay the subsidy.

It was no secret to the Gorbachev leadership that decontrol of prices was the key to economic reform. "In the USSR, we need to come to the sober realization that until [market] price relations are attained," wrote reform economist Nikolai P. Shmelyov in 1988, "we will always be living in an economically unreal world, in a kind of 'kingdom of distorting mirrors,' in which everything is inverted from an economic standpoint." Gorbachev's personal economic advisers, including Abel Aganbegyan, a rotund Armenian with a keen sense of politics, began to discuss prices in public as early as 1985. They generally used a suitably inscrutable euphemism, such as "reform of the system of price formation," so as not to alert the citizens too early on that it meant the end of two-ruble meat and twenty-five-kopeck bread. As early as October 1987 Gorbachev committed himself to price reform. In June 1988 the 19th Communist Party Conference decreed: "After broad popular discussion, carry out a reform of price formation and a review of wholesale and retail prices." But it qualified that declaration with a characteristically unrealistic corollary: "Changes in prices should cause no harm whatsoever to people's living standard."

The momentous decision was postponed again and again; in fact, even the discussion failed to get going. Some of the economists who had cavalierly spoken in 1986 or 1987 about freeing prices were speaking much more cautiously a couple of years later. The regime seemed to recognize that decontrol of food prices and apartment rents would, at a single blow, shatter one of the most important props of the Soviet illusion. It was one thing to free photocopiers and *Doctor Zhivago*, quite another to free retail prices. Gorbachev appeared to have lost his confidence that the Communist system could survive such a blow.

𝕎

In 1931 a venturesome twenty-year-old American named John Scott graduated from the University of Wisconsin, pondered his possibilities—and headed for the Soviet Union.

It was not an irrational choice. The United States was in the grip of a deep depression that seemed to betray a fundamental flaw in capitalism. Millions were out of work, and plants were closing every day. Scott was intrigued by what he heard of the Bolshevik experiment. In once-backward Russia, plants were opening, not closing, in a breakneck industrialization drive unprecedented in history. Soviet factories were owned by the workers and not subject to the whims of absentee, coupon-clipping capitalists. In the Soviet Union there was neither inflation nor unemployment. The economy was not rocked by mysterious and terrifying cycles of boom and bust. It was ruled by the Plan, a scientific blueprint that would tell managers how much to produce and what to sell it for.

To Scott, as he wrote in his memoir, *Behind the Urals*, "something seemed to be wrong with America. I began to read extensively about the Soviet Union, and gradually came to the conclusion that the Bolsheviks had found answers to at least some of the questions Americans were asking each other. I decided to go to Russia to work, study, and to lend a hand in the construction of a society which seemed to be at least one step ahead of the American." He embarked for the Ural Mountains to join thousands of workers building the world's biggest steel plant at Magnitogorsk.

Marxism-Leninism was going to replace the maddening unpredictability of capitalism with solid science. Surely the visible hand of Gosplan would prove superior to the invisible hand of Adam Smith. Surely an intelligent manager in a centralized system could calculate what kinds of shoes and how much laundry soap to produce. Certainly he would do better than leaving such matters to the uncontrolled permutations of the market.

In theory it is always better to control everything in a rational way. In practice, with a complex system, it is not better because it is impossible. Soviet industry produced some 25 million different items, more than any central bureaucracy could price individually. Gosplan's and Goskomtsen's and Gossnab's attempt to plan an economy as large and complex as that of the USSR was as hopeless as if a human being tried consciously to control all the muscles directing his breathing, blood circulation, and digestion, deciding just when to contract his right ventricle and how much insulin should be released by his pancreas. The Columbia University economist Richard Ericson cited to me the example of ball bearings, a critical part in nearly every modern machine. Considering the various combinations of size, material, and design, about 100,000 types of ball bearings are in use in developed countries. But Gosplan set production quotas in only fourteen categories of ball bearings; after all, there were so many other things to plan. The consequence was that ball-bearing production was only nominally subject to planning. Even doing their very best, bureaucrats and factory managers could hardly hope to duplicate the subtle controls of the marketplace for so complex a product. Some kinds of ball bearings were always oversupplied, others in constant shortage, others simply unavailable. The resulting domino effect in the manufacture of items as diverse as combine harvesters, vacuum cleaners, and swivel chairs is not hard to picture. Imagine the ball-bearing problem repeated for screws and bolts, transistors and capacitors, house paint and sewing thread, and you can begin to imagine the inefficiency of the Soviet economy.

It became fashionable among both Soviet and Western journalists in the late 1980s to write that, economically speaking, the Soviet Union was a Third World country. The comparison was fundamentally misleading. In fact the Soviet economy had achieved a great deal that was far beyond the reach of any Third World nation. When we arrived in Moscow in early 1988, one of the most talked-about shortages was the shortage of soap powder for automatic washing machines. It was a revealing complaint, not one you'd be likely to hear in Botswana, because to run short of soap powder you have to have a washing machine. Most Soviet families did. Ownership rose from four washing machines per hundred families in 1960, to fifty-two by 1970, and to seventy by 1980, and kept climbing. In 1987, 5.2 million washing machines were sold to Soviet consumers.

But the soap-powder story also revealed the fatal flaw in the Soviet economy. Responding lethargically but mightily to the public outcry—there was a volume level at which even Gosplan could hear the consumer—the state struggled to correct the shortage. A year and a half later there was laundry soap everywhere—stacked up in boxes in every urban and rural store and abandoned to the rain in snow-white mountains outside factories because trucks could not carry it away fast enough. Doctors identified the cause of a strange malady affecting many Muscovites: the watering eyes and sore throats were the result of sharing little apartments with huge stockpiles of laundry soap. The problem was the inevitable clumsiness of managing supply and demand without prices. The soap industry was like a huge truck with no steering wheel, careening from one curb to the other.

Something always seemed to happen somewhere along the road between impressive production statistics and long-suffering Soviet consumers. The Soviet Union had surpassed the United States in milk production by 1960, and in 1989 produced 43 percent more milk per person than the United States, despite a stunning inefficiency of production. But as with shoes, the big production figures did not pay off on the street. In the United States, despite lower production, I could go to perhaps twenty stores within a mile of my home and be confident of finding fresh milk—skim, 1 or 2 percent fat, or whole, in four or five different sized containers. Yet long before the economic disintegration of the late 1980s, even a Muscovite could not count on finding fresh milk every day in a nearby store, to say nothing of small towns or rural areas. Even if he found it, he might not want to drink it. Like most foreigners, my family came to rely mainly on milk imported from Finland, because most Soviet milk was either sour by the time you bought it or went sour within a day or two. You could figure out the reasons easily enough. One state farm manager outside Moscow told me that about 10 percent of the milking facilities in the region had no refrigeration, so their milk always went sour, and it was mixed in with the rest. In addition, there weren't nearly enough refrigerator trucks, modern processing plants, or even refrigerators in retail stores. But why *weren't* there refrigerators at those 10 percent of the farms? Why *was* the sour milk mixed in? Again, the real customer, the state, was largely satisfied by the big milk production figures; there was no feedback via prices to make the satisfaction or dissatisfaction of those who actually drank the milk count for much.

The newspaper *Izvestiya* a few years ago ran a photograph of the huge, three-liter, wide-mouthed glass jars in which most juice was sold, with an angry caption noting how impossible the heavy, unwieldy, breakable containers were for Soviet shoppers to wrestle home by foot, bus, and Metro. The newspaper rightly concluded that the jars served the convenience of the producer, not the consumer. But nothing happened; there were neither market-hungry competitors to introduce cardboard juice-packs, nor information for Soviet consumers about the packaging used in Western countries, nor prices falling in response to unsold stock to worry the Soviet juice cartel.

When a problem could not be ignored, the system's Stalinist instinct was to find a culprit. In a remarkable report on television and in *Pravda* in 1989, the Party Control Committee, a sort of discipline board for wayward Communists, announced that it was tackling the problem of shortages. It was chaired by none other than Boris K. Pugo, the hard-line Latvian Communist who would go on to head the Soviet Ministry of Internal Affairs and to lead the August 1991 coup attempt. Pugo's committee took up the question of why "there had disappeared from sale many goods, first of all soap, laundry powder, toothpaste, razor blades, school notebooks and pencils, and batteries." In all, the report said, 243 of 276 designated common household products were frequently or constantly unavailable. The committee's solution? It picked out eight economic bureaucrats, ranging from the minister in charge of the "chemical wood-processing complex" to the minister of construction for the western and northern regions of the Russian Federation. It gave each an official reprimand, the severity of the reprimand varying with the gravity of their offense. Could even Pugo have believed that such scoldings would put more goods on the shelves? The mind boggles. But it was always worth the sacrifice of a few bureaucrats, of whom there was no shortage, in order to protect "Her Majesty, the System," as *Izvestiya* once eloquently put it.

The failure of the fortress economy that Stalin built became critical only at a certain point in its development and the development of the world outside. Had the industrial age merely churned on, without plastic, without semiconductors, without microprocessors, without fiber optics, the crisis might have been put off indefinitely. In 1987 the Soviet Union produced 102 percent more steel than the United States—but just 19 percent as much synthetic resins and plastic. It produced 462 percent more woolen fabric than the U.S.—but just 32 percent as much synthetic fibers and threads. By 1979 the annual volume of plastic produced in the United States had overtaken the volume of steel, offering huge advantages in weight and flexibility to automakers and many other manufacturers. But the Soviet economy stuck doggedly to its Stalinist roots, glorified in 1930s novels whose names leave little to the imagination, such as *How the Steel Was Tempered*, by Nikolai Ostrovsky, and that solid tome endured by every student of Soviet literature, *Cement*, by Fyodor Gladkov.

The command economy was capable of many things, but one of them was not achieving a modern consumer market, shifting daily to meet demand. Even when the state was moved to try to satisfy consumers—bureaucrats too, after all, drink juice and wear shoes—trying to do it with Gosplan and Gossnab was like trying to type with boxing gloves on: you could hit plenty of letters, but not the ones you needed to hit and not in the order you needed to hit them.

This economy without markets and their constant flow of information, this strange species so fraught with paradox, did not spring magically into existence after 1917. It was built, on orders from the state, with brutal force and at great cost in human lives. The origins of the command economy were vivid memories in certain places in Russia. One such place was a speck on the map of central Russia called Plosko-Kuzminka, an overnight train ride south of Moscow. From the rail station in the city of Lipetsk, there was a half-hour bus ride to the tiny village of Bruslanovka, followed by a mile's walk on a rutted, muddy track through wheat fields to the still tinier village of Plosko-Kuzminka. In June, when I visited, the edges of the trail were bursting with weeds and wildflowers of every description, for this was the incomparably fertile soil of the *chernozyom*, the black earth. As I stepped gingerly around the biggest potholes and tried to skirt the deepest muck, a question repeated itself over and over in my mind: How can it be that such land does not feed its people?

As in thousands of other semiabandoned villages, people in Plosko-Kuzminka remembered well how Russia had been hammered into the first country of collectivized agriculture, a place of factory-farms where laborers traded a farmer's varied dawn-to-dusk labor for shift work at a single task. Plosko-Kuzminka demonstrated how Stalin had supplanted the myriad individual decisions that make up a market with a rigid hierarchy and top-down control, effectively locking the peasantry into a new form of the serfdom they had escaped seventy years earlier, in 1861.

This collection of perhaps one hundred little houses seemed to survive only due to the magnetic field of the two-hundred-year-old yellow-painted Church of the Archangel Mikhail and its white-bearded eighty-year-old priest, Father Ioann. Some six decades earlier, then a simple country carpenter, he had spoken out against collectivization and spent several years in a labor camp as a consequence. Now the Gorbachev leadership was coming closer every day to acknowledging that he had been right, but it gave him no satisfaction. The disaster around him was too stark. "There's no hope, because there's no faith," he said. "People don't believe in God. They don't believe in the Communist party. They've forgotten how to work."

On the glassed-in porch of the little house of a widow named Maria Yakovlevna, with flies buzzing, I sipped her cow's still-warm milk from a glass jar and listened to war stories. The unhealing wound of Plosko-Kuzminka was not the Great Patriotic War, World War II. Though it had taken the lives of many villagers, that war had been a just cause. No, the villagers interrupted one another telling the only foreigner they had ever seen about de-kulakization, the "liquidation of the kulaks as a class" at the beginning of the 1930s. The kulaks were the "rich peasants" who had managed to make a go of farming, build up a small herd of livestock, perhaps hire a laborer or two. Naturally, they resisted the hardest when the Soviet regime ordered all peasants onto collective farms. In Stalin's determination to break the resistance, millions of kulaks were arrested and executed or sent into exile, along with countless ordinary peasants caught in the frenzy of score-settling and denunciation. "It was tearing everything down and building nothing in its place," said Ivan Fyodorovich, fifty-four, a big, open-faced man who had grown up hearing the horrors of the time recounted by his parents and grandparents.

"The kulaks, they were the *rabotyagi*," the hard workers, agreed Maria Yakovlevna, at sixty-seven just old enough to remember herself.

They told of families broken up, neighbors hauled away, houses burned, children going hungry as agriculture was devastated by the war on the kulaks. They told the long, sad story of the failure of the local *kolkhoz*, or collective farm, with its succession of grand plans from Moscow and its succession of hapless chairmen. Officials had tried the old Bolshevik name magic to will the kolkhoz to a "glorious destiny." What started as the First of May Collective Farm faltered and was recast as the Lenin Collective Farm. Later it was reorganized and renamed the Victory Collective Farm. In defeat, Victory was reorganized yet again to become the 50th Anniversary of the October Revolution Collective Farm. Finally Gorbachev ended the fashion for sloganeering names, and the local kolkhoz became the State Variety Testing Station. But none of the succession of names had conjured crops from the rich black earth. Now Moscow was moving hesitantly toward offering the land back to the peasants. But Stalin's factory metaphor had worked: most of the *kolkhozniki* commuted from apartments in Lipetsk, worked eight-hour shifts, and had no interest in taking on the long hours and risk of their own farms.

Ivan Fyodorovich was fifty-four, and he could count only four men younger than himself left in the village. "Who's going to take the land?" he asked me. "If they finally are ready to give back the land, who's going to take it?"

ℵ

Hundreds of thousands of kulaks forced from their land in the 1930s had been forced from places like Plosko-Kuzminka into exile at one or another of Stalin's industrial mega-projects. In the Ural Mountain city of Magnitogorsk, the quintessential Stalin-era factory town, I asked older residents how they had come to live there. Again and again I heard the same answer, from the mother of the Communist party ideology secretary, from a curator at the local history museum, from a grimy-faced steelworker: Their parents, or grandparents, had been de-kulakized, thrown off their land, and shipped here involuntarily. So there was an eerie historical fraternity between a place like Plosko-Kuzminka and one like Magnitogorsk, between collectivization and industrialization. Stalin had squeezed grain for export from the peasantry to earn the hard currency necessary to build Magnitogorsk—using Western technology purchased from firms such as McKee Corporation, the Cleveland engineering company for which my grandfather worked. At this steel combine, once the world's largest, some of the agony, ruthlessness, and heroism of crash industrialization remained. You could understand the steep upward curve of steel production on the 70-Years-of-Soviet-Power charts that had become a staple of propaganda.

It was here that young John Scott, the American idealist, had landed to build socialism. He had quickly learned that those building "Magnitka" were not just young enthusiasts but exiled kulaks and prisoners, many of them framed on trumped-up charges. Gradually he fell into disillusion. When his friends were arrested for nothing in the great purges of the late 1930s, a survivor justified the terror by telling him, "We are at war." It was a class war, the man told him. Collectivization was war; industrialization was war; Stalin seemed to require the discipline, sacrifice, and fanatical loyalty of war to build the economy he sought. Indeed, when real war came in 1941, Magnitogorsk seemed to reflect brilliant foresight, since it supplied the Soviet armaments that defeated Hitler even after his troops had occupied the older industrial areas of the Ukraine and Russia.

By the time I visited in 1991, the plant was a dinosaur, the 1930s allowed to live into the 1980s under the protection of the state. It reminded me in many ways of Bethlehem Steel's huge Sparrows Point plant in Baltimore. But for decades Sparrows Point had been painfully, gradually adjusting to the changing world market and to tightening environmental regulation. Magnitogorsk had been protected from both. The town was an ecological catastrophe: the clouds above the plant alternated between blue, red, and yellow, and residents said they got headaches whenever they went on vacation to a place with clean air. Now Magnitogorsk suddenly seemed confronted with both the urgent need to cut its pollution and the prospect of having to compete on the world market. The world hardly needed huge quantities of low-quality Magnitogorsk steel. Stephen Kotkin, a Princeton University professor who did a detailed study of Magnitogorsk, concluded that such smokestack-era monsters would remain "a daunting stumbling-block for all who would dare to lead the country out of crisis."

This, then, was the Brobdingnagian economy Stalin had built on the bones of kulaks and prisoners, an economy subject to state command and control. It was an economy designed not to generate the stream of information necessary for self-regulation but to respond to orders from the regime. It was an economy planned for total control. But especially in the absence of terror, control cannot be total.

When he retired in early 1990 at the age of thirty-two, Valentin Fomin was doing rather well for himself. He was taking home about thirty thousand rubles a month, or more than one hundred times the average Soviet salary at the time.

Fomin was a slightly shy, acne-faced man from a small Ukrainian city who looked considerably younger than his years. Only the Camel or Marlboro cigarettes in his shirt pocket hinted at his wealth. But he had followed what in America would have been a textbook path to business success. He had identified a product people wanted—an electronic "decoder" that would enable Soviet

VCRs to play European videotapes. He had found a way to produce the decoders in quantity. He had priced them competitively, virtually cornered the Moscow market, and watched the money pour in.

In the West Fomin might have been profiled by a financial magazine or invited to lecture at a business school. In the Soviet Union he considered himself fortunate to stay out of jail. His electronic components were purchased on the black market, undoubtedly after having been stolen from state enterprises; there was no legitimate source. The decoders were assembled by technicians at state factories who used state-owned equipment during working hours and simply ignored their official assignments. Fomin and his partner made as many decoders as they could, working with no quota from Gosplan; they set their own prices, without help from Goskomtsen; and they distributed the decoders via word of mouth and, later, discreet classified ads in the Moscow evening paper, not according to the decrees of Gossnab. There was no end to the laws they had broken. Their activity was what Soviet law referred to as "speculation," also known as buying cheap and selling dear.

When the state's command economy of heroic steel combines and grandly named collective farms failed to meet demand for a particular good or service, there was often an enterprising citizen ready to plug the gap. On a good day in front of the consignment shop on Komsomolsky Prospekt, you could buy or arrange to buy any brand of imported beer or cigarettes or perfume; a huge range of electronics and clothing; even a foreign car. The service was good, and the prices were out of sight. "Black market" is too paltry a term for the scale of unofficial commerce; "shadow economy," the favored term in Soviet parlance, came closer to the truth. Even though it was against the law, it was everywhere, involved everyone, and served everyone. "May you live on one salary" was a jocular curse almost as old as the Soviet Union.

They might not have thought of it this way, but the decoder makers, and the cab driver who moonlighted as a car repairman, and the machinist who traded in stamps on Saturdays, were really economic dissidents. By exercising economic freedom, they were challenging the state's monopoly on the economy, just as a political dissident who asserted freedom of speech or of the press challenged the state's monopoly on ideology. And if they were caught by the state, the moonlighters could be sent to a labor camp just as political dissidents were.

A prisoner returning from the Gulag in Vasily Grossman's essay-novel of 1963, *Forever Flowing*—banned along with *Life and Fate* until the late 1980s—comes to understand the parallel restraints on mental and physical labor. "I used to think freedom was freedom of speech, freedom of the press, freedom of conscience. But freedom is the whole life of everyone," the ex-prisoner declares. "Here is what it amounts to: you have to have the right to sow what you wish to, to make shoes or coats, to bake into bread the flour ground from the grain you have sown, and to sell it or not sell it as you wish; for the lathe operator, the steelworker, and the artist it's a matter of being able to live as you wish and not as they order you to. And in our country there is no freedom—not for those who write books nor for those who sow grain nor for those who make shoes."

The ban on free press and the ban on free enterprise sometimes conspired to make risk-taking entrepreneurs rich. The economics writer Vasily Selyunin told me in 1990 that he had been pleased to find a couple of years earlier a reliable samizdat photocopying service that could produce high-quality copies quickly at five kopecks a page, the price of a ride on the Metro. As in most such arrangements, Selyunin had only a first name and phone number, though he assumed the reproduction was being done illegally at night in some state institution. One day he was given an envelope that he expected to contain the copy of a foreign journal article he had requested. But there had been a mix-up. Inside the envelope was a document prepared for the next meeting of the secretariat of the Communist Party Central Committee, the country's top leaders. He called, and the envelopes were exchanged with due apologies. But Selyunin was delighted to learn by accident that his illicit photocopy service was run by moonlighting employees of the Central Committee, who would gladly reproduce the most subversive stuff as long as they got their money. "Hey," Selyunin said, "they have to live too."

Valentin Fomin, the decoder man, had gotten into the shadow economy gradually, via the unofficial street markets that had developed alongside the state stores. There were unofficial but well-known sites around the city for specialized retail commerce in the areas where the state system failed most egregiously; apartment exchanges, videotapes, cassettes and records, books, auto parts, and many other items. As a rock music fan in his early twenties, Fomin said, he had begun to hang out at a street music mart that developed in a park on Tsvetnoy Boulevard, just down the street from our apartment building. Like most of the black markets, the Tsvetnoy market was raided off and on by police, in the manner that U.S. police occasionally sweep an urban drug corner. "The police would come and we'd scatter like cockroaches when you turn on the light," Fomin recalled.

At first he just traded records. But he gradually learned subtleties that few rock aficionados in the West knew. A Beatles record from England, for instance, went for fifty-five rubles, while a disc with an identical cover but manufactured in Greece with inferior vinyl brought only forty rubles—prices set by the market and carrying information about quality and demand. As a buyer, "if you didn't see that 'Made in Greece' label you lost fifteen rubles," Fomin said. Later he graduated to making and selling cassette copies of rock records, either from his own growing collection or rented from street dealers for five rubles a day. The cassette business grew until he was working twelve-hour days and grossing eighteen hundred rubles a month, he said. That compared with the seventy-three rubles a month he made in his official job, sweeping a stretch of sidewalk near the Chinese embassy, or the two hundred a month he earned later as an emergency repairman for elevators. Both jobs were *khalyavy*, sinecures requiring few hours and little effort, but they served to keep him from prosecution as a "parasite."

From cassette recording, Fomin moved on to buying foreign-made electronics equipment from sailors and other travelers and reselling it. In 1988, as video boomed on the shadow economy, he started making the decoders. The parts for one decoder cost him about forty rubles on the black market. He paid another ruble for a printed circuit board and five rubles to the factory technician who soldered the parts to the board. But getting the microchip that was the heart of the device was the stickiest job. Such microchips were not sold to the public in the USSR, so Fomin, who had never been abroad himself, supplied acquaintances who were going to Western Europe or the United States with Soviet military watches and Cuban cigars. The travelers sold the goods and used part of the proceeds to buy the microchips. When Fomin started out, the street price for a decoder was 250 rubles. Once Fomin and his partner got their manufacturing down to a reliable system, they began to offer the decoders for 125 rubles, half the going price. The business prospered. Unhappy competitors threatened him. "People called when we cut the price to 125 and said, 'We'll burn your apartment out,'" he said. Such threats were not necessarily idle; even then, some of Moscow's black marketeers played by gangland rules. But Fomin said he and his partner called the competitors' bluff: "We answered very simply: 'Call again and we'll cut our price another five rubles.'"

Earning twenty-five times what a Politburo member made, Fomin spent lavishly. He had a state-of-the-art imported compact disc player and two hundred discs, bought on the black market, of course. He never took the bus or Metro, preferring always to flag a private taxi. He smoked only American cigarettes, an expensive status symbol. He amassed a big collection of the black-market philosophy and economics books he liked to read. He capitalized some black-market businesses for friends. But he grew worried about violence in the shadow economy, which was increasingly controlled by organized gangs. And he was tired of being viewed by the law and by many of his fellow citizens as a criminal. "If the government pays 10 rubles for jeans and sells them for 100 rubles, that's normal. If a *fartsovshchik* [black marketeer] buys the same pair for 100 and sells them for 130, that's speculation," he said. Despairing over the Gorbachev regime's refusal to move dramatically to legalize the private economy, Fomin joined the queue at the American embassy and left for the United States in late 1990. "Commerce should be respected in society," he told me before he left. "Here, it's not. There, it is."

Fomin's engaging entrepreneurship was one side of the shadow economy, but there was another. It was on spectacular view in Uzbekistan when the Soviet government decided to crack down on official corruption in the cotton industry. A short, balding, grandstanding detective named Telman Gdlyan, along with his sidekick Nikolai Ivanov, kept pulling on the thread of bribery even as it began to unravel the Communist party and government of this Central Asian republic of twenty million people. By falsifying cotton statistics on a grand scale, officials from Communist party boss Sharif Rashidov on down had diverted millions of rubles to their private use. The cotton swindle was protected by an elaborate hierarchy of bribery reaching from local police precincts up to top Ministry of Internal Affairs officials in Moscow including Brezhnev's playboy son-in-law, Yuri Churbanov. At first, Gdlyan and Ivanov—a phrase that became nearly as familiar to Soviet ears as "Marx and Lenin"—were lionized by the press for their courage in exposing "the Uzbek affair" in the face of death threats and tempting bribe offers. Then, suddenly, they were denounced for using blackmail, deceit, marathon interrogations, and even torture to wring confessions from suspects. Clearly there was some substance to the charges; after all, they were part of a police state with Stalinism in its past. But just as clearly their "impermissible methods" were not the real reason the probe was shut down.

The problem was that the snowballing investigation had decimated the entire power structure of Uzbekistan, revealing that the cotton scam and associated bribery was not an ugly residue of capitalism but rather an organic part of the Communist economic system. Power was for sale, and its cost had even become more or less stable and standardized: the post of first party secretary of a district in Uzbekistan could be purchased for ten thousand rubles. Russians who wrote about the Uzbek affair often emphasized its roots in the Asian culture of gift-giving. But Lev Timofeyev, a brilliant dissident writer who got interested in the case when the Uzbek cotton minister turned up as his cellmate, argued that the real key to the scandal was the bureaucratic control of prices. Timofeyev's subtle and complex thesis can be summarized as follows: Bureaucrats who are given the ability to control prices exercise so much economic power that their own offices become a desirable market commodity, and they themselves end up being bought and sold. "The price is a most important instrument of power. To set prices is the privilege and right of the bureaucrats of the ruling apparat. Or not simply a privilege, but a sort of fundamental, sacred principle of Communist doctrine," Timofeyev wrote in a powerful article in 1991, long after he had been released from a camp and his cotton-minister friend executed. "Behind the 'cotton affair,' behind the modest fact of the overvaluing of cotton that we have discovered, is revealed an epoch-making phenomenon: the logical and historically inescapable overvaluing of power itself," he wrote. "With historical inevitability, the Communist doctrine is turning the country into a huge black market, and its ruling apparat into a criminal mafia." Corruption was not in the system, he argued; corruption *was* the system. Between 1984 and 1987, 90.4 percent of Communist Party Central Committee officials in Uzbekistan were dismissed in connection with the probe, the new party leader, Inamshon Usmankhodzhayev, reported after being brought in to clean house. Then Usmankhodzhayev himself was arrested and charged with taking tens of thousands in bribes.

"Acceleration" was Gorbachev's first economic reform slogan, and the first to be abandoned. It is not difficult to see why. Accelerate the production of steel and concrete? Of shoes? Of soap powder? Of sour milk? Of nonexistent cotton? It was not the gas pedal but the steering wheel that was failing. Fixing the steering mechanism would mean freeing prices and breaking up the state monopoly. Taking those steps would mean abandoning the propaganda claims on which the regime based its legitimacy and abandoning the levers of power. No wonder Gorbachev and his prime minister, Nikolai Ryzhkov, preferred to keep tinkering. In regular Saturday-night TV interviews with a fawning Soviet journalist in 1990, Ryzhkov played the benign corporate president to his audience of state employees, reviewing quarterly results and urging them to greater efforts. His general approach was: first stabilize, then reform. But the tendency was to get stuck at the stabilization phase.

Sometimes the solution seemed so tantalizingly obvious. A couple of hours south of Moscow I visited Vladimir Gusenkov, a thirty-nine-year-old man who had become a media star in late 1988 by leasing, with official approval, fifty cows and 150 acres from the Vereysky State Farm and starting his own operation. Soviet journalists were charmed by the farm-family saga, a banal piece of bourgeois life to us bourgeois correspondents but a sensation to *Pravda* and Central Television. There was twelve-year-old Alyosha, a daredevil behind the wheel of the tractor; seven-year-old Olya, who had penciled the cows' nicknames above their stalls; and Vladimir's wife, Galina, who cheerfully served reporters and photographers tea from a huge samovar and studied a book of blueprints for additions to their little house, including one with an indoor swimming pool. Gusenkov had raised his cows' productivity from 3,200 liters per year—already above the Soviet average—to 5,200 liters and was widely viewed as a farming genius. Gusenkov himself knew better, and so did Viktor Ninkonenko, the reformist state farm director who was actually trying to get his workers to lease land. American cows produced 6,000 or more liters per year, Ninkonenko noted. The real miracle was not 5,200 liters but 3,200, he said. In a disarming confession, Ninkonenko said the state farm had such a low yield because the workers assigned to milk the cows didn't always bother to milk them. "He gets his pay, he goes on a drunk, and the cows may not get milked, may not get cleaned for days. There [on the state farm] every cow has a dozen masters. Here," he said, gesturing at Gusenkov, "there's one master, and he's interested in profit."

It was a beautiful picture, one that gave hope that a few million Gusenkovs would soon turn Russian agriculture around. But there were catches. One was the 210,000 rubles the state farm had invested in creating the Gusenkovs' model farmstead—building the house and barn, providing a tractor and other equipment. Where would the capital come from to replicate it everywhere else? Moreover, the Gusenkovs' milk was still being dumped into the same storage and distribution system that produced the milk that soured so quickly in Muscovites' refrigerators. Although his cows' productivity was admirable, the real milk problem was not gross production but preservation and transportation. Gusenkov's farm was a Potemkin village in the sense that it cheered up the press and public without threatening the power structure of the countryside. Until the *fermeri* (the Russians borrowed the English word for the specific meaning, "private farmer") were truly competing with the collective and state farms for land and customers, no political battle had been won, or even fought. Despite the atypical encouragement from Ninkonenko, the state farm director, Gusenkov's former co-workers on the state farm next door had not rushed to follow his example and lease their own farms. Most of them seemed to prefer their shift work, their modest pay packets, and their occasional vodka binges to the responsibility and risk of a private farm.

The Russian-born American economist Wassily Leontief, a Nobel laureate, visited his native land a few times to offer encouragement and advice. But he always emphasized the scale of the task. Once, asking the people's patience for growing economic chaos, he compared perestroika with the total renovation of a house while the family remained in residence. On another occasion he said reforming the Soviet economy was "like teaching penguins to fly." What became increasingly clear after 1988 was that the Stalinist economy, still essentially intact, could not be reformed. It could only be dismantled, and a market economy grown in the ruins.

4

The KGB,
Father of Perestroika

The ubiquitous, omnipotent state police.... This is the
hideous spider whose invisible web runs right through the
whole of society; this is the vanishing point where all the
lines of fear ultimately intersect; this is the final and
irrefutable proof that no citizen can hope to challenge the
power of the state. And even if most people, most of the
time, cannot see this web with their own eyes, nor touch its
filaments, even the simplest citizen is well aware of its
existence, assumes its silent presence at every moment in
every place, and behaves accordingly—behaves, that is, so as
to acquit himself in those hidden eyes and ears.
> —Vaclav Havel, "Dear Dr. Husak," 1975

From the KGB—To the Children
The children of the F. E. Dzerzhinsky Orphanage in Omsk
now have their own transportation. The employees of the
Omsk Region branch of the KGB have given their young
charges Bus No. PAZ-672, declared surplus by the KGB
fleet.
> —Caption to photo of smiling KGB officer
> standing with a group of children in
> front of a bus, *Izvestiya*, February 27, 1990

He who has the information calls the shots.
> —retired KGB Lieutenant Colonel Vladimir
> Rubanov, *Moscow News*, April 21, 1991

In November 1987 the city of Sverdlovsk saw some of the first spontaneous political demonstrations in Soviet Russia since the 1920s. They were modest affairs—a few dozen people, mostly intellectuals, gathering on a downtown square to demand in the name of glasnost the facts about the resignation of Boris Yeltsin, the populist Moscow party boss and a native son of Sverdlovsk. But the rallies were more than enough to rivet the attention of the KGB.

As the agency whose mission was to maintain political control, and first of all information control, the Committee for State Security was suddenly facing unprecedented challenges to its habitual mode of operation. Reform, we shall see, had been launched with the crucial support of the KGB. But as the process of change picked up momentum and a grassroots constituency, the KGB leadership would shift to skepticism, alarm, and finally, in 1991, open resistance. The Sverdlovsk rallies are a window on the security police at a revealing moment in the early stages of the gathering information battle.

A year or two earlier such effrontery on the part of the public would have been ended swiftly and unceremoniously. The would-be demonstrators would have been hustled instantaneously into police vans and rushed to jail, restoring the streets to their accustomed political silence.

Now things were more delicate and complex. Yeltsin, previously party boss in Sverdlovsk for ten years, had in his twenty-two months as Moscow's party leader recast himself as a populist and the Politburo's most radical reformer. Then, at a closed Central Committee plenum in October, he had mysteriously resigned. At a Moscow party meeting a few weeks later, Yeltsin was savaged by officials from Gorbachev on down, all the way to neighborhood functionaries. When the transcript of the session ran in *Pravda*, the unanimous denunciations had an eerily Stalinist cast and transformed Yeltsin into a martyr of reform. Telegrams, letters, and petitions poured into newspapers and Kremlin offices defending Yeltsin and demanding publication of his still-secret plenum speech.

In Sverdlovsk, a tough, industrial city of 1.3 million in the Urals, the KGB was in a quandary. Forcefully breaking up the tiny demonstrations and arresting their participants might spark even bigger protests. Moreover, the political rules were changing. Gorbachev was talking all the time about glasnost. Andrei Sakharov had been released from exile in Gorky the previous December. Scores of political prisoners had been freed. True, Gorbachev had blasted Yeltsin in the party's whipping session as "politically immature." But what did that mean? What was the KGB to do? Break up the pro-Yeltsin protests? Or sit back and applaud the expansion of democracy?

The Sverdlovsk KGB chose to use what was, in the absence of outright terror, the agency's most potent weapon and the source of its unmatched power over Soviet lives: information. One rally took place November 22. By November 23 KGB agents had turned in a detailed report on the identities of the thirty-two demonstrators. Each entry on the report, which was leaked to me much later, included the protester's name, year and place of birth, place and nature of work, address, and other relevant facts. For instance:

Polozov Gennady Dmitrievich
year of birth 1939, native of Kamyshin, Kuibyshev region
singer in the chorus of the Opera and Ballet Theater
lives on Lenin Street, house 64, apartment 148
member of the Historical-Cultural Society "Fatherland"

In the next two columns the agents listed times and places where the individual had participated in public meetings ("1905 Square, Regional Communist Party Committee building, Sverdlov House of Culture"), revealing at a glance which demonstrators were most active. Since the protests were spontaneous, the speed and completeness of the report suggests that the local KGB had ample files, plenty of men for street surveillance, and a wide net of informants, including agents infiltrated into activist circles.

Notations penciled on the report in the days that followed revealed the KGB's diverse and imaginative tactics in trying to prevent or minimize the size of future rallies while doing nothing publicly at odds with Gorbachev's proclaimed glasnost. The agents spoke to protesters' parents, job supervisors, or, in the case of a few Communist party members, leaders of their party units. In some

cases they arranged for obligatory duties at a demonstrator's workplace to coincide with the scheduled time of the next rally. In others
they sought weak points for pressure or blackmail.

"Rehearsal," said the note on Gennady Polozov's entry, indicating
that the KGB had arranged for a choral rehearsal to be scheduled at
the time of the next planned protest. "Business trip" had been
arranged for another. For a woman working in a pharmacy who
had proven "Uncontrollable" the KGB men noted: "Arrange inspection with OBKhSS"—in other words, organize a police vice-squad
inspection of pharmacy drug records at the time of the planned
demonstration, necessitating her presence at her workplace. For a
thirty-eight-year-old man officially categorized as disabled by epilepsy, the note said: "We will request hospitalization." Of another
demonstrator the note said, "Engages in speculation [i.e., black
market activity]," suggesting a possible area for KGB leverage.

Some activists were given character sketches: "Sticks up for
himself, sociable, communicative" for one man, "Blabbermouth!"
for another. Other notations summarized the more active protesters'
speeches to the crowd: "Actively agitated in favor of organizing a
demonstration 29/11. Proposed walking in organized columns, carrying flags at the head and rear of the columns, walk along the sides
with red armbands, that way no one will have the right to stop the
demonstrators. There will be megaphones, we won't disperse, bring
with you relatives and acquaintances."

The lists leaked to me are incomplete, but the KGB campaign
seems to have had temporary success. Many names were marked,
"Gave in," suggesting they had succumbed to pressure and agreed
not to attend future rallies. Scrawled at the top of one list, as on a
scorecard, was the notation: "of 34, 12 can say for certain will not
participate."

The Sverdlovsk rally notes represent, if not quite omniscience on
the part of the KGB, at least a good try. By knowing everything, the
KGB would increase its chances for controlling everything. That was
the theory, and for a time it worked.

Before the Bolshevik coup, the yellowish stone building with the columned façade and the clock below the roofline had been the office of the All-Russia Insurance Society. Since 1917 it had housed an agency that provided a different kind of insurance to the select clientele who worked down the street in the Kremlin.

Facing a busy square next to the Children's World department store, the Lubyanka, headquarters of the KGB, was nondescript— indeed, its architecture was less intimidating than many newer, Soviet-era buildings. But few Russians walked past without an involuntary shudder at the history it stood for. "Every time I pass by the solemn façades of the buildings occupied by the KGB," a Muscovite wrote to the magazine *Ogonyok* in September 1988, "I experience a feeling of vague alarm, perplexity and, I admit, fear. I don't think I threaten in any way the security of the Fatherland—yet there were so many who never threatened it...." Behind the heavy wooden doors to the Lubyanka, faceless men had overseen terror unprecedented in human history. To its cells party leaders, eminent scientists, brilliant writers had been spirited from their homes for long nights of interrogation and sometimes torture. In its cellars thousands had been executed without trial. In less bloody times, the KGB had shattered careers, forced some of Russia's greatest citizens into exile, and intimidated all who challenged the system.

Yet it was the ultimate paradox of perestroika that from behind these doors, in the early 1980s, came the original impetus for reform. Yuri Andropov, KGB chairman for fifteen years, had imparted a sense of crisis about the Soviet position in the world when he succeeded Brezhnev in 1982. He had anointed as his heir Gorbachev, who with the KGB's tacit support would launch the most daring reforms since the Revolution. Thus the most important institutional sponsor of change was the very agency that seemed most reactionary, most threatened by democracy. In fact, it probably could have been no other way: any reform that lacked the blessing of the security police would have been swiftly and quietly snuffed out.

Information in any society is power. In the Soviet Union the KGB had the information. When so much information was stopped at the borders, scissored out of the press, and hushed on the airwaves, no institution benefited more than the *Komitet Gosudarstvennoi Bezopasnosti*, the Committee for State Security. Entrusted with the data kept from everyone else, the KGB could determine to a considerable degree which facts were for the broad public and which for secret archives, who was to be praised as an innovator and who arrested as a subversive, which policies would be propped up and which demolished with fact-packed, eyes-only reports.

Officially, according to Soviet doctrine, the secret police were the "sword and shield" of the Communist party, its "armed detachment." As the agency's name changed over the years—ChK, OGPU, NKVD, NKGB, MGB, finally KGB—it remained, in theory, a powerful instrument, but merely an instrument, of Communist power. But in practice, where did the Politburo get its inside information? Who reported to local party bosses about corrupt factory managers or unreliable journalists? Who decided which information would be highlighted for the general secretary, which information provided but without emphasis, and which information omitted from the leader's daily reports?

A high KGB official in the 1960s told the Soviet sculptor Ernst Neizvestny that Norbert Wiener, the inventor of cybernetics, "was completely correct when he said in his book *Cybernetics and Society* that without feedback, society cannot survive," as Neizvestny recalled years later, after he had emigrated. " 'But Wiener was wrong in thinking that our society has no feedback,' the general said. 'We do have feedback,' he continued, 'because the KGB is a kind of feedback. In the USSR, the KGB realistically reports to the upper echelon the actual situation in the country.' " The story reflects the KGB's awareness of how its influence was magnified by the information-control system it administered. At the same time it is just another facet of the glittering gem that was the Soviet illusion: the belief that a vast multinational superpower in the late twentieth century could be governed on the exclusive basis of reports to the leadership from a spy-and-police agency.

Unquestionably, if anyone could be expected to spot the economic disaster looming for the USSR in the face of the world's information revolution, it was the firm-jawed overseers of the Lubyanka. This mammoth agency, CIA, NSA, and FBI rolled into one, was an information monster, sucking up data and then parceling it out discreetly to party bosses. Information poured in from hundreds of domestic offices, which in turn received reports from approximately one million domestic informants. *Chekisti*—the romantic name for KGB agents, comparable to "G-men" for FBI agents, derived from the original abbreviation for Dzerzhinsky's secret police, the "ChK" or Cheka—were in place in every large factory, every university, every research institute, every government agency. Letters from citizens suspected of dissenting views were intercepted and opened. Their telephone calls were monitored. If other government agencies struggled along with outdated or worn-out equipment, the KGB could count on the best: a KGB cameraman with a portable video camera, usually a Panasonic, was a fixture at every unsanctioned political gathering in Moscow.

The resulting mosaic portrait of Soviet reality could be compared with economic and social data provided by several thousand agents posted all over the world. KGB analysts read the Western analyses of Soviet affairs that were kept from others. They monitored the "radio voices" that they also jammed. They read and studied the samizdat critiques of official policy that they were paid to track down and stamp out.

For KGB officers, all of whom were required to be in the 7 percent of the population that belonged to the Communist party, the Soviet illusion naturally was a powerful and durable molder of perceptions, as it was for others. But exposure to more information nonetheless seems to have brought a certain realism to the KGB's analysis of the information predicament.

If the party under Brezhnev, in the years before his death in 1982, seemed almost oblivious to the eroding Soviet economic position, the KGB under Andropov was acutely aware of the deepening quicksand. As head of the agency from 1967 until 1982, Andropov had a clearer idea than almost anyone else in the leadership of how serious and fundamental were the causes of Soviet economic malaise. Eager to focus the Kremlin's attention, Andropov set up a secret department for economic analysis in the KGB in the late 1970s or early 1980s. Such a department would undoubtedly have highlighted

Soviet technological backwardness and focused on the enormous role played by West Siberian oil in financing such economic progress as there had been in the 1970s. Understanding that the oil-fueled joyride was coming to an end, Andropov would have known that the Soviet Union's very status as a superpower, already reduced essentially to a big collection of nuclear warheads, could soon be jeopardized altogether. The KGB wanted to be the secret police and intelligence agency of a superpower—not of some oversized Third World country, "Upper Volta with missiles," as the sardonic saying went.

So it was, after all, logical that the KGB should have been a force in favor of economic reform, particularly as the full implications of reform for ideology, party power, and national unity were not yet evident. "Really, who else in the country other than the KGB, with its exclusive channels of information, knew what in reality was happening in the expanses of the Fatherland, including in the economy?" wrote Yevgeniya Albats, a *Moscow News* reporter and one of the most penetrating Soviet students of the secret police, in 1991. "The Central Committee? The Politburo? From whom? If from local areas flowed the touched-up, cleaned-up, prettied-up reports that suited the top leaders?.... In short, only the KGB had a full enough picture of a) the state of affairs in the Soviet Union; b) the success of Western military technology, to come to the conclusion: the economy had reached the point where it was already losing its ability to meet the demands of the military-industrial complex and, it followed, posed a threat to the existence of the very system of power. That meant reforms were needed. But what kind? Obviously within limits preserving the security of the State Security Committee itself."

Albats was a courageous and outspoken young woman who took on the KGB partly because for her it embodied the moral degradation which the Communist regime had imposed on her country. During the day she tracked down elderly Stalin-era investigators for her own interrogations about their crimes and developed sources within the KGB to track its shifting position in an era of reform. In the evening she read from the Bible to her uncomprehending infant daughter, hoping that the habit would somehow shield the baby from the sordid world of party and KGB. Her research and interviews led her to conclude that under Andropov, the KGB's control of information had turned it into an independent political force in some ways more powerful than the party. (Such a development had been foreseen in the emigré novelist Vladimir Voinovich's comic anti-utopia *Moscow 2042*, where the country is ruled not by the Communist party [KP] or the State Security Committee [KGB] but by the KPGB, the Communist Party for State Security.)

When Andropov became too sick to work less than a year after becoming Communist party general secretary, he designated Gorbachev to take his place at leadership meetings. Palace intrigue thwarted Andropov's designated heir from succeeding him immediately, as Konstantin Chernenko, Brezhnev's shadow, maneuvered into the general secretary's chair with the backing of the party's old guard. But Chernenko lived only a little more than a year. And when the Politburo chose a successor to Chernenko in March 1985, the KGB played a decisive role in Gorbachev's favor.

Gorbachev's chief rival for the job was Viktor Grishin, the aging, conservative Moscow party boss. According to a number of authoritative accounts, Viktor Chebrikov, Andropov's longtime associate and successor as KGB chief, undermined Grishin's candidacy and guaranteed Gorbachev's selection by citing KGB evidence of corruption against Grishin's playboy son.

Gorbachev acknowledged the status of the KGB in his administration by giving Chebrikov the key speech on November 6, 1985, at the Kremlin ceremony on the eve of the first Revolution Day under his leadership. Chebrikov reciprocated by expressing strong backing for Gorbachev and his nascent reforms. In fact the KGB chief used in his speech the Russian word *reforma*, still pronounced infrequently and timidly in Gorbachev's first year. He spoke of "the extension of personal rights and freedoms" and called the current moment a "turning point."

Confirmation for Chebrikov's and the KGB's crucial support for Communist reform has come from unlikely sources. The liberal theater director Mark Zakharov, who had frank conversations with the young KGB men who accompanied his troupe on foreign tours in the guise of "employees of the Ministry of Culture," wrote in

1991: "I'm convinced: it was the KGB that exerted the greatest effort to change the state's situation after the death of Chernenko. Judging by certain hints, the leading role in the decision to name Gorbachev to the post of general secretary, which was so fateful for the whole planet, was played by the most farsighted and enlightened people in our secret institution. It was precisely they who pushed aside the undoubted candidate to that post, Grishin. Precisely they, with the help of the works of American Sovietologists that had been seized at customs, established a scientifically objective opinion of the condition of the Soviet state. They knew better than other leaders...the negative dynamic of our economy and the popular mood, and palpably felt the extreme spiritual degradation of society."

On March 21, 1988, KGB chief Chebrikov gave Gorbachev and the rest of the party leadership a revealing status report on the agency's information-control mission. "In 1987, the measures implemented in the country for economic perestroika and the broadening of democratization and glasnost resulted in a 29.5 percent reduction in the distribution of anonymous materials of an anti-Soviet, nationalistic, or politically harmful content as compared with the previous year," Chebrikov wrote. "However," he went on, "the number of persons who took part in their preparation and distribution (1,663) increased by 9.4 percent because of some growth of certain cliquish, negative occurrences among the youth of the Kazakh SSR and Latvia." He appended such helpful details as a breakdown of the occupations of the "authors of pamphlets, letters, and graffiti": 37.2 percent students, 18.6 percent workers, 16.8 percent office workers, 9.5 percent retired.

Here it is: the KGB performing the role of feedback to the leadership from the entire country. The secret report—made public only in 1992—betrays a breathtaking self-confidence, by which the KGB chief assumes his agency can know what is happening, down to a tenth of a percentage point, from Minsk to Kamchatka. But it also demonstrates Chebrikov's conception of reform—his implicit assertion that relaxed political controls are somehow leading to a *reduction* in anti-Soviet activity. It shows how party and KGB leaders believed, for a time, that with the kind of behind-the-scenes prophylactic work the KGB was doing in Sverdlovsk, they could relinquish the grossest tactics of political persecution but still avoid real changes. The Gulag would be gone, they thought, but the system would survive.

Perestroika was a capacious and ambiguous term. The prefix *pere-* corresponds to the English *re-*, as in repeat or redo, while the root *stroika* comes from the verb *stroit*, to build. Literally, perestroika meant "restructuring" or "rebuilding," conveying the idea of change without specifying the nature of the change. In the short run that was its virtue as a slogan, since such strange political bedfellows as KGB generals, former political prisoners, and Baltic nationalists could line up behind it. In the long run the vagueness of perestroika would be its undoing, as three distinct notions of reform came more and more sharply into conflict.

For Chebrikov and the KGB, as for Andropov and for Gorbachev at the time he came to power, reform meant technological modernization, greater discipline, and an end to the flagrant corruption and embarrassing luxury of officialdom that characterized the Brezhnev era. Pressed by the postindustrial global economy, the regime would have to ease controls on information and information technology that had made it inefficient, backward, and isolated. It would remove the absurdities. Such policies, the leaders believed, would serve to accelerate Soviet economic development, thus strengthening the fifteen-republic Soviet empire, the socialist fatherland. Reform would vindicate, not vanquish, Soviet ideology. In short, this blueprint for perestroika can be called Communist reform.

But for ordinary people, as they received new information about their history and about life in the outside world, reform came to mean something very different. A phrase that recurred in conversations beginning about 1988 captured the populist conception of the goal of reform: *normalnaya strana*, a normal country. A normal country would be one where the stores offered a reasonable choice of food and consumer goods without long lines and constant shortages. And it would be one where people could say, write, or read what they wanted without fear that they would be punished for it. To most people it was of secondary importance whether this normal country consisted of all fifteen republics or whether it could be called "socialist." This vision of perestroika can be given the name of populist reform.

For non-Russians, reform had a third interpretation. They too wanted to live in a normal country. But to the Russian's criteria of an adequate living standard and a measure of political freedom, many non-Russians added full sovereignty or outright secession for their republic. Few Lithuanians, for instance, would accept that they were citizens of a normal country until they were citizens of an independent Lithuania, and the same went for Estonians, Latvians, Georgians, Armenians, Moldavians—the list grew with every passing month. Call their vision of perestroika nationalist reform.

As the Gorbachev era unfolded, the three versions of reform would diverge, as the "internal contradictions"—that favorite phrase of Marxist ideologists analyzing capitalism—in the original conception of perestroika came to the fore. Gradually the limited KGB version of Communist reform would be overtaken by populist and nationalist reform, or to put it differently, Communist reform would be overtaken by democratic revolution. Ultimately the KGB, which had helped give birth to perestroika, would turn on its own offspring.

In retrospect the seeds of KGB disillusionment with reform are evident in its labor-intensive tactics against the pro-Yeltsin demonstrators in Sverdlovsk in 1987. Such tactics could work only as long as demonstrators remained few, and demonstrators would be few only as long as fear of the KGB was intact. In the old days the investigation, arrest, trial, and sentencing of a rebel such as Andrei Mironov cut a wide swath of intimidation through society. In his case more than fifty people were interrogated or had their apartments searched, and his fate was an indelible lesson for all of them and for hundreds of their friends and relatives. The example of a four-year prison camp term was plenty of deterrent for most of those who might otherwise be tempted to get involved in samizdat or political protest. Fear was the key to the KGB's efficiency, since making examples of a few dissidents served to keep most everyone else in line.

But if Andrei Mironov's imprisonment had been unforgettable, his release in February 1987 was an even more memorable lesson. As prisoners of conscience were freed, as demonstrators avoided arrest, as the newspapers became more outspoken, fear began to dissipate. Andrei Mironov, plunging back into protest and agitating for the release of the remaining prisoners of conscience, discovered that in the ambiguous atmosphere of 1987 and 1988 his status as ex-prisoner had become a powerful shield. When a policeman or KGB plainclothesman stopped him and demanded *"Dokumenti!"* in the arrogant tone known to petty power around the world, Andrei obediently handed over his internal passport, the fundamental ID every citizen was required to carry. Ordinarily, surrendering one's passport was an act of submission and defeat, since the cop could learn where the holder lived and worked and bring the resources of the state to bear against him. But Andrei's passport was his trump card. Folded inside were his release papers from the camp, revealing to the policeman that he had done time under Article 70—and been released, with other political prisoners, by the decision of Gorbachev himself. The system already had done its worst to this fellow, in other words, and he had been forgiven by the highest authorities in the land. What was some poor slob of a cop, or for that matter even a KGB street officer, going to do to him?

Like most human rights advocates, Andrei was scornful of the Soviet government-organized peace campaign and exasperated by the Westerners he saw as its dupes. The Soviet Peace Committee was riddled with KGB agents, ever-ready to denounce whatever Western action the Communist party told it to denounce and reliably silent about Soviet militarism. Genrikh Borovik, smooth-talking chairman of the Peace Committee, had close ties to the KGB and had dutifully attacked Alexander Solzhenitsyn in the 1970s. Yet in the official peace movement and the naive Americans who visited the Soviet Union under its auspices, Andrei Mironov spotted a grand opportunity for creative mischief.

In June 1987, when the Soviet press reported that a Soviet-

American peace march from Leningrad to Moscow was underway, he traveled to Leningrad, inquired about the route the marchers had taken, and caught up with it in Tosno, a town near the beginning of the route. He approached the Americans and introduced himself in English. He was a Soviet citizen who wanted peace as much as anyone else, he said, but he had not been permitted to sign up for the march. The Americans—perhaps as naive about dissidents as they were about the KGB—received him warmly, and as they walked he answered their myriad questions about Soviet life. Gradually he shared his views on the political situation in the Soviet Union and the true character of the official Soviet peace movement.

The Peace Committee organizers understandably were furious. "The KGB guys were all over the place, like mosquitoes," Andrei recounted. "But there were always Americans with me, so they couldn't just grab me." After a few days, at a camp near the ancient Russian capital of Novgorod, Peace Committee marchers drew Andrei away from the crowd, and he was immediately arrested by the handiest KGB agents. Locked in the local jail with a bunch of petty criminals ("I was used to thieves"), Andrei announced to his bemused audience of pickpockets and burglars that he was beginning a hunger strike. By the next day the authorities apparently had calculated that he was causing more trouble than he was worth. They released him and put him aboard a plane to Moscow. Resistant as always to the lessons the system was trying to teach him, Andrei quickly caught a train to Kalinin, about ninety minutes from Moscow, caught up with the peace march, and resumed his cat-and-mouse act with the peaceniks from the KGB. "I had come to understand that the worse I treated the KGB, the more they would respect me," he said. "They depend on fear. When you're not afraid of them, they are much less effective."

By the time of the peace march Andrei had become a familiar figure in the growing community of Moscow human rights activists. Official glasnost was beginning to supplant the underground book photocopying he'd done before; several of Shalamov's *Kolyma Tales*, for which he'd been sentenced to a labor camp in 1986, were published in the literary monthly *Novy Mir* in June 1988. But Andrei and a number of other ex-political prisoners nonetheless understood that information remained the weapon to which the system was most vulnerable. Just as Gorbachev was using information against political rivals and conservative opponents of change, the dissidents could use information against the regime as a whole. While the KGB used its information for controlling and dampening demonstrations like those in Sverdlovsk, the dissidents could use information to stir up protest.

Andrei was one of the few Moscow activists who got along with both of the rival former political prisoners who ran the two most prominent of the new samizdat publications, Sergei Grigoryants and Alexander Podrabinek. Grigoryants, who had been denounced by Gorbachev himself for his ties to the West, named his weekly periodical *Glasnost*, defiantly taking the Soviet leader at his word. It tended to longish political essays, but the ragtag collection of dissidents who put it out often had up-to-the-moment information on KGB arrests, republican independence movements, and other matters ignored by the official press. Alexander Podrabinek, Grigoryants's rival, put out *Ekspres-Khronika* (Express-Chronicle), a fact-packed weekly with a growing network of correspondents in every republic. Every Sunday Podrabinek and his fellow editors would hold court near the statue of the writer Nikolai Gogol in downtown Moscow, distributing copies of their latest issue and collecting news of rights violations and other injustices. Police would occasionally sweep the area and arrest those hawking the newspaper, and on more than one occasion the KGB tracked down the places where it was surreptitiously photocopied. But the setbacks were temporary. Once, when the KGB shut down the moonlight photocopying at a Moscow music school, Podrabinek traveled to one of the Baltic republics—he wouldn't say which—and found an offset printer who could handle far more copies. "Every time they shut us down, our circulation goes up," Podrabinek told me with a grin.

When he wasn't gathering news for *Glasnost* or *Ekspres-Khronika*, Andrei was often promoting to foreign correspondents the causes of various victims of Soviet injustice. He understood that in the atmosphere of warming East-West relations, a mere mention in the Western press conveyed a considerable measure of protection to any Soviet citizen. One afternoon at a clandestine meeting in a park,

Andrei introduced me to Leonid Dobrov, a wood sculptor whom the KGB had put in a mental hospital for demanding schools, newspapers, and television in his native language, that of the Gagauz, a small ethnic group in Moldova. Another evening he led me to the Aerovokzal, the bus station serving Moscow's five airports, to meet a homeless woman trying to free her son from prison; she and her younger son were among a semipermanent community of about fifty homeless people living in the bus station. Another time it was Naum Slobodsky, a bureaucrat and party member given forced psychiatric treatment after he complained in a long letter to Politburo conservative Yegor Ligachev about *pripiska*, falsification of statistics, on agricultural production. Another time it was Sergei Kuznetsov, a Sverdlovsk activist and contributor to Grigoryants's *Glasnost* who had been jailed for his political activities. On a trip to Helsinki, away for a few days from the relentless pageant of Soviet politics, I switched on CNN on my hotel television just in time to catch Andrei and a few compatriots handing over a petition in defense of Kuznetsov at the gate of the British embassy in Moscow. If only for a few seconds, they had succeeded in placing this obscure dissident's case before the eyes of the world. It was enough: Kuznetsov was released.

Sometimes Andrei was so persistent in his quiet advocacy that he drove me crazy; here I was trying to cover a superpower going through a revolution for a daily newspaper, and he wanted me to drop Gorbachev, drop arms control, drop the Supreme Soviet, and focus all my attention on some nobody from Irkutsk who supposedly got a raw deal. Vengeance may have been part of his motive, but guilt played a role as well, he told me later. "It was very uncomfortable for me, because they had freed me, but there were others still locked up. I wanted to raise a scandal about all the rest, in part, I suppose, to justify my own freedom," he said.

In the warm early autumn of 1988, what the Russians call *babye leto*, woman's summer, Andrei recounted to me an incident that captured the way fear of the KGB was eroding. Andrei was strolling the Arbat, the storied Moscow street where Pushkin had once lived, now blocked off to cars and with a pleasant bohemian atmosphere that took visitors by surprise. Artists offered instant pastel portraits or caricatures of the tourists, peddled Palekh lacquer boxes of dubious authenticity or the nested Soviet-history dolls that began with a tiny bearded Lenin and grew to the bald Gorbachev. Folk singers, amateur comedians, and street poets performed for spare change. Andrei was a connoisseur of political folk songs and sometimes took a tape recorder to the Arbat to collect them.

That evening he stopped to hear a young guitarist named Alexei who had drawn a few dozen listeners as he tested the new permissiveness. One of his songs ridiculed Yegor Ligachev, the conservative No. 2 to Gorbachev and every Moscow liberal's favorite bête noire. Another song made flagrant fun of the KGB's thuggish rank and file, with the refrain:

I'm an agent of the KGB,
Aren't you scared?

This proved to be too much for one of the beat policemen who walked the Arbat, collaring drunks, shooing away prostitutes, and sometimes hauling away Hari Krishna devotees jangling tambourines or soapbox comics who made light of Gorbachev. The cop unceremoniously halted the impromptu concert and ordered Alexei to accompany him to the local precinct station, a few minutes' walk away on a side street.

For Andrei this was meat and drink. He stepped forward and told the policeman that the kid was not violating the law. The policeman replied uncertainly that singing about Politburo members and the KGB was forbidden. By what law, Andrei wanted to know? Forbidden, and that's all, the policeman said. Tell me the statute, Andrei persisted. You want to make trouble, you come with me to the precinct too, the policeman said. So the three of them set off down the Arbat—trailed by most of the listeners, who were angry that the music had stopped and fired up by Andrei's challenge to authority.

Inside the station the cop demanded Andrei's passport and discovered his release paper. Seeming flustered, he held a muttered consultation with a superior, then abruptly informed the singer and his defender they were free to go.

The crowd received them with the cheers of victory. Alexei

thanked Andrei, saying that normally singers who were detained were roughed up in the station. The procession went back to the Arbat, the concert resumed, and a few dozen Soviet citizens pondered a lesson in sticking up for their rights.

The night of November 2, 1989, Soviet Central Television offered sensational fare: five top KGB officials on a live, call-in interview show. "Today it is not officers of the KGB who are asking questions," said the evening's host, a well-known TV anchorman named Vladimir Tsvetov. "Today they are being asked the questions."

This was the new face of the KGB, the glasnost KGB, the KGB of Vladimir Kryuchkov, who had gone to work in the "organs," as Russians said, before Stalin's death. He had advanced under the wing of Andropov and headed all the KGB's foreign operations for fourteen years before being tapped by Gorbachev in late 1988 to replace the aging, cranky Chebrikov. Unlike Chebrikov, who never gave interviews, the balding, unsmiling Kryuchkov was liberal with his comments. You could collar him without much trouble in the foyer at parliamentary sessions or between acts at the Bolshoi Theater, as I once did. At the same time Kryuchkov gave the impression of superhuman self-control; when he answered questions you could almost hear his mind whirring as he calculated what to say and what not to say. When you filtered out the rhetoric, there appeared to be three major changes Kryuchkov had made to reform the KGB: he had abolished the notorious Fifth Directorate, which had been responsible for monitoring and prosecuting dissidents; he had begun to permit cooperation of local KGB units with activists and citizens who were researching Stalin-era arrests and executions; and he had opened up the secret agency to regular contact with the press and public. In a way, the changes were a remarkable break with past practice. I could—and did—call the KGB press office for comment and information on various matters, even if their most frequent reply was, "No comment."

But in all respects there was considerably less to the Kryuchkov reforms than met the eye. The Fifth Directorate had been abolished, to be sure; but its place was taken by a new Directorate for the Protection of the Soviet Constitutional System, which happened to have essentially the same personnel and nearly identical functions. Support for research into Stalinism consisted largely of confirming what public groups had already found out; only slowly and grudgingly were actual records admitted to exist. As for the KGB's glasnost campaign, it was a Potemkin village if ever there was one. The agency went in for high-profile, image-shaping moves, such as the TV call-in show, the creation of a KGB Center for Public Relations, a beauty contest for female *chekisti* to bestow the coveted title "Miss KGB," and the publication of KGB newspapers with cute names such as "Top Secret." But while Kryuchkov made a splash by ordering his PR men to answer the public's questions, he did not insist that they answer them truthfully.

A memorable example from the 1989 TV show was the KGB's answer to a question on KGB persecution of religion. The question was taken by Alexander Nikolayevich Karbainov, a veteran of the Fifth Directorate who later would become the KGB's chief public relations man. His answer was unequivocal and to the point. "The state security bodies," Karbainov said in the reassuring voice of authority, "do not concern themselves with any religious movements, they never have, and they probably never will." In fact, as even the most superficial student of the Soviet secret police knew, they had, did, and probably always would. In creating their officially atheist state the Bolsheviks quite naturally feared that the Russian Orthodox church and other religious organizations would become centers of opposition. They responded by slaughtering thousands of priests, destroying thousands of churches, and infiltrating the church with agents. Monitoring, harassment, and infiltration of religious groups was one of the most important domestic missions of the secret police.

Despite Gorbachev's use of the 1988 celebration of the one thousandth anniversary of Russian Christianity to launch a political rehabilitation of the church, the KGB retained its role. A few weeks after the KGB TV show I happened to hear a lecture by Konstantin Kharchev, who had revealed in an interview with the magazine *Ogonyok* that he had been forced out as chairman of the government's Council on Religious Affairs because of his poor relations with "the neighbors," one of many euphemisms for the KGB. In his talk Kharchev went further. He disclosed that among his deputies at the Council on Religious Affairs had been one known in-house as "the Deputy for the KGB," a KGB employee assigned full-time to supervise the council's oversight of Soviet religion. As chairman, Kharchev said, he had to make every decision "with one eye on the door of the office of the deputy for the KGB."

When I got the opportunity to interview Karbainov in his spacious office in the Lubyanka in May 1990 I asked him about the KGB's control of religion. At first he repeated his assertion on television, though this time he qualified the statement in windy style. "If, to some degree, there were questions connected with the interests of the security organs to be put to certain representatives of various religious movements, it was connected first of all with the ties of these representatives of various religious movements with anti-Soviet centers overseas or with their underground activity inside the country," Karbainov said. When I pressed the point, Karbainov retreated: "I'm not a specialist on religion."

Was there an assistant to Kharchev from the KGB? I asked. "Honestly speaking, I don't know of such a person," Karbainov replied. "I don't know that there is one. I simply don't know. I just haven't come across such a thing. In general I'm a person who's kept his distance from religion, although I think it's right that there has been such a turn [in government policy] toward the rebirth of human spirituality."

The Center for Public Relations would be another Bolshevik exercise in language over reality. It would be not a sign of real change inside the Lubyanka but rather a means of resisting real change by dressing the agency up in new, perestroika-colored camouflage clothing. "The new image of the KGB is cosmetic," said Oleg Kalugin, a former KGB major general who went public with searing criticism of the agency a month after my interview with Karbainov, "and just consists of applying rouge over the quite flabby face of the old Stalin-Brezhnev system."

Gorbachev did not forget his debts to the KGB, nor did he lose sight of the power of the Lubyanka. Long after East German Stasi agents had left their headquarters to be ransacked by demonstrators and former Czech secret policemen were pumping gas and driving cabs, their mentors and teachers at the KGB were feeling just fine. If the KGB was taking some direct hits in the liberated media, its Center for Public Relations was ducking the punches and swinging back with TV newsclips of agents swooping down on black marketeers and films portraying KGB officers who wrote poetry and loved to cook. If the agency's scope for arresting dissenters was curtailed as a result of glasnost, Gorbachev gave it important new jobs: policing interethnic disputes, battling organized crime, rooting out "economic sabotage." Many experts argued that such jobs should be handled by the Ministry of Internal Affairs, leaving the KGB to concentrate on intelligence and counterespionage. But Gorbachev shrank from any wholesale reorganization that would shake up the KGB or cut its power.

Apart from gratitude to the KGB for its role in bringing him to power, Gorbachev clearly was wary of the danger of making the KGB unhappy. The agency had played no small role in the ouster of Nikita Khrushchev in 1964, an episode revisited frequently in the liberated press. The power of the Soviet leadership had traditionally rested on a triad: party, army, KGB. Under economic pressure to slash military spending and reduce the party's role in economic management, Gorbachev needed institutional support from the third leg of the triad, and he knew it. When Gorbachev removed KGB chief Chebrikov in September 1988, he did it gingerly, taking pains not to offend the KGB as an institution: Chebrikov was named to the Central Committee and put in charge of a party legal commission where he retained considerable control over the KGB and other law-enforcement agencies. Kryuchkov, Chebrikov's replacement, was the ultimate KGB insider. A year after he was made KGB chairman, Gorbachev gave Kryuchkov a full seat on the Politburo.

On the surface, at least, the loyalty ran both ways. When the Communist party finally lost its constitutional monopoly on power in March 1990, Kryuchkov wasted no time in stating that while the KGB previously had served the general secretary of the Communist party (Gorbachev), now it would serve the president of the USSR (Gorbachev). "The preparation of information for the Soviet President will be the most important function of the KGB," Kryuchkov told Tass on April 29, 1990. "In the present complicated and volatile situation, the importance of information for state bodies engaged in decision-making has grown," Kryuchkov said. "The President needs precise, verified and reliable information."

A crucial question went unasked at the time: who would check the information the KGB provided to the president? How would Gorbachev know he was being kept objectively and promptly informed? In August 1991, after the abortive coup, that question would finally be posed, but only in hindsight.

Gorbachev's relationship with the KGB was probably the only bargain that could have initiated serious reform of any kind in the early 1980s. But it was nonetheless a Faustian bargain, fraught with unintended consequences. Lining up the KGB as your key ally in democratic reform was a little like hiring the mob to encourage support for your campaign for nonviolence: you got clout, but at considerable expense to principle.

Those puzzled by Gorbachev's on-again, off-again embrace of democracy and markets, his vacillation, his frequent lapses into crude tactics against Boris Yeltsin or liberal journalists, and his paradoxical preference for party hard-liners over anti-Communist democrats, might have learned much from studying his relationship with the KGB. It doesn't matter so much whether the core of this relationship was Gorbachev's fear of the KGB, his gratitude to the KGB, his acceptance of much of the KGB's worldview, or his dependence on KGB information. The relationship was extremely important, and it constrained and tainted Gorbachev's words and actions.

Unlike Brezhnev, Gorbachev demanded accurate, objective information. But like Brezhnev he was to a considerable degree dependent on the information the KGB gave him. In return for his soul, the story goes, Faust received not only all pleasures but all knowledge. Faust's information, at least, was accurate.

5

The Press and the
Restoration of History

The Soviet Union—the only country in the world with an
unpredictable past.
                    —Soviet proverb

For half a century they had kept the secrets they knew from
childhood, when they swam in the pond next to Kalitnikovsky
Cemetery. Now they were telling the secrets to this man with the
spotted tie, the big nose, the respectful smile, the courtly manners,
and the burning core of hatred for what had happened. Alexander
Milchakov was a master at drawing out the eyewitnesses.

They told him how they crouched behind the gravestones and
watched the trucks pull up at dusk—ordinary blue-green trucks
with "Meat" or "Bread" painted on the side, so as not to alarm the
public. They watched as uniformed men in jackboots, wearing long
rubber gloves, balanced in pairs on the back of the truck, gripped
the naked corpses of men and women by arms and legs and threw
them into the pit. When the truck was empty, other workers would
climb down beside the bodies and shovel over them a layer of sand.
Many nights the children returned to watch this incomprehensible
spectacle, despite nightmares and admonitions from their frightened
parents. They saw how the bullet holes in the skulls had been

plugged with newspaper or cotton to keep the trucks clean. They saw how rainstorms washed away the sand, revealing random legs and arms. They saw the stray dogs that lived around the meat-packing plant next door descend into the pit to dig. And on holidays, at the meat workers' Palace of Culture, they saw the huge portrait of Josef Stalin, surrounded by electric lights.

This was the image, of all those drawn for him by all the witnesses of all the mass graves around Moscow, that seemed to Milchakov most succinctly to capture the terror. "The empty grave-yard, the dogs digging in the pit for the scent of blood, and this giant face with the mustache overseeing it all," Milchakov said to me one day, the smile gone, looking out across the graves and back in time. "That, in Stalin's understanding," he said, "was socialism."

Alexander Milchakov was in his late fifties and had already had a fairly successful career in journalism when he found his calling. Driven by his own family's shattering history, he began to find and interview elderly Muscovites who had glimpsed the secret disposal of the thousands upon thousands of bodies of those executed in the capital during the Stalinist terror. He located the unmarked graves, estimated the numbers, questioned aging NKVD retirees. His research, he told me, "started with what is really a child's question: What did they do with all the bodies?" For Milchakov it was not a matter of morbid curiosity but of immense political consequence. "We have to know exactly how it was done, where it was done, by whom it was done," Milchakov said. "We have to learn all this while we still can. Because only by knowing that terrible history can we avoid repeating it."

A veteran television and radio correspondent, Milchakov had plenty of media connections. But when he set out in 1988 to publish his material on Moscow's secret mass graves, he was turned away by a number of major publications. Most of what was being printed about the terror was still abstract; editors were wary of Milchakov's graphic accounts of the machinery of slaughter in the heart of the capital. He found an outlet in a relatively obscure, weekly tabloid called *Semya* (Family). Nervous Central Committee officials insisted on reviewing the publications, and Glavlit censors cut out some of the most horrifying recollections. But when "Ashes of the Executed" finally appeared in September 1988 Milchakov began receiving hundreds of calls and letters from people who remembered other grave sites. Another article appeared a couple of months later, and another, and another, and another. Later his writings would begin to appear in *Vechernyaya Moskva*, the capital's evening newspaper, and he would take on the KGB in print, with millions of readers cheering him on, and begin to pry open its archives. In the end Milchakov and his eyewitnesses would have mapped and documented the hidden history of terror in Moscow.

"There was so much we didn't know," was the refrain of many Soviet citizens, face to face for the first time with information about their country's murderous past. In the space of three years, from 1987 to 1989, the official history that had been twisted, dressed up, and invented gave way before memories, documents, and photographs which first trickled, then flooded onto the pages of newspapers and magazines. Soviet journalists, for so long the cowardly mouthpieces of half-truths concocted by their party overseers, suddenly had the chance to be heroes, returning historical memory to a people from whom it had been stolen. A wrenching shift of worldview began, as facts such as those literally unearthed by Alexander Milchakov struck at the durable edifice of Soviet legend, the "glorious destiny" which citizens had for so long been assured was theirs.

By mid-1988 so much had been published that contradicted the textbooks that school history exams for the year had to be canceled. In their place, shell-shocked teachers whose entire curriculum had been exposed as a string of half-truths and falsehoods led classroom discussions based on press clippings. "Everyone—teachers, parents, students—cannot but feel relief and gratitude toward those who had the courage to say no to the exams," *Izvestiya* wrote. "But this feeling is mixed with another—a feeling of enormous shame. Huge, immense is the guilt of those who misled generation after generation, giving them falsehood of the intellect and of the soul." In its front-page commentary the paper declared: "Today we blush and don't know what to say to our own children. Let's teach them in such a way that when they become fathers they won't have to blush in front of our grandchildren."

ñ

Naturally, in this country where for so long the state had handled information as a hazardous material, the restoration of history had not begun as a grassroots movement, the whim of a thousand Alexander Milchakovs. It was authorized from above, by decision of Gorbachev and the Communist party Politburo. Artists, rather than historians, were the first to respond to the signal from above. In 1986 and 1987 there was the release of the film *Repentance*, a phantasmagoric allegory about a Georgian dictator that left many who had lived through the Stalinist terror in tears; there were the historical plays of Mikhail Shatrov, *Dictatorship of Conscience*, *Onward...Onward...Onward*, and *The Brest Treaty*, with their controversial reopening of the debates among the early Bolsheviks; there was Anatoly Rybakov's novel *Children of the Arbat*, a popular treatment of Stalin and Moscow on the eve of the great purges, whose serialization in *Druzhba Narodov* helped drive the monthly's circulation seven times higher. As the return of history gathered momentum, it divided the Politburo between those such as Alexander Yakovlev, who favored a complete airing of the grisly past, and others, such as Yegor Ligachev and KGB chief Viktor Chebrikov, who worried about the consequences of this unrestrained "blackening" of Soviet history. In November 1987 Gorbachev marked the seventieth anniversary of the Revolution by delivering a compromise speech, balancing Stalin's achievements against what Gorbachev called his "real crimes." The speech disappointed many liberals, but it nonetheless had the effect of freeing the press for a more aggressive exposure of Stalinism. In 1988 newspapers and magazines took up the task with a vengeance, and hardly a day passed without a major article rehabilitating some figure erased from the history books or exposing another crime of Stalin and his secret police chiefs.

By then the Kremlin was running to keep up with the campaign it had unleashed. Gorbachev appointed a Commission for the Additional Study of the Materials Related to the Repressions of the 1930s, 1940s and Early 1950s. Mikhail Solomentsev, the undistinguished Politburo old-timer who chaired the commission, assured the readers of *Pravda* in August 1988: "Our work is based on a well-considered plan and proceeds in strict compliance with the norms of party and state life. Before making a decision on a specific case or a specific trial we instruct the USSR Prosecutor General's office and other competent agencies to conduct a thorough check of the case and prepare corresponding law-based decisions, to provide an exhaustive, well-documented, and demonstrative conclusion." In the ensuing months the commission's stilted announcements via the Tass newswire would mark its tedious progress through the late 1920s and early 1930s. The NKVD case against the Union of Marxist-Leninists, Solomentsev's commission found, had been concocted; its victims were hence posthumously rehabilitated. The United Anti-Soviet Trotskyite-Zinovievite Center and the Parallel Anti-Soviet Trotskyite Center had—surprise!—been framed. So, by coincidence, had the Workers' Opposition and the Leningrad Counterrevolutionary Zinovievite Group of Safarov, Zalutsky and Others. The commission plodded onward, failing to find anyone who did not deserve rehabilitation, but nonetheless exercising case-by-case care to reassure the public of the party's born-again devotion to the law.

But with every month the Kremlin fell farther behind the press in the de-Stalinization drive. The Kremlin's Communist reformers, with their goal of strengthening socialism, treaded cautiously; populist reformers among editors and writers, who cared only about getting the facts out, rushed forward. In his *Pravda* interview Solomentsev was asked whether the mass graves of terror victims could be found. "The question, let's say frankly, is not only sad, but truly lamentable and, if you please, leads to a dead end in terms of its solution," he replied. "To establish the burial place of people who perished while incarcerated is unfortunately practically impossible." A few weeks later the first of Milchakov's articles was published in *Semya*, illustrating how a solo journalist with no access to secret archives could himself establish the location of such burial sites.

What set Milchakov's reporting apart not only from the Kremlin's official pronouncements but from the generalities of many press reports as well was its insistence on the physical reality of the terror.

He laid bare the whole industry that had torn the country's heart out in the late 1930s. He told how the NKVD recruited its executioners, by approaching strong young men from the villages who were about to end their army service and offering them unimaginable prizes: a Moscow residency permit and apartment, an officer's rank in the NKVD, a princely salary, and a top-secret mission. Some drove trucks, gunning their engines on command to mask the sound of nearby gunshots. Some marched prisoners to the cellar execution chambers. And some had the gruesome task of pulling the trigger, hundreds and thousands of times. The executioners, Milchakov wrote, were kept plied with vodka and often did their jobs in a state of deep inebriation. Milchakov did not spare readers. He told how one pensioner who had watched from behind the gravestones at Kalitnikovsky Cemetery, Zinaida Filippova, described the sound made when the NKVD men tossed fresh bodies onto the already bloated, decomposing piles beneath: it was "a strange sound, like a bursting volleyball or inner tube." Her account made it past Glavlit, but such details were often cut by the censors, Milchakov said. One witness, for instance, told Milchakov of seeing in a pile of corpses a young mother with her arms still around her dead baby; the passage never made it into print.

Alexander Alexandrovich Milchakov, like thousands of other citizens who brought a fierce devotion to the restoration of history, had personal motives. They could be traced to the sprawling, grey jumble of an apartment complex on the Moscow River that had been immortalized as *The House on the Embankment* in Yuri Trifonov's novel of that name, a child's view of Stalinism so gentle and subtle that it was officially published in 1976. Here the Bolshevik brass had settled into big, luxurious apartments, and among them was Milchakov's father, also Alexander, who served in a number of top jobs in the 1930s, including as first secretary of the national Komsomol youth organization. As the Moscow elite began to topple before the bullets of NKVD executioners, the younger Milchakov recalled how his teachers directed the children to censor their own textbooks. "They made us blot out the eyes, then the face, then the whole picture, then the words, 'Marshal of the Soviet Union,'" he said.

"We all knew they were enemies of the people, traitors to the country, agents of capitalism."

But soon the night visitors from the Lubyanka began to carry off neighbors, playmates' fathers, from the house on the embankment. Finally, in 1938, the terror reached Milchakov's father, by then an official in the gold industry. He was charged with "sabotage." His son was seven. "I remember how relieved my mother was when he got 'fifteen years with right of correspondence,'" Milchakov told me. The alternative was "ten years without right of correspondence," a thin camouflage of legal-sounding words for immediate execution. When a person was exposed as an enemy of the people, his disgraced family was swiftly evicted from the privileged apartment building on the river. Milchakov remembered the crowded rooms in a nearby building where several of the evicted families sought shelter, making daily journeys to the Lubyanka or to Moscow prisons to get word of their loved ones or to try to hand over a food parcel or letter. One woman on such a mission was arrested herself and never came back; another hung herself one night from the heating pipes.

Alexander did well in his studies; he said all the children of the "repressed" worked hard, to redeem themselves in the eyes of their country. His father survived and was released after eighteen years in the camps. In 1960 Milchakov was working on a short story based on a real epidemic and visited the Moscow crematorium in Donskoy Cemetery to collect some realistic details about the disposal of bodies. He began interviewing the employees. "Suddenly," he recalled, "an old woman said, 'That's the way it was in 1937. They brought the bodies every night, still warm. Each with a little hole in the skull.'" He pressed for more information, but others were listening and the woman clammed up. Milchakov filed the information away. Twenty-eight years later he decided the time had come to pick up the thread. He returned to the Donskoy crematorium and made it the basis for the first of his articles.

Two months after Gorbachev came to power he mentioned Stalin in a speech commemorating the fortieth anniversary of victory in World War II—and touched off prolonged applause from the audience of veterans and party and military brass. After nearly a year in office he told the French Communist newspaper *L'Humanité* that "Stalinism" did not exist; it was "a concept made up by opponents of communism and used on a large scale to smear the Soviet Union and socialism as a whole."

Certainly his family history—the arrest of both grandfathers, his childhood in what he would later call a "plague-house" of a purported "enemy of the people"—would have given Gorbachev reason to doubt that Stalinism was a mere capitalist smear tactic. But even in more thoughtful moments he seemed to accept the cost-benefit theory of the Stalin era, in which collectivization, industrialization, and military victory are placed on the scales to counterbalance the terror. His 1987 book *Perestroika* reflects such an approach. "Yes, industrialization and collectivization were necessities. Otherwise the country could not have improved its position. But the methods and ways of carrying out these transformations did not always and in all respects correspond to socialist principles, socialist ideology and theory," he wrote. There were, Gorbachev wrote, "excesses," "administrative pressure"; "people suffered."

Later the same year, in the long-awaited speech on the seventieth anniversary of the Bolshevik Revolution, Gorbachev inched farther. The text, entitled "October and Perestroika: The Revolution Continues," was a document negotiated by the entire Politburo, and its qualified language showed a committee's touch. Collectivization was marred by "a deficit of the Leninist considerate attitude to the interests of the working peasantry." Likewise there had been "excesses" in the "basically correct policy of fighting the kulaks." The speech denounced "the personality cult, the violations of legality, the wanton repressive measures of the thirties. Putting things bluntly—those were real crimes stemming from an abuse of power. Many thousands of people inside and outside the Party were subjected to wholesale repression." It is necessary to face this "bitter truth," the speech said, "in order to assert Lenin's ideal of socialism once and for all." Gorbachev put Stalinism on the "balance sheet" and concluded that "contradictions and complexities" did not outweigh the "truly heroic" nature of Soviet history: "Neither gross errors nor departures from the principles of socialism could divert our people, our country from the road it embarked upon by the choice it made in 1917."

Gorbachev's first calls for glasnost, his condemnation of Stalin, his candor about Soviet problems all had a galvanizing effect on the public. But as time passed people grew weary of Gorbachev's weighing of Stalin's faults and virtues, his insistence on the infallibility of Lenin, his invariable references to the "choice" the people allegedly had made in 1917. Soviet intellectuals, frustrated by what they saw as credulous Western Gorbymania, used an analogy. It was as if, they said, Gorbachev had inherited a country where for decades the leadership had insisted that two plus two was six. He had stunned and enthralled the people by boldly announcing that this was not true. Now it was necessary to muster the courage to face the truth, he said. Two plus two was not six, Gorbachev said: Two plus two was five.

Meanwhile a more accurate mathematics of Soviet history was being offered to a public hungry for the facts of their own past. One memorable instance came on a late afternoon in a chilly rain in November 1988 when I found a huge line, more like an elongated crowd, outside the House of Culture of the Moscow Electric Lamp Factory.

The civic group Memorial had been born a year earlier when a ragtag group of young students and dissidents had started a petition in support of building a monument to the victims of Stalinist terror. Their first forays onto the Arbat in 1987, petition in hand, had ended in arrest. But by mid-1988 the *malchiki*, the boys, as they were known, had attracted to the board of Memorial most of the biggest names of Soviet liberalism, including Andrei Sakharov, the historians Yuri Afanasiev and Roy Medvedev, poet Yevgeny Yevtushenko, ousted Politburo member Boris Yeltsin, and a number of prominent editors, writers, and filmmakers. The board conveyed clout and respectability, and local branches of Memorial sprang up around the country during the latter half of 1988. In many places their first

activity was to search out the mass burial sites used by the NKVD in
their cities during the 1930s.

Now, in this factory building, after overcoming the considerable
resistance of the bureaucracy, Memorial had managed to organize a
"Week of Conscience" to remember the victims of Stalinist terror.
Just inside the entrance was a striking map of the Gulag, constructed of brick and marked with the locations, names, and
numbers of camps spanning the continent from the Baltic to the Sea
of Japan. In a little side room a remarkable amateur historian,
Dmitry Yurasov, collected material for his card index of victims of
the terror. He had started his research at the age of thirteen out of
innocent curiosity, when he stumbled across the word "repressed" in
an encyclopedia and set out to find its meaning. Now, at nineteen,
his hobby suddenly had put him on the cutting edge of the new
history. It was a sign of the sorry state of official history that one of
the largest compilations of facts on Stalinist repression had been put
together by an amateur in his spare time; his cards, files, and books
were threatening to squeeze himself and his mother out of their tiny
apartment. Grey and white heads surrounded the lanky teenager,
offering and asking for information about the fate of fathers, wives,
brothers, husbands, aunts, cousins.

In another hall a two-story interior wall was covered with
memorabilia of those whom the camps had ingested: their photographs; their arrest papers; their sentencing papers; their rehabilitation papers, stating tersely that a review had found no crime had
been committed; a brief, falsified death certificate declaring that
so-and-so died of a heart attack in Kolyma; a prisoner's letter of
hope, explaining that he was the victim of a big mix-up that
undoubtedly would soon be set straight; another prisoner's letter of
despair, acknowledging that his middle-of-the-night parting from
his family was a parting forever. More people every day added their
families' contributions, preserved in secret for so long, or pinned
memorial carnations to the board.

Beside a staircase in the first hall stood an old woman in a grey
knit cap, holding up a hand-lettered piece of cardboard with
"MINLAG" in Cyrillic letters on one side and "Shch-270" on the
other—the identifying name and number of her arctic camp. A knot

of people would gather around her, listen for a while, then move on, to be replaced by others. In a loud, clear voice, sixty-five-year-old Yevgeniya Vrublevskaya was telling the story she had kept to herself for thirty-four years.

She had been born in what was then Poland, she said, detained by the Germans and held during World War II in a Nazi prison camp, and finally freed by the Red Army in 1945, when she was twenty-one. She found her family and spent three weeks with them. Then, grateful to the country whose soldiers had saved her life and captivated by the Stalinist vision of heroic construction, she boarded a train east "to help build socialism."

She was arrested by the NKVD before she left the train. Vrublevskaya was shipped to a labor camp in the Russian far north where 37,000 prisoners were building an entire city, to be called Inta. Using hand tools at temperatures as low as fifty below zero, she and her fellow prisoners dug a sewer system and constructed government offices, apartments, even an airport. They survived on cabbage soup and porridge, she said, and slept in cold barracks on wooden bunks. The frozen bodies of those who did not survive were stacked like firewood until the brief summer, she said, when the ground thawed enough to permit burial. She recounted all this in a tone of outraged anger; occasionally she would have to stop, overcome with emotion. Then the people crowding around to listen would call out in empathy: *"Svolochi!"* The bastards!

In a way, what was most compelling about Vrublevskaya's story was the fact that she had never before told it. After her release in 1954 she had married a fellow prisoner, moved to a little town in Byelorussia, worked as a telephone operator—and never breathed a word about her imprisonment outside her family. In that fall of 1988 she had heard on a Russian-language broadcast of the Voice of America about plans for the Week of Conscience. She boarded a train to Moscow and asked her way to the exhibit. And after three decades of silence Yevgeniya Vrublevskaya told her story, patiently answering the questions of young people, comparing memories with fellow camp survivors, and sparring with the occasional skeptic. For a week she was transformed, a babushka become a prophetess whose power was to reveal not the future but the past, which in this country was almost as unknown.

Appropriately, the Week of Conscience in Moscow was sponsored jointly by two publications: the tabloid *Moscow News* and the color magazine *Ogonyok*. It was an irony worth savoring that precisely these two weeklies had become the pathbreaking, iconoclastic voices of 1987 and 1988, shattering taboos and showing the way to the rest of the media. For no periodicals had more shamelessly dedicated themselves, through the years, to the painting over of Soviet reality.

Published by two institutions firmly in the hands of the KGB—the Novosti Press Agency and the Union of Soviet Societies for Friendship and Cultural Relations with Foreign Countries—*Moscow News* had since its founding in 1930 been a clumsy propaganda sheet published in several languages for gullible foreigners. A typical edition, dated exactly one year before Gorbachev took power, had Konstantin Chernenko on the cover, casting his ballot in an election in which, the accompanying story stresses, "more than 99.9 percent of the electorate have cast their votes for the nominees." At that time the editor was the man who would become the witty chief spokesman for the Soviet Foreign Ministry and one of a handful of internationally known Soviet faces, Gennady Gerasimov.

Ogonyok, meanwhile, printed only in Russian, was a knockoff of *Life* magazine. Its cover was graced with children in folk dress, smiling factory workers, and military parades. Inside, along with upbeat features, were official speech texts and photographs of officials in suits at long tables with captions such as "The Reception of N. Kinnock by K. U. Chernenko" or "Arrival of the Delegation from the Supreme Soviet of the USSR in the Sovereign Republic of Vietnam." Many people subscribed mainly for the crossword puzzle.

Like their publications, the two new editors who took over after Gorbachev came to power were unlikely revolutionaries. Yegor Yakovlev was known as the author of uninspired books on Lenin. Vitaly Korotich had been a Brezhnev-era literary toady and none-too-liberal secretary of the Ukrainian Writers Union. But both were, like Gorbachev, "children of the 20th Party Congress," who had come of age in the spirit of de-Stalinization. Both, it seemed, had been waiting for the return of the thaw, and when it came they seized their chance. Both Yakovlev at *Moscow News* and Korotich at *Ogonyok* recruited liberal commentators from their own generation along with young, aggressive reporters who gave their editions a tone of skepticism, irony, and moral outrage. On Wednesday mornings, when *Moscow News* was hitting the capital's news kiosks, many would open at 8 a.m. with fifty or more people in line.

Much of the publications' soaring popularity and authority derived from historical articles that filled in the *belye pyatna*, the white spots or blank pages, of the Russian and Soviet past. Nothing in official history could survive reassessment unscathed: not the ritual portrayal of tsarist Russia as a land exclusively of brutal poverty and backwardness; nor the glossing over of the Red Terror of 1918; nor the legends encrusted on the character of Lenin; nor the silence about Nikita Khrushchev and his removal from power in 1964; nor the alcoholism and senility of Brezhnev in his last years. But it was Stalin's three decades in power that were the core of the problem of the restoration of history. The traditional word-magic of Soviet propaganda had hidden history behind one bland euphemism or another: the "mistakes," "miscalculations," "excesses," "contradictions," or "costs" of "Stalin's cult of personality"—as if the main problem had been the glut of statues and images of the leader. A story an enterprising Soviet reporter uncovered about Yegor Ligachev, the Politburo member so worried about journalists' "blackening" of the Soviet past, seemed emblematic of the old approach to history. In 1979, when Ligachev was a Siberian party boss, a mass grave from the 1930s had been uncovered by rising waters on the River Ob. Ligachev ordered the skeletons firehosed into the river; when some floated to the surface, workers were ordered to weight them with stones until they sank from sight and mind.

The result of this firehosing of history was that many people had only the vaguest notion of the Stalin years. For older people who had experienced terror themselves or in their family, Stalinism remained unexamined, a dark secret, a national trauma repressed like a horrible childhood memory. And it was a widely shared memory. In a poll of 1,953 adults in three regions of Russia and five other republics in 1991, 26 percent said they had relatives who had been "repressed" (arrested or executed); another 16 percent were not sure. If the percentage held up for the rest of the country, some 75 million people had lost relatives to the terror. But until the late 1980s they could not publicly discuss the disappearance of a brother or the execution of a father. They could make no official inquiries; they could conduct no research.

"Our history became as smooth as an office desk, as red as the cloth of a presidium table at a ceremonial meeting," Galina V. Klokova, who was in charge of commissioning new textbooks, told an interviewer in 1989. "Not a single superfluous hue, not a single indentation. No pain, no mistakes, no desperate struggle—everything that created doubts had disappeared. Even many famous people seemed to have disappeared from our past without a trace."

Now those who had disappeared were brought back. There were revolutionaries such as Nikolai Bukharin, who some argued had offered a humane alternative to Stalinism before his show trial and execution in 1938. Bukharin's face appeared in the newspapers more frequently than those of some Politburo members, and his writings and legacy were discussed everywhere. His widow, Anna Larina, miraculously still alive, published her memoirs in the literary journal *Znamya*. There were scientists such as the geneticist Nikolai Vavilov. Yevgeniya Albats, of *Moscow News*, tracked down an NKVD investigator who had interrogated and beaten Vavilov; turning the tables, Albats interrogated the former NKVD man about his half-century-old crime. There were poets such as Osip Mandelstam. *Ogonyok* wrote of Stalin's cat-and-mouse game with the great poet, Mandelstam's bitter poetic portrait of the dictator, and the poet's subsequent death in the Gulag.

Literary works by the score reappeared—not only those of authors whose entire oeuvre had been banned but the missing works and missing passages of authors whose official Soviet editions resembled Swiss cheese, including Anna Akhmatova, Boris Pasternak, Mikhail Bulgakov. As long-prohibited works appeared they were often accompanied by a note on when they were written and first published abroad. "This novel was first published in 1978 by the YMCA Press in Paris," said a typical footnote, to the first installment of Yuri Dombrovsky's novel of the terror, *The Faculty of Unnecessary Things*, when it appeared in *Novy Mir* in 1988. "*Life and Fate* was published in Switzerland in 1980," noted the first Soviet edition of Vasily Grossman's novel in 1988. A collection by the exiled poet Josef Brodsky, published in Leningrad in 1990, remarked in an introduction that he was the author of eight books of poems, a book of plays, and a book of essays. "All have been published in the West," the introduction said, "for the most part in the U.S.A., where Josef Brodsky has lived since 1972, when Party ideologues and the KGB forced him to leave his homeland." Such notes tainted with bitterness many Russians' discovery of their own literary masterpieces. Gorbachev often stressed that the party itself had launched perestroika, implying that the people should be grateful. But even a person exhilarated by the opportunity to read *Doctor Zhivago* might find it difficult to be grateful to the authorities who had banned it for thirty years.

Gorbachev, in his seventieth-anniversary speech, had spoken of "many thousands" of victims of repression. A year later historian Roy Medvedev, himself just emerging from official disfavor, came up with a rough estimate of 35 million victims of terror or organized famine, about half of whom had been executed or starved to death. He published his calculations in *Moscow News*. Article after article tackled the difficult, still unresolved problem of the numbers; but they invariably began from the assumption of not thousands but millions of victims.

Many older Soviet citizens who could accept the new reports of the scale of the terror or the cost of collectivization found it most difficult to revise their view of Stalin's war record. Yet the press subjected the generalissimo to scathing examination. Readers of *Ogonyok* learned in early 1988, for instance, that in the years immediately before the war the NKVD had imprisoned or executed three of the five marshals of the Soviet Union, thirteen of the fifteen army commanders of the first and second ranks, all sixteen army commissars of the first and second ranks, sixty of the sixty-seven corps commanders...and so on down a staggering list. They read that Stalin had so trusted in his deal with Hitler that he ignored repeated, credible warnings of Germany's impending invasion. They learned that when the invasion came Stalin was so shattered that he secluded himself at his suburban Moscow dacha and refused visitors for three days as the German war machine roared across Byelorussia.

This restoration of military history, which produced euphoria in some, caused intense pain in others. Outside the Bolshoi Theater on Victory Day, May 9, veterans traditionally gathered to swap stories and show off their medals. But in 1988 I found as much bafflement as pride. A sixty-five-year-old veteran named Pyotr Ivanovich, surrounded by a small crowd of the curious, recalled the battle of Stalingrad. "We all believed in him then," he said, "and I think our faith saved us. Our generation was with Stalin. We didn't know about the repressions. Now I don't know what to think." Across the park, eighty-three-year-old Alexander Svistov acknowledged that Stalin was a "despot" but insisted that was not the whole story. "He was a great military leader," Svistov said. "He kept the price of bread low. He fed the people. He built our industry. He was severe, but he was a friend of the people." Younger people, who by tradition were expected to offer respect and support to veterans on this day, muttered objections. A man of about forty, wearing a beret, called out, "What about the millions who were sent to the camps?" Svistov replied, "Well, there were mistakes." A woman clutching a bouquet of roses said loudly, "Too costly mistakes." Svistov, looking befuddled, returned to his original thesis. "He was a despot," he said. "As for Beria," he added, referring to the head of Stalin's secret police, "he was a son of a bitch."

In their zeal to spill out the truth before someone again curbed them, both *Moscow News* and *Ogonyok* seemed to outstrip Gorbachev's plans for them. Every few months after late 1988 would see a new Gorbachev outburst at the most radical publications. On occasion, infuriated by some article, he would sarcastically refer to *Moscow News* by its English title rather than as *Moskovskiye Novosti*, as if to imply it must be a foreign publication. Gorbachev spoke often of "glasnost in the interest of socialism and of the people." Korotich, by contrast, remarked in a 1988 television appearance:

"For me, glasnost is simply a return to the norm, nothing special. We have already started saying it's some feat to print Pasternak, a feat to print [the great poet Anna] Akhmatova. But what the hell kind of feat is this? The hero is the one who banned them, and what we are doing is a normal act.... They still try to convince us that if we speak the truth a lot, then something will come crashing down in our country. I will be terribly glad if everything that collapses because of the truth collapses immediately." Already in 1988 the gap was widening between Communist reform and populist reform, between defenders of "socialism" and those who sought only "the normal." Gorbachev was staving off the collapse; Korotich was welcoming it.

In this country where politics had always remade history, history now was remaking politics. In no sphere of life was the process clearer than in the revival of nationalism and the growth of republican independence movements. No tenet of the Soviet illusion would collapse more violently and more completely then the notion of the happy family of nations. But no one predicted the spiral of secessionism nor the related epidemic of tribal violence that began in 1986. Kremlin autocrat, samizdat dissident, and Western Sovietologist alike had looked at the multiethnic Soviet Union before that year and seen no ticking bomb, no looming disaster, no real crisis.

Surely with a hundred-plus identifiable ethnic groups—one meticulous Soviet scholar counted four hundred—the country had its share of the usual street prejudice and institutional discrimination. A foreign visitor quickly picked up on Russians' disdain for darker-skinned southerners (*chyorni*, blacks, Russians called them) or Balts' feeling of superiority toward Russians. The predominance of Russians in important political jobs—including the party's second secretary in each republic—and in sensitive security posts in the army and KGB showed clearly who was boss. Yet open conflict was almost nonexistent, and in many parts of Transcaucasia or Central Asia multiethnic communities seemed genuinely free of serious tensions. "We live in a multinational state. This quality is an element of its might, not of weakness or disintegration," Gorbachev wrote in *Perestroika*. The national question, he suggested with the unmistakable hubris of a member of the dominant ethnic majority, had been "resolved": "Every unbiased person cannot but admit that our Party has carried out gigantic reform work in this sphere....Our state could not have held together if there had not been a factual equalizing of the republics, if a commonwealth had not arisen on the basis of brotherhood and cooperation, respect and mutual aid." The view from the West was certainly not so sanguine, but the fact that Hedrick Smith's 1976 best-seller about this half-Russian country could be called *The Russians* suggested that ethnicity was not seen as a crucial issue.

But at the end of 1986 young Kazakhs rioted to protest the replacement of the Kazakhstan party chief with an ethnic Russian. In February 1988 Azeris in the bleak town of Sumgait went on a brutal anti-Armenian rampage that took thirty-two lives. Gradually it became clear that the constant threat of brutal repression by the state, more than "brotherhood and cooperation," had kept the ethnic peace for so long. Russians, Gorbachev among them, were taken aback as *Moscow News* and other publications reported the atrocities from Sumgait. "How could we, who were brought up to believe that we are a unified family, have reached such a point?" asked a writer in *Izvestiya* in May 1988. "We had to admit bitter, fantastic, incomprehensible things: People had been killed and maimed physically and morally just because they were of a different nationality."

Many non-Russians were less shocked because they had tasted discrimination and worse at the hands of the Russian "elder brother." In the Baltic republics older people had vivid memories of the brutal Soviet occupation of 1940 and the murderous mass deportations that had crushed nationalism and decimated the population. In Estonia, Latvia, and Lithuania, therefore, the reopening of history was by no means of merely intellectual interest. The heart of the Baltic question, which would loom large over perestroika and eventually become the wedge that would shatter the union, was a dusty document a half-century old, the long-suppressed secret protocols to the Molotov-Ribbentrop Pact, the 1939 deal between Stalin and Hitler.

Official Soviet history had taught that, by a miracle of simultaneity, genuine popular revolutions had occurred in 1940 in all three independent Baltic republics, in which the people had risen up against their respective bourgeois governments and invited the Red Army in to ensure socialist victory. This Soviet fairy tale had no place for an inconvenient fact—that in the Molotov-Ribbentrop protocols Hitler and Stalin had actually divided Eastern Europe and the Baltic countries between them, with Stalin claiming Estonia, Latvia, and Lithuania as well as Western Ukraine and Bessarabia, which would become part of Soviet Moldavia. So Soviet diplomats and historians had simply denied the existence of the protocols, copies of which had long been published and authenticated in the West.

Even as glasnost toppled other myths of Soviet history in 1988, Gorbachev clung to this one. On the eve of the forty-ninth anniversary of the Molotov-Ribbentrop Pact, Valentin Falin, a former ambassador to Germany and politician of legendary flexibility, told foreign journalists that the versions of the secret protocols published in the West were "copies of copies.... It is hard to say accurately what in those copies corresponds to reality and what has been forged." But even as Falin offered this more sophisticated version of the traditional Soviet denial of the existence of the protocols, the Baltic media were publishing incontrovertible evidence of their authenticity. Two weeks before Falin's press conference, Vilnius radio broadcast in Lithuanian a detailed account of a 1940 meeting in which V. M. Molotov, Stalin's foreign minister, lectured the Lithuanian prime minister on how Russia since Ivan the Terrible had rightly demanded access to the Baltic. Five days before Falin's press conference the Estonian newspaper *Rahva Haal* became the first Soviet publication to print the actual text of the secret protocols. A week later *Sirp ja Vasar*, another Estonian paper, declared that "it is no longer tolerable to juggle with lies or half-truths" on the protocol question. "Proclaiming the whole truth about what led the Estonian people in August 1940 into the Soviet Union," the paper said, "is the crucial political problem of perestroika; even more—it is the prerequisite for perestroika and glasnost to continue in Estonia."

By embracing the principle of historical glasnost Gorbachev had given the Balts a tool they wielded relentlessly against the sanitized Soviet version of the annexation of their republics. A little more than a year after Falin's press conference the Kremlin finally was forced to acknowledge the existence of the protocols and declare them illegal and void—in effect granting the republics' argument that they never had legally joined the Soviet Union. The admission was made by Alexander Yakovlev, the Politburo's most scholarly and most radical figure, in a resonant speech. Yakovlev wryly noted that the secret protocols had first been published as early as May 1946—in the *St. Louis Post-Dispatch*. He said the Soviet leadership had been guilty of "ideologizing history to the extent that it loses its true content," and insisted that "the whole truth, even the bitterest one, must be told some time." He said the protocols "reflected precisely the inner essence of Stalinism. This is one, and not the only one, of the delayed-action mines from the minefield which we have inherited, and which we are now trying to clear with such difficulties and complexities." Finally Yakovlev declared, in remarkable language from a Politburo member: "Sooner or later the truth will out on God's earth; deception is unlocked; without such moral cleansing the development of civilization is inconceivable." Yakovlev insisted that the historical facts had no bearing on the Baltic republics' current status, but he also said that "battles for truth are the motive force of history." A few months later the "delayed-action mine" of Molotov-Ribbentrop would explode, and Lithuania would become the first republic to declare its independence.

The pursuit of history also led directly into politics in Byelorussia, long viewed as the sleepiest of the republics. In a wooded area on the edge of Minsk where people often took picnics, a young archaeologist named Zenon Poznyak carried out the same kind of work being done in Moscow by Alexander Milchakov. Minsk's Kuropaty Woods were documented to have been the grave of tens of thousands of people trucked to a fenced NKVD compound for execution between 1937 and 1941; the secret police abandoned the killing only when Hitler invaded.

Poznyak's revelations, first reported in a small-circulation Minsk literary magazine, were picked up by *Moscow News* in the summer of 1988. Then, in September 1988, *Ogonyok* published photographs of the rows of unearthed skeletons at Kuropaty—the first photos in the Soviet national press of a Stalinist killing field. In October, when activists organized a peaceful memorial march to Kuropaty, police attacked with dogs and firehoses. The overreaction radicalized many people and led directly to the founding of a Byelorussian People's Front. The People's Front, led by Poznyak, became the first organized opposition to the party and accomplished what many thought impossible: it awakened a Byelorussian national identity distinct from the dominant Russian culture and language. More than two years later, when wildcat strikes suddenly broke out at the huge, placid factories of Minsk, it was the People's Front that would channel the workers' inchoate anger into an organized, effective anti-Communist political movement. An obscure archaeological publication had planted the seed that grew into political rebellion.

In other republics, too, the unearthing of history produced a growing feeling of resentment against Soviet rule, a rediscovery of indigenous culture, and a new insistence on national sovereignty. In Ukraine article after article reconstructed the brutal famine of the early 1930s, building the case that Stalin had directed it deliberately against Ukrainian peasants to crush their resistance to collectivization. In Moldavia the press showed how Stalin had set out to disprove the obvious fact that the "Moldavians" were ethnically and linguistically indistinguishable from the neighboring Romanians by banning the Romanians' Latin alphabet and forcing scholars to invent a distinct "Moldavian" language and ethnicity. In Central Asia journalists documented the devastating effects of Moscow's demand over the decades for greater and greater cotton production, which had poisoned water supplies, dried up the Aral Sea, created a class of impoverished seasonal laborers, and corrupted the government.

The movement to restore history even provided camouflage for the formation of a prototype opposition party. In January 1989, though the Communist party still firmly held its constitutional monopoly on power, the Memorial society managed to hold its first national conference. Over a snowy weekend, in a gathering of unofficial activists unprecedented in Soviet history, 505 delegates from chapters in 108 cities throughout the country met in the Moscow Aviation Institute auditorium.

Sensing the danger, party officials had unsuccessfully pressured the institute not to permit the use of the hall. The conference demonstrated that the official nervousness had been justified. Speakers moved fluidly between 1938 and 1989. Stalinism was treated not as a historical phenomenon but as a political platform, one very much alive in the party and government bureaucracy. When Memorial managed to publish its own newspaper a couple of weeks later, its front page carried a long-banned excerpt from Anna Akhmatova's poem of the terror, "Requiem," and a Gulag story by Varlam Shalamov. But the rest of the issue had a distinctly political tone, and the back page carried Andrei Sakharov's platform for the upcoming parliamentary elections.

In fact, nearly all the Memorial leaders would be elected to the first Congress of People's Deputies, where they would at first be called the "Moscow Group" and later the "Interregional Deputies Group." Ultimately they would become the core of the anti-Communist reform movement that would launch Boris Yeltsin into the Russian leadership and direct competition with Gorbachev. Information about history was galvanizing people, turning them into organizers and demonstrators. The exercise in historical truth-telling that was supposed merely to cleanse the system was threatening to sweep it away.

Alexander Milchakov inevitably was caught up in the move from history to politics. When a reform-minded Moscow City Council was elected in 1990, one of its moves was to appoint him chairman of an official commission investigating Moscow's mass graves. He challenged the KGB to open its archives and was rebuffed, but the newspaper *Vechernyaya Moskva* covered the conflict: "Duel: Alexander Milchakov vs. the KGB," said its front-page headline. "Our past has not become past, it is not behind us, as many believe, but remains with us," he told the paper. In the Lubyanka, where the terror had been directed and where its records were still locked, was where the past and present met, he said. "Whether we like it or not," he said in one interview, "from the building on Dzerzhinsky Square stretches an historical trail of millions of crimes, a sea of blood. And when in the KGB they claim that the documents have disappeared, that there are no employees to search for them, I don't believe it." A few months later Milchakov told his millions of readers that anonymous sympathizers inside the KGB had informed him precisely where the lists of those executed and their burial sites were preserved in the agency's central archives: Archive No. 7, Inventory No. 1. The KGB, so informed, again had denied that such documents existed. The duel went on. Finally, in October 1990 the KGB suddenly announced it had discovered full lists of those executed—in Archive No. 7, Inventory No. 1.

At Milchakov's suggestion, *Vechernyaya Moskva* began reserving a column of space every day to publish a half-dozen or so names from the lists of the condemned: the small black-and-white photos of the victims, their names, ages, and professions. It was a haunting device, a dark counterpoint to the news. The faces stared out at readers looking for parliamentary debates and sports scores, theater announcements and lottery numbers, a daily reminder of the exhumed past.

On the crisp afternoon of October 30, 1990, just about the time the KGB began turning over to Milchakov the lists of the executed, thousands of Memorial activists and elderly Gulag survivors rallied in a park a half-mile north of the Lubyanka. By dissident tradition it was the Day of the Political Prisoner, which Andrei Mironov had marked with a hunger strike four years earlier in Dubrovlag. Now a woman's somber voice read over a public-address system from a seemingly endless list of the victims of terror: "Ivan Dmitrievich Leskov, carpenter, shot. Alexander Pavlovich Smirnov, collective farm worker, shot. Lyudmila Alexandrovna Berogaya, engineer, shot...." The list went on as the crowd marched down Dzerzhinsky Street, surrounded by the KGB's ever-expanding office complex, which incorporated everything from ultramodern concrete-and-glass buildings with antennas bristling from the roof to a spectacular, blue, nineteenth-century palace. Memorial had finally won permission to establish the monument it had first petitioned for in 1987: a large chunk of grey granite from the Solovetsky Islands in the White Sea, site of the first large-scale camps for political prisoners after the Bolshevik Revolution. The granite had been unloaded in the little park of spruces on one side of Dzerzhinsky Square, about equidistant from the statue of Iron Felix and the Lubyanka doors. The Politburo had approved the idea of a memorial to the "thousands" of victims of the repression "of the 1930s, 1940s, and early 1950s." But the inscription on the granite, as thousands of people filed past and laid down their roses or carnations, quietly insisted on two facts: that the victims could not be counted in the thousands, and that the repression did not begin in the 1930s nor end in the 1950s. "To the Memory," the inscription read, "of the Millions of Victims of the Totalitarian Regime."

Among the speakers as the stone was dedicated was ninety-year-old Oleg Volkov, a white-bearded writer who could testify to the fact that terror had begun before 1930. He himself had been brought to the Lubyanka by horse-cart after his first arrest in 1928, and he had begun his odyssey through the Gulag of nearly three decades in the Solovetsky camp. "I never thought I'd live to see a time when I could not only tell the truth about what happened, but see a monument to those who will never return," Volkov boomed into the microphone. But then he turned and pointed to the Dzerzhinsky statue, overlooking this memorial to the very men and women whom Iron Felix and his successors in the Lubyanka had condemned to imprisonment, exile, and death. "He was one of the main organizers of the state's ruthless policy toward its own people," Volkov said. Repentance for the terror could not take place while the statue was still standing, he declared. The crowd roared its agreement. "Don't forget the lessons of the past!" he cried. "Don't forget the victims of the terror!"

6

Television and the Revival of Politics

The TV image is everything.
          —Alexander Yakovlev

The lanky, grey-bearded man who strode to the podium of the first Congress of People's Deputies on May 31, 1989, was one of the few among the newly elected legislators whose name and face were known across the country. He was Yuri Petrovich Vlasov, a former Olympic weight lifter whose exploits with the barbells had thrilled Soviet sports fans. But it was now that he would perform his greatest feat before the biggest audience of his life.

The unveiling of Stalinism had helped drive circulations of the boldest publications to unheard-of heights: between 1985 and 1989, for instance, *Ogonyok*'s subscribers had quintupled, from 596,000 to 3 million and climbing. *Komsomolskaya Pravda*, the lively national youth newspaper, reached 20 million; the fact-packed weekly *Argumenti i Fakti*, which a few years earlier had been distributed to just 10,000 party propagandists, would top out at 35 million, becoming the most widely circulated periodical in the world. But the biggest television audiences still dwarfed the draw of the press, and the live broadcast of the Congress of People's Deputies was among the most-watched broadcasts of all time. It is likely that roughly 200 million people, nearly the entire adult Soviet population, watched the live broadcast of Vlasov's speech or saw its replay that evening.

A few days earlier Mikhail Gorbachev had approached the weight lifter during a break in the Congress to introduce himself and make some friendly comments about Vlasov's athletic achievements and his fame. Vlasov mentioned his intention to ask for the floor at the Congress. Gorbachev said he agreed completely with Vlasov's published criticism of bureaucracy and corruption in Soviet athletics, suggesting, Vlasov thought, that he expected the retired sportsman to make athletics the subject of his maiden speech. Vlasov did not correct the mistaken assumption.

Now Vlasov peered out across the more than two thousand deputies in the marble-and-glass Palace of Congresses and began to speak. When he got to the phrase "Deputy Gorbachev," deputies stopped chatting and started listening. Gorbachev was customarily referred to by first name and patronymic, in the Russian form of respectful address, or by his lengthy titles as chairman of the parliament and party leader. Calling him "Deputy Gorbachev" was a calculated slight, something like a British member of parliament referring to the prime minister as "MP." Next Vlasov tore into what he claimed was politically motivated censorship of reports of the Congress on the evening news program *Vremya*. Radical speeches were cut or dropped while loyal speakers got full coverage, he charged. Then he proposed that what the country needed, in the wake of Gorbachev's comments on the killing of sixteen demonstrators by the army in Georgia the previous April, was a good impeachment law. If Gorbachev hadn't known what his troops were doing in Tbilisi, "what sort of head of state is he?" If he did know and approve of the violence, the same law would be necessary, Vlasov said.

By this point some deputies were grinning, thrilled by Vlasov's outrageousness; others were shaking their heads and murmuring disapproval. Vlasov moved on to Soviet Prime Minister Nikolai Ryzhkov and his government. "One of the richest countries in the world, in peacetime, is making ends meet with food coupons, which are the same as ration cards," he said. "Elementary foodstuffs are unavailable. Our ruble is pitiful as compared with other currencies."

Those responsible should resign "along with their entire staffs," because that's how governments behaved in the rest of the world.

By now there were yells of encouragement and shouts of anger echoing across the huge hall. But everything Vlasov had said amounted to merely hors d'oeuvres, designed to whet the appetite for the main course of his speech. In the next ten minutes he savaged the KGB: "crimes unknown in the history of mankind...millions killed...threat to democracy...most closed, most secretive of all state institutions...." It was as if, with every sentence, he was adding another fifty kilograms and pressing the barbell above his head. He contrasted the "enormous ultramodern" hospital the KGB had built for its employees in a Moscow suburb to the "rundown" tuberculosis hospital next door. "When the first steps are being taken on the path of democratization, and at the same time there is a desire to crush it, a force such as the KGB takes on special meaning.... This committee exercises all-encompassing control over society and over each person individually.... The KGB is not a service," he declared, "but a real underground empire that has still not yielded its secrets." The KGB must surrender the Lubyanka and the surrounding buildings as a symbol of a break with its past: "For decades, orders for the annihilation or persecution of millions of people were issued from that building. This institution sowed grief, lamentation, and torture on our soil. In the bowels of this building, people were tortured—people who were, as a rule, the best, the pride and flower of our peoples. Then there is the very complex of these buildings, which are so unaccountably and monumentally immense, as if to indicate to whom power in this country really belongs." Finally, Vlasov dipped into history to end his tirade: "One hundred fifty years ago, Pyotr Chaadayev, an original Russian thinker and friend of Pushkin, wrote about Russia, 'We are exceptional people; we are among those nations that, as it were, are not members of mankind but exist only to give the world some terrible lesson.'

"Let there be no more," Vlasov concluded, "of this terrible lesson."

It is not easy to convey the power of Vlasov's attack on the KGB. Even in mid-1989 many people still preferred not to name it in conversation; they would call it "the neighbors" or "the committee" or just knock three times rather than pronounce aloud those three letters. Vlasov had not only pronounced the name of the KGB, he had pronounced it with venom and contempt, given it an unprecedented, unimaginable tongue-lashing.

The evening of May 31 I rode the Metro home from the Congress, and that night I went to a Soviet friend's birthday party. On the street and in my friend's apartment people were talking excitedly, incredulously, about Vlasov's speech, repeating his phrases, reliving what they immediately felt to be a triumphant, historic event. People savored the fact that the truth had been told about the most fearful of Soviet institutions, and that it had been told not by an obscure intellectual, the most abundant species in the reformist faction at the Congress, but by good old Yuri Vlasov, practically a working-class hero. They assumed correctly that his prominence and legal immunity as a parliamentary deputy would protect him from retaliation. There was a sense of a people's victory over an enemy of overwhelming strength. It was David versus Goliath, live on the tube.

If Vlasov's message was striking, its medium was extraordinary. In this land where information had for so long been handled as a hazardous substance to be entrusted only to the elite, this diatribe, which compared with the most fierce passages in Solzhenitsyn, went instantly to everyone. A random telephone poll in six cities on the day of the speech found that about eight of ten urban adults were following the Congress either "constantly" or "more or less constantly": 77 percent in Moscow; 75 percent in Leningrad; 88 percent in Kiev; 69 percent in Tallinn, the Estonian capital; 93 percent in Tbilisi, Georgia; and 78 percent in Alma-Ata, Kazakhstan. Nearly everyone else reported watching the Congress "from time to time." In the three biggest Soviet cities only 1 percent said they were "practically not following" the sessions.

A few weeks after Vlasov's speech, when the Supreme Soviet, the smaller, working parliament, started its session, the live, unedited coverage was dropped, replaced by a few hours of excerpts. Though interest in the tumultuous debates was still huge, there were few protests. During the two weeks of the Congress so many workers had walked away from assembly lines to cluster around TV sets that Soviet manufacturing production had fallen by 20 percent.

If the KGB was the Soviet institution working to control, curtail, and distort information in the Gorbachev years, television was the institution that disseminated it most widely, most powerfully, most democratically, and most subversively. The print media had pioneered the opening up of history that was the first wave of glasnost, starting in 1987—though supplemented, to be sure, by TV broadcasts of newsreel and archival footage from the Stalin period. As the history boom subsided and the country focused on politics, television came into its own.

Television operated as a catalyst and amplifier for the first, powerful wave of political enthusiasm that began with the election campaign of 1989. The last contested national elections in Russia had been held just after the Bolsheviks seized power in 1917. But the Bolsheviks won only 24 percent of the seats and naturally lost the first votes in the Constituent Assembly when it met in January 1918. So after one day, Lenin, to whose concept of socialist democracy Gorbachev so often said the country was returning, sent over two hundred heavily armed sailors and forcibly dispersed the parliament. Since that time, for seven decades, Soviet citizens had trooped regularly to the polls, been handed a ballot with one name for each open seat, and dropped the card into the urn. If they chose they could vote against a candidate by crossing his name out, but few people bothered. Turnout was high: those who didn't vote were questioned about their lack of civic consciousness and sometimes disciplined at work; plus, the authorities put desirable delicacies on sale at the polling-place snack bars. The soviets (Russian for "councils") thus elected at the local, republican, and national levels were nominally the foundation of "Soviet power"; in fact they were powerless, decorative organs, a fig leaf for party decision-making.

Now Gorbachev was seeking to shake up the system while ending the embarrassing election charade. In 1987 and 1988 there were a few local experiments with contested elections. The first national election, to choose the Congress, was set for March 26, 1989. It was egregiously flawed democracy: one-third of the seats were set aside for "public organizations," most of them subject to strict party control. Gorbachev himself and his Politburo colleagues simply awarded themselves seats from the party's quota of one hundred seats. But in many places there were genuine races for the contested seats. Many Moscow voters followed the campaign with passionate interest, and the neighborhood meetings held to nominate candidates invariably drew overflow crowds.

One such meeting was hastily organized on the last possible day to nominate Vitaly Korotich, the controversial editor of the pioneering magazine *Ogonyok*. Korotich had been rejected by the official writers' and journalists' unions for their set-aside seats, and right-wing goons from the anti-Semitic organization *Pamyat* (Memory) had broken up an earlier neighborhood meeting to nominate him. On this snowy evening in north Moscow the hall was filled more than an hour before the scheduled beginning. Some five hundred people were still outside, many with campaign posters, trying to push through the entrance. Someone with a megaphone kept repeating, "The hall is full! No one else will be allowed in!" People shouted in reply, "It's a trick!" and pushed harder, actually shattering one of the heavy glass doors. The crowd was overwhelmingly behind Korotich, but lots of others were on hand: shaggy young men from Pamyat; workers from a nearby electronics plant, obediently turned out to nominate their boss; party loyalists; KGB watchers; and curious neighbors. Inside, after five hours of tumult, manipulation by party bosses, shouting matches, and name-calling, Korotich was nominated, one hour before the midnight deadline. Most striking was the ferocious interest of people who, according to the cliché of Western Sovietology, should be passive and subservient to authority. Many were deeply grateful to Korotich for what he had done with *Ogonyok*. "*Ogonyok* used to lie around at the hairdresser's," said Maria Andreyeva, an elderly woman who had come to support the editor. "Now the whole country reads it. Korotich has uncovered all kinds of evildoing by Stalin. He's telling us the truth." Maria Andreyeva was eighty-two—old enough to remember the Revolution and to have cast her meaningless vote in dozens of meaningless elections. "You know what's good?" she said. "These people aren't standing in line for sugar, not for bread, not for meat. They're standing in line for ideas."

Television carried this urgent and unfamiliar feeling of political involvement to a far broader audience. Many urbanites chose their candidates based on televised debates broadcast live, evening after evening, in Moscow, Leningrad, and many other cities. One night I watched a half-dozen candidates competing for the Timiryazevsky District seat in north Moscow debate issues for more than two hours. I was amazed to hear one candidate, a polite young man with a mustache, explain calmly that the Communist party's monopoly on power was the reason for all Soviet woes. That was still considered a dangerous heresy, and I reran that section of the debate on my VCR several times to make sure I had heard it right. I had. The man, Arkady Murashyov, a boyish physicist, went on to win the seat and became a leader of the parliament's radical faction, the Interregional Group. Without the televised debate the unknown Murashyov might well have lost to older, better-known, and more conservative competitors.

When the elections were over it was television that brought the spectacle of the first Congress of People's Deputies, with such bracing speeches as that of Yuri Vlasov, into people's homes. The televised Congress introduced the Soviet public to a new cast of political characters; it legitimized debate in a political culture where public unanimity had always been the highest value; and it went a long way to banishing fear. If an elected official such as Vlasov could savage the KGB on TV, maybe an ordinary citizen didn't have to keep his mouth shut about his bosses' thievery or the long wait to buy a car, or even the president's mistakes or the party's ideology. Through 1989 and in 1990, the year of the first contested elections at the republican and local levels, television used talk shows, parliamentary reports, and meet-the-mayor programs to bring people close to the new politicians. Television turned the *vlasti*, the authorities, for so long faceless bureaucrats eager to please only their superiors in the party hierarchy, into personalities who suddenly seemed both responsive and vulnerable.

Any Westerner who in the 1980s managed to visit a village in the Russian *glubinka*—the depths, in other words, the sticks—was struck first by the nineteenth-century backwardness. The Russian word *bezdorozhiye*, roadlessness, captured the long slog through the mud often necessary to reach a village. Even on the few paved roads the most common transport was the horse-drawn cart, the bicycle, and the infrequent, jam-packed, smoke-belching bus. There was never plumbing inside the little wooden houses, often decorated with brightly painted carvings around the windows and along the roofline, and generally only wood heat. Any visitor quickly grew accustomed to seeing old women drawing water at a village well, lugging away two buckets in their hands or suspended from a wooden yoke across stooped shoulders. Yet sprouting from the roof of even the humblest cottage was a TV antenna, linking this Tolstoyan world with the biggest television transmission system in the world.

Why had the government invested so much more in television than in plumbing? The answer was obvious: the Soviet leadership had recognized the importance of television as a medium for propaganda and political control. Lenin had pronounced film to be "for us, the most important of the arts" and in his last years had grown very excited about the political potential of radio broadcasting. In 1922 Lenin wrote to Stalin about the possibility radio offered for transmitting propaganda from Moscow "over hundreds, and under certain conditions, over thousands of versts" (a verst being about two-thirds of a mile). There were lots of "bourgeois social science professors" still around, Lenin complained, and only a few "Communist professors." But with the new reach of radio, a Communist professor at a microphone in Moscow could reach "every corner" of the country, he wrote. Despite the famine and hardship of that year, the party allocated up to 100,000 rubles from the gold reserve to set up a radio laboratory. In 1925 the first shortwave station in the world began broadcasting from Moscow's Sokolniki Park. At about the same time the government showed its concern about the subversive potential of the new medium. It prohibited "the recording or dissemination of the output of foreign radio stations" and designed most radios to receive only Soviet stations. Astonished foreign tourists discovered that the radio in their Soviet hotel room often could not be tuned or even switched off; only the volume was adjustable.

Experimental television transmission began in the 1930s, and the number of television sets soared from ten thousand in 1950 to 4.8 million a decade later. But a party decree in 1960 declared that TV had to move faster. "Television," the decree said, "is called on to play an important role in the education of Soviet people in the spirit of Communist ideals and morality, irreconcilable opposition to bourgeois ideology and morals, and in the mobilization of the workers to successful fulfillment of the seven-year plan." The Central Committee declared "extremely insufficient" the current exploitation of TV "for the propaganda of the achievements of the Soviet people in political, economic, and cultural life and for displaying Soviet man, builder of Communism."

A crash expansion program followed. In time for the fiftieth anniversary of the Revolution in 1967, the huge television tower in Moscow's Ostankino neighborhood had gone into operation, complete with restaurant on top. It was intended to be a symbol of Soviet technology, though in later years dissidents spoke of it as a giant hypodermic needle for the ideological vaccination of the Soviet people. An expensive satellite relay network was constructed to take TV almost anywhere, from Central Asian deserts to Siberian tundra. By 1988 there were 8,828 TV broadcasting stations in the country; together they covered territory where 96 percent of the population lived. There were ninety million television sets—more per capita than in Italy, the Netherlands, or New Zealand, in sharp contrast to the status of other common technology, such as telephones, in which the Soviet Union lagged far behind almost every developed country.

Figuring an average of three people per television household, it is safe to say that nearly everyone could watch TV. And long before glasnost, even at a time when shows such as For You, Cattle Breeders; factory-exceeds-plan movies, and interviews on scientific communism were standard fare, nearly everyone did. TV drew a huge audience, especially for news. By the mid-1980s an average of 150 million people were watching the main evening news show *Vremya* (Time) every night, more than 70 percent of the adult Soviet population. By comparison, according to Ellen Mickiewicz, an American expert on Soviet TV, the three U.S. networks' news shows were being watched by just 60 million people, about a third of U.S. adults. One reason for the huge audience, Mickiewicz has noted, was the state's monopoly: though most people could receive two, three, or even four channels, Vremya was shown on all channels.

The power of the new medium to persuade naturally demanded that it be treated with the utmost ideological care, and censorship of the airwaves was thorough. Not only was Glavlit, the usual censorship bureaucracy, able to red-pencil scripts before broadcast; another in-house censor had the job of watching all recorded shows just before they went on the air, to catch the *nuansi*, the subtly subversive or corrupting moments. For many years the word "vodka" was banned from the air; even a film of Gogol's "Inspector General" had to be doctored to fudge a famous scene in which the main character is drunk. Cynics sometimes combined the name of the KGB with the name of the state broadcasting monopoly, calling the State Committee for Television and Radio the "State Security Committee for Television and Radio," which implied both the importance and danger the leadership was seen to attach to the small screen.

Certainly Gorbachev understood the tool his predecessors had put in his hand. His adviser and media overseer, Alexander Yakovlev, was quoted in 1987 as declaring, "The TV image is everything." The same year the revered elderly historian of Russian culture, Dmitry Likhachev, generally no fan of new technologies, remarked on television's paradoxical ability both to leap national borders and to achieve intimacy: "Television permits us to see things not only at great distances but at tiny distances, too. It replaces the telescope and the magnifying glass, allows us to see other countries and to see the face, the living face of a man point-blank, when that face can neither lie nor pretend. Television is the great exposer of lies, pomposity, stupidity." He did not say so, but Likhachev may have had in mind the live television coverage accorded to speeches by Brezhnev, which had dramatized the leader's frailty and senility before a huge audience. People remembered seeing him continue reading a speech when, because a page was missing, it made no sense; they also saw him stumble approaching a podium and hesitate in momentary incomprehension of his situation. In this sense, without ever trying, television inadvertently became "the biggest dissident of all" in the late Brezhnev years, TV official Eduard Sagalayev told me. "Television showed who Brezhnev and Chernenko were—the flagrant lies, the flagrant hypocrisy, so I think for many people a reverse effect was achieved by television," he said. To show the ailing Brezhnev awarding himself a fifth star of the Hero of the Soviet Union for his modest World War II record—"that was the destruction of ideals and not their creation," Sagalayev said.

Already in 1986 Gorbachev was capitalizing on the contrast by using television to cultivate his image as a youthful, dynamic, democratic leader, able to ad-lib a speech and quote figures from memory, unafraid to plunge into a crowd of ordinary citizens for an exchange of views. Even for an American, the television coverage of Gorbachev's walkabouts during domestic trips was strikingly unfamiliar and unpredictable. If the Soviet viewer was accustomed to seeing his leaders reading woodenly from lengthy texts, the American viewer was used to hearing his president either in ten-second sound bites on the evening news or in TelePrompTer-assisted imitations of spontaneity from the Oval Office. On his trips Gorbachev would be shown for twenty, thirty, or forty minutes lecturing, cajoling, arguing, and explaining, without podium or text, sometimes barely visible in the midst of a pushing, swirling crowd, with his wife Raisa usually standing watchfully but silently at his side. TV newsman Alexander Tikhomirov, who covered many Gorbachev trips for Vremya, recalled: "It was completely out of the ordinary how he would walk out into the crowd—and a real crowd, not a faked one."

On a trip to the Siberian city of Krasnoyarsk, Tikhomirov recalled, Gorbachev stopped his motorcade in a little settlement on the road from the airport and began conversing with those who quickly gathered. One man told Gorbachev local officials wouldn't show the president how people really lived—"there's no water, they don't deliver bread, you can't breathe for the gas fumes." Another yelled skeptically: "What we're saying now, will it be shown on television?" Gorbachev replied that he did not dictate television coverage. The man replied: "What you say won't happen, you'll see, none of this will be shown." When Tikhomirov went to the local TV studio to edit the videotape and send it to Moscow, his superiors wanted to cut the sharpest moments, including these. But Tikhomirov told them Gorbachev had implied that the coverage wouldn't be emasculated, and they gave in. "They watched it in Krasnoyarsk that night," he said.

But Gorbachev's impact as master of his own TV image was quickly dwarfed by the impact of the television shows he permitted on the air. As in Eastern Europe, his greatest achievement with television was not to intervene. Or, to be more precise, to intervene only when it was too late.

The twelfth floor of Central Television's main office building near the Ostankino tower was for youth programming, and it was there that television's movers and shakers congregated under the direction of a shrewd television veteran, Eduard Sagalayev, who would become the most important single influence at Ostankino in the liberation of Soviet TV. For some years before Gorbachev, publications and broadcasts aimed at young people had been permitted a little more of a freewheeling tone; even mossbacked ideologues could see that something lively would be necessary to compete with Western pop culture. Glasnost made for a still longer leash, and from this division in 1986 and 1987 came the shows that would soon conquer the airwaves: Give Me the Floor, The World and Youth, Cast of Characters, Twelfth Floor, Up to 16—and Over, and, most important of all, *Vzglyad* (Glance, or View), carrying as well the metaphorical sense of "point of view" or "opinion." Sagalayev dated television glasnost from the summer of 1985 when Give Me the Floor went to the little Moscow suburb of Balashikha for a preannounced meeting with the public. Tens of thousands of people showed up, many took their turn at the microphone to complain or urge their solutions to various problems—and the whole tape was aired without cuts.

Later youth-division shows were equally spontaneous but more sophisticated. Though they had their peculiarities, most of the division's hits were variety programs with no precise American equivalent, mixing crusading exposés, star interviews, and pop music. They were substantive enough to draw not just the young people who were their ostensible target but older people as well. At its peak between 1988 and 1990, Vzglyad was so universally popular that it was considered rude to invite anyone to do anything else during its time slot late on Friday night. Despite the fact that it often began at 11 p.m. and ran as late as 2 a.m.—one man from Rostov wrote to *Ogonyok* that he watched the show standing up to avoid falling asleep—Vzglyad drew audiences even larger than Vremya's. Anyone who missed the show had cause to regret it, because in many Russian circles it was the main topic of weekend conversation.

Journalist Tatyana Khloplyankina captured the way Vzglyad and other new shows gripped people's attention in a piece written for *Moscow News* in early 1989: "Having bought a new TV set a few years ago, we didn't get rid of the old one but put it in the kitchen. And yesterday (the date doesn't matter, such evenings are now commonplace) the whole family was running back and forth between the living room and the kitchen, because the Leningrad channel was showing 'Public Opinion,' and the all-union channel was showing Vzglyad, and both were a must. In Leningrad people were literally tearing the microphone out of one another's hands in order to speak, while on Vzglyad they were showing the latest political rally—the pain and despair sometimes prevented people from speaking, and sometimes it was hard to listen to. But that pain and those differences of opinion are a hundredfold more valuable than the unanimous rejoicing shown in newsreels from the 1950s."

Vzglyad's young, hip hosts, mainly English-speaking products of
Radio Moscow's World Service, were like surfers riding the advanc-
ing wave of glasnost, masterfully judging just where the edge of the
permissible was located and trying to stay just ahead of it. Whether
the topic was AIDS and its spread in hospitals by unsterilized
needles, or the neglect of injured veterans of the war in Afghanistan,
or newly opened archives shedding light on the Stalinist terror, or
the secret privileges of party officials, or the lives of Moscow's
hard-currency prostitutes, or unusual military maneuvers that might
suggest preparations for a crackdown—Vzglyad was first with the
story in the Soviet media, or nearly first. When it was not first, the
show often was picking up a theme from the small-circulation
Moscow News or from a highbrow literary monthly and broadcasting it in simple, emotive, illustrated form to Stavropol tractor-drivers
and Arctic coal miners.

But unabashed sensation-seeking in a sensation-starved society
was only one key to the show's popularity. Another was the fact that
although portions of the show were taped in advance and beamed to
eastern time zones, Vzglyad almost always went live to the European
USSR, a circumstance underscored by the clock hanging in the
studio and the repetition of the studio telephone number for calling
in comments and questions. Live broadcast meant unpredictability
and spontaneity, a characteristic the hosts underscored with their
casual, unrehearsed commentary, their interruptions of one another
and occasional on-air disagreements. In many respects Vzglyad
was trying to be anti-Vremya, counterposing its youthful hosts in
jeans to the news show's stolid middle-aged readers in neckties,
its wide-open studio shots (with cameras and technicians often
glimpsed) to Vremya's dull man-reads-text format, its informality to
Vremya's pompous ceremony, its Western orientation to the news
program's socialism-is-best bias, and its candor to Vremya's prevari-
cating.

In a Vzglyad show from September 1988, early in its triumphant
run, the hosts are the handsome blond Sergei and his strikingly
beautiful actress partner, Yelena, both about thirty. Brief clips flash
by, bouncing from the trivial to the solemn to the ridiculous, always
with a sense of urgency and a passionate, sophisticated point of view:

an Afghan-war veterans' folk-song festival in Leningrad; a Hungarian rock group singing in English "Clap Your Hands for Mikhail Gorbachev," the slinky songstress cooing about Gorbachev's "sexy smile"; Soviet pop stars at a Latvian music festival talking about their pay, artistic freedom, and aspirations ("I want my own apartment," says one famous performer); an exposé on a long-unfinished children's hospital, with the reporter reading the list of guilty officials ("I think this is simply a crime," remarks the host); shots of the trial of the Ovechkin family, Siberian musicians whose hijacking attempt ended in a bloody assault by security troops, with the strong implication that the troops' violence was excessive. Then comes a clip of the late counterculture balladeer Vladimir Vysotsky, singing a song with the lines, "I don't like it when they shoot in the back, I don't like it when they beat the innocent"; an exposé of a pipe-laying project in Magnitogorsk that dug up the cemetery where the city's founders were buried; an Afghan-vet physician announcing an upcoming conference of medics who served in the war; a boy of about eight years in Smolensk giving an impressive rendition of a comic Russian folk song; an elderly Artists' Union conservative answering an artist's attack on him in an earlier Vzglyad program; a weird Soviet rock video ridiculing a hard-drinking middlebrow father figure; and excerpts from a one-man show portraying the late folksinger Alexander Galich, with a sampling of his swipes at communism, bureaucracy, and anti-Semitism to show viewers why he became a magnitizdat star and why he was forced to emigrate in 1974.

Lasting from thirty seconds to ten minutes apiece, these short subjects frame the show's main topics, which occupy fifteen to thirty minutes apiece. One is an interview with historian V. L. Danilov on the famine of 1932–1933, a cataclysm in 1988 still virtually unknown to most Soviet citizens, which he says "by Western estimates" cost from three million to seven million lives and was "the very worst crime of Stalin." Danilov describes the "barbers"—the peasant women who took scissors into already harvested grain fields in a desperate search for food for their families, and the penalty for such "theft of state property"—execution. The emotional force of Danilov's facts is magnified by the archival film that accompanies the interview: shots of hollow-faced, starving peasants alternating with shots of Stalin waving to smiling, athletic demonstrators pushing huge floats bearing his likeness across Red Square on May Day. Compulsive about record-keeping, the Soviet government filmed everything and locked the films away, inadvertently creating a mother lode of material for television glasnost in the 1980s.

Vzglyad's second major topic of the evening is a new documentary film, *Limita*, which shows the squalid lives of Moscow's *limitchiki*, people who come from the provinces to the capital to take the factory and construction jobs that Muscovites shun. They get their pejorative nickname from the fact that they live in the city under a quota, *limit*, for those who do not have a permanent residence permit. Excerpts from the film, never played widely in movie theaters, show how these migrant workers are vulnerable to exploitation because of their desperation to hang on to the more interesting life and fuller shops of the capital. There are heartrending shots of families sharing single rooms in leaky, run-down dormitories as the parents grow old with no hope of achieving their dream—a residence permit and an apartment. The sound track, a sardonic rock song singing the praises of the capital's cushy lifestyle, provides a constant ironic counterpoint. After one excerpt the film's director is interviewed and notes that despite an official decision not to permit the recruitment of more limitchiki, Moscow's Leninist Komsomol Automobile Factory has just brought in a group of Central Asian workers who, she says fiercely into the camera, are "working in slavery-like conditions."

The third major item is the evening's main live guest, eye-surgeon-turned-entrepreneur Sviatoslav Fyodorov. Known in the West as the inventor of radial keratotomy, the operation to correct nearsightedness, Fyodorov had built an empire of state-of-the-art medical clinics and become a Soviet millionaire. He was such a dynamo that few of his admirers realized he had lost one leg in a childhood accident and walked on a prosthesis. His status as a Communist party loyalist and his gift for dressing capitalism in a flimsy negligee of socialist terminology made him one of the earliest prominent spokesmen for market reforms. His can-do style and high standards gave the lie to many Russians' belief that their country was doomed to inferiority. He radiated energy and confidence, and his rapid, articulate, quotable speech—he sometimes was reminiscent of Jesse Jackson—made the crew-cut Fyodorov an extremely effective TV figure. As chairman of the country's new, unprecedented Charity and Health Fund, Fyodorov was not so vulnerable to accusations that he was a money-grubbing, heartless exploiter.

The Vzglyad hosts lean forward with intense interest as Fyodorov, their elder by at least twenty years, describes how he has turned his state eye clinics into an employee-operated "concern" that will pay 3.5 million rubles to the state in rent each year in return for "economic freedom, which is such a pleasure, when you can do good for people and depend only on that, not on any bosses." As the show goes on, the hosts return to Fyodorov from time to time for comments, and he proselytizes, alternating scathing criticism of the existing economic system with tantalizing visions of the prosperous and friendly future offered by the market. "We've forgotten what kindness is, humanism, nobility, self-esteem. We've been turned into an appendage of a huge bureaucratic machine," he says. His eye clinics now are going to lease their own farm to supply fresh milk and meat for staff and patients; the farmers will be sent to Switzerland or the U.S. to learn new methods. Later Fyodorov counters Sergei's timid suggestion that the move to economic self-sufficiency at every enterprise may make people more callous. No, says Fyodorov, on the contrary—market relations create mutual dependence and strengthen "normal human relations." In the new economy, Fyodorov gushes, the people now so desperate to leave the grim life of the village for Moscow will be able to "work intensively" and keep the profits. "They could earn fifty thousand rubles a year"—this at a time when farm workers were lucky to be earning two thousand—"and go to the city, have a great time, travel to Switzerland, see Paris, walk the Champs Elysées—if there's the basis for normal economic life."

This absurd vision of Ivan Ivanovich, peasant, abandoning his milking barn near Lipetsk for a quick tour of the Louvre is almost persuasive in Fyodorov's winning patter. "I believe that," Sergei replies, hesitatingly, then adds: "But so far, unfortunately, economic perestroika is not working at a very fast pace...."

This was 1988, when Vzglyad was still relatively generous to the old order. But the cumulative effect of these fast-alternating subjects is to paint a dark portrait of a country run by heartless, brainless bureaucrats: where fifty-five years ago millions of farmers were deliberately starved to death; where nineteen years ago a talented artist was driven into exile; where today unskilled laborers are mercilessly exploited. At the same time there is the promise, just beyond the horizon, of abundance, creative fulfillment, travel to exotic places, all brought by the magic of the market—"normal" life, the life lived in the West.

How could the authorities allow such stuff on the air? What were they thinking? Many officials were thinking, in fact: How can we allow such stuff on the air? "It was a terrible battle, a terrible battle," Eduard Sagalayev told me in 1991 of Vzglyad in 1988 and 1989. "People just don't know about it. They tried to shut down Vzglyad many times." The battle over TV was raging inside the Politburo, with Alexander Yakovlev often the only defender of the daring new shows, Sagalayev said. But the reach and power of television had already been so dramatically demonstrated, he said, that many party conservatives were wary of attacking television for fear of being exposed by it themselves. "There were always people who wanted to shut it all down, but they were afraid it might cost them their career. They were afraid of the guys from Vzglyad, they were afraid of Sagalayev, they were afraid of [news correspondent Alexander] Tikhomirov," Sagalayev said.

In the constant, running battle between party factions over Vzglyad and the new TV, Gorbachev at first stayed above the fray, then gradually shifted to the side of the outraged conservatives. The fights took place for the most part behind the scenes, but the public caught striking glimpses from time to time. One famous occasion was on Lenin's birthday in April 1989, when Vzglyad's live guest, the liberal theater director Mark Zakharov, gently offered his opinion that Lenin's body should be removed from the Red Square mausoleum and buried. Zakharov emphasized that he made his proposal out of respect for Lenin, who himself had expressed the wish to be buried with his mother in St. Petersburg and whose wife, Nadezhda Krupskaya, had begged the leadership "not to make an icon" of him. The Vzglyad host that night, Vladimir Mukusev, endorsed Zakharov's idea. Zakharov said it was "dangerous" and one of Stalin's "evil deeds" that Lenin had been turned into a demigod whose portrait hung everyplace. "I believe of course that we want to mark the commemorative spots associated with the personality and life of the great leader," Zakharov said. "But there's absolutely no need, let's say, to put up a plaque on the fence of the Moscow Zoo saying, 'Lenin was here.'"

All tasteful, tactful, polite—and heretical. When the party's Central Committee met a few days later, there was hell to pay. "Why would our television—state television, Party television—allow itself to make a statement of that kind?" sputtered eighty-year-old Georgy Zhukov, a veteran *Pravda* correspondent. Zhukov was a slightly comical figure with his musty references to the "soldiers on the ideological front." But he understood, and stated precisely, the implications of Zakharov's modest proposal and the slippery slope on which Gorbachev had placed the system. As usual it was the conservative Communists who understood and articulated the fatal threat posed by the liberated media to the survival of Soviet communism. The press and TV had moved off the approved territory of Stalinism for exposés and truth-telling and were heading both back in time, to examine Lenin, and forward in time, to examine the recent past and the present. Gorbachev's recasting of Soviet history, the Good Lenin/Bad Stalin theory, was eroding. "I think that while condemning everything that was bad and criminal throughout our history, we should not forget about the sanctity of the gains of the October Revolution," Zhukov said. The West, he warned, was "stepping up its onslaught on us.... Not long ago, for example, *Figaro* magazine published an article under the headline, 'Will Lenin Follow Stalin into the Dustbin of History?' which said, 'It's good that Stalin has been debunked, but it's bad that the Soviet Union doesn't dare to debunk Lenin, too.'" Other conservatives, reeling from their recent losses in the first contested parliamentary elections, joined the attack on Zakharov. "As if this were a private enterprise and not state-run television!" fumed Ratmir Bobovikov, party boss in the Vladimir region east of Moscow. "Lingering over such issues is simply immoral. Literally the next morning people were phoning party committees and asking in bewilderment how it was possible to understand this." "Comrades," said Alexei Myasnikov, a miner from Irkutsk and one of the token workers on the Central Committee, "a lot has been heard under our current democracy and pluralism, but what was said on Vzglyad about the most sacred thing—about Lenin—is worse than incomprehensible."

Sheltering himself from this rain of blows, the chairman of Gosteleradio, the State Committee on Radio and Television, Alexander Aksyonov, offered a fascinating defense. In the best Communist tradition of self-criticism, Aksyonov first agreed that Zakharov's remarks had been "shocking" and that on TV "political mistakes are especially inadmissible." Then he offered his excuse: "Many people try to use every opportunity to get across [on television] their own special views and opinions, which are often unsound and tendentious, particularly because most sociopolitical programs are broadcast live, that is, without first being taped.... This accents the specific and complex nature of the work of television and radio as opposed to the written press, where it is possible to reach an agreement with an author, and, should he disagree, not publish an unsound article."

Despite his valiant explanation of how tough it was to censor broadcasts, Aksyonov was gone within a month of the Zakharov appearance, sacrificed to the cause of ideological purity on the airwaves. The new head of Gosteleradio, the veteran apparatchik Mikhail Nenashev, told an interviewer that he hoped to curb the "destructiveness" of Vzglyad. Vzglyad, Nenashev said, attracted mainly "people of radical orientation, who want to destroy everything.... I want Vzglyad to show, right beside bad people, people who say: 'Despite those scoundrels, I'm creating something, I'm doing something....' In Vzglyad, I don't want to say there are no good people, but it's 90 percent destruction."

Not surprisingly, the political battles over television in general, and Vzglyad in particular, grew ever sharper. The censors began to prevail more often; Vzglyad lost more and more material to the scissors—pieces on the Bolsheviks' execution of Tsar Nicholas II and his family, satire on the government's economic bungling, a comedian's imitation of Gorbachev. One Friday night in October 1989

Vzglyad viewers saw a little notice superimposed on the screen every few minutes: "Tonight's broadcast is not live for reasons beyond the editors' control." I called a friend who worked for Soviet TV, who told me an amazing tale: The usual early version of the show had been taped in the morning for broadcast in the Far East. Then authorities got wind of Vzglyad's plan to invite Andrei Sakharov to appear on the live version of the show that night—and panicked. Just hours earlier Gorbachev had given a severe tongue-lashing to top editors in a closed meeting, news of which was flashing across Moscow from shell-shocked participants. In a memorable image he told the editors that the country was "knee-deep in gasoline" and accused the more daring newspapers and TV shows of tossing around matches. One particular target of Gorbachev's ire was the weekly *Argumenti i Fakti*, which had just published the results of a count of readers' letters that ranked Sakharov as the most popular member of the Congress of People's Deputies. Gorbachev himself was not even on the chart; the editors told me they thought it less offensive to leave him off the chart than to give him ranking in the lower half. Gorbachev denounced the popularity ranking, told *Argumenti i Fakti* editor Vladislav Starkov he should resign, and suggested that such radical deputies as Sakharov were getting altogether too much publicity. In this context Sakharov's uncensorable appearance before millions of TV viewers that very night would have been interpreted as direct defiance of the president and party leader. TV bosses sent the police to seal off Ostankino's Studio 2 where Vzglyad was to be broadcast, preventing hosts Alexander Politkovsky and Vladimir Mukusev from entering. A rock musician who had performed for the earlier, taped version of Vzglyad was not even permitted to collect his instruments from the studio. The angry Vzglyad team's only comeback was the cryptic announcement flashed repeatedly on the screen, which they hoped would at least raise some questions in viewers' minds.

"It's Gorbachev battling Gorbachev," Starkov told me a few days later in an interview in his apartment. The forty-nine-year-old editor, a Communist party member like every editor of an official publication in 1989, was hurt and bewildered by Gorbachev's turning on the media he had liberated. *Argumenti i Fakti*, the largest-circulation publication in the world, was a flagship of glasnost; Gorbachev seemed intent on strangling his own offspring. "He cooked the *kasha* [porridge]," Starkov said, applying homespun Russian to the media boom under Gorbachev, "and it didn't turn out the way he had expected." My television acquaintance said that the makers of Vzglyad and every other progressive show were engaged in "guerrilla warfare" with the bureaucrats in charge of TV.

Both print and broadcast journalists fought back in the spring of 1990 in an unorthodox manner: they ran for the new Russian parliament. Unlike most of their competitors, they had familiar names, or at least were associated with familiar publications, and a remarkable number were successful. No fewer than five *Argumenti i Fakti* editors, Starkov included, ran and won. So did Politkovsky, Mukusev, and Alexander Lyubimov from Vzglyad. The new politics, and the new information media that fueled it, seemed almost to be merging. The reporters' new clout as members of parliament slowed the pressure on the TV show.

I have another tape of Vzglyad from late April 1990, about a month after the republican and local elections, hosted entirely by the stocky, sincere Vladimir Mukusev—now Deputy-elect Mukusev. It illustrates how sharp the show's tone had become despite the best efforts of TV boss Nenashev to tame it. The theme was the economy; the public's focus, which had shifted from history to politics, now was expanding to encompass economics, as the debate over a transition to market relations heated up. Vzglyad's contribution begins with a sheepish administrator of Moscow's Institute of the International Workers' Movement, who acknowledges that, yes, the meaning of the slogan still at the top of most Soviet newspapers— "Workers of the World Unite"—now had primarily, ahem, historical meaning. Then, without introduction, we are suddenly in the United States, hearing how automation has cost manufacturing jobs but how services have taken up most of those laid off by factories. A union official explains that his autoworkers earn $1,500 to $2,000 a month, usually own a four- or five-room house, and own one or two cars—"but not new ones." Of course, the correspondent says, there is exploitation in America; he explains briefly the status of undocumented Mexican migrants. But this, he says, is far from the world of middle-class America. To understand better how the "proletariat" is faring, we see a detailed profile of the life of a young construction worker named Sean Avery, who is shown in a hard hat, installing drywall. The place is never named, but it looks like southern California. Sean earns $3,000 a month, works from seven to four, and comes home to the modest, two-story tract house he has bought with a friend. They relax over beer in the living room, flipping channels on the big TV-video with the remote control. We see Sean shooting baskets indoors, playing baseball on a local team, socializing at a sports bar. We hear him say he'd like to start his own construction business in about five years, when he has more savings and experience. "Do you consider yourself exploited?" he is asked. "Personally, me, no," he replies. "What would you consider exploitation?" Tough one. Sean thinks. "Well, when you have to work on Saturday and you don't get doubletime." More shots of Sean's sunny life. "Sean, is there something you lack in your life?" Sean is stumped. "Well, no, no, I guess not, not desperately." Sean explains why it doesn't bother him if someone has more money then he does—either they inherited it ("that's fate") or they worked for it ("more power to 'em"). Correspondent Mikhail Taratuta, whose reports from the U.S. were generally lively and fair, draws the conclusions: "Sean doesn't resemble the proletariat of the times of classic capitalism—not in his attitudes, not in his living standard, not in his feelings about those he would have been expected to hate. [Cut to Sean saying he has "pretty good relations" with his bosses.] ...Unquestionably this country has come a long way from barbarous capitalism as it was known in the classics to today's relative abundance and comfort—at least for the majority of those who live here."

Next Vzglyad goes to Bonn, where a group of Soviet entrepreneurs and managers is in a training seminar. Several of them gripe about their troubles with the Soviet bureaucracy. "I crossed through all the circles of hell in the foreign trade bureaucracy, all the way to a deputy minister," says a frustrated would-be businessman from Kazakhstan, trying to make VCRs with foreign partners. "I understood you can only solve the problem through politics." The narrator draws the lesson—that ideology must not interfere with normal market relations. As he speaks the camera does a slow pan of the shelves of West German shops: a meat counter that seems to go on forever, jammed with T-bones, pork loins, bratwurst; rows and rows of boxes of strawberries; a huge pile of bananas; shoes, cameras, VCRs. . . .

From Bonn we hop back to an old factory near Moscow that is still churning out plaster busts of Lenin. The segment is handled with delicate irony. A worker brags how they have always filled the plan; they used to do a lot of Marx busts, but now it's just Lenins. The camera shows rows and rows of completed Lenin busts. A boss explains that the army is their biggest customer. A woman, apparently a manager, explains with a puzzled expression that demand has been falling recently, she's not sure why.

On to a dilapidated Moscow metallurgical plant with peeling signs everywhere warning workers of the dangers on the job. Vzglyad's Vladimir Mukusev reminds viewers of the pre-Revolutionary factories they had seen in their school textbooks and in films. "Murderer-factories" they were called, because they were so dangerous for the mercilessly exploited workers. This too could be called a murderer-factory, Mukusev says: inside air pollution exceeds safety standards by twenty times. We see a stooped woman shoveling dusty cement, and an angry workers' meeting where the traditionally meek labor union seems to be awakening. Next, for contrast, we visit a plant taken over by a cooperative—in effect privatized—where pay has climbed from three hundred to five hundred rubles a month and workers say they feel like owners.

As usual in Vzglyad, these main subjects are set off against a score of quick reports and music videos. The sharpest consists of shots of a Radio Liberty evening in Moscow, where a packed hall turns out to meet and hear the young Soviet correspondents of the U.S.-financed, Munich-based shortwave station. The Vzglyad correspondent explains how the Radio Liberty reporters have said they are under no restrictions except that they cannot call for violence or air obscenity. He then turns to the camera and says, in a pointed jibe at the censorship still operating for Soviet broadcasting: "So let's hope that in Moscow, not only 'Liberty' will be free."

To appreciate the force of such a program it is necessary to recall how drastically it constrasted to what the audience was being told and shown even three years earlier. In 1987 pictures of Western store shelves were taboo, and the bulk of reporting on the United States still emphasized poverty and homelessness. Lenin, and everything associated with him, was treated reverently. *Pravda*'s notion of glasnost was a ghoulish interview with the doctor in charge of the annual rehab job on Lenin's corpse—a story made to order for ironic treatment by Vzglyad of 1990, but one *Pravda* was still treating with absolute seriousness in 1988. While a particular problem at a particular Soviet factory might have been pointed out, there could have been no implication that workers were widely mistreated or exploited. And certainly Radio Liberty, long denounced in the Soviet media as a CIA front, could never have been acclaimed as "free."

In short, Vzglyad, with the whole country tuned in, was taking the world as portrayed by Soviet television for decades and turning it 180 degrees: We are the ones who are exploited, impoverished, and censored, it said, and they are the ones who live the good life and are free. It was a shocking, embittering, disillusioning message that came from Ostankino every Friday night. The reverberations reached all the way to the Politburo.

Gorbachev's outburst at the media in the fall of 1989 was just one of the first strong signs of his deep ambivalence toward the information revolution he had touched off. His statements to Soviet audiences about the media show a gradual but dramatic shift in late 1989. Before that time he is urging glasnost, as in his 1987 book, *Perestroika*: "People should know the good and the bad, in order to multiply the good and do battle with the bad.... The masses should know life in all its contradictions and difficulties. What are our achievements and what delays our development, hinders us, throws us off the path—about all that the working people should have full and reliable information." These statements can easily be mistaken for an endorsement of a free press. But Gorbachev is reflecting a very utilitarian view of the press as an instrument of social, political, and economic change, implicitly in the hands of the state. Gorbachev's "we" is not far from the royal "we." People must know "what we are striving for, what plans we have"; apparently it is less important for him to know what the people's plans are.

This is not nit-picking, because a subtle reading of Gorbachev on glasnost in 1987 anticipates his growing anger at the media by late 1989 and his outright fury by early 1991. He began by challenging and encouraging the media, but when the media responded with a volcano of criticism he switched to scolding and threatening. His ambiguous behavior often puzzled those Westerners who had pegged him as a free-speech democrat, and they sometimes persuaded themselves he was simply maneuvering to avoid the ire of conservative colleagues.

In fact, in light of the original goal of Communist reform—a stronger, socialist Soviet empire led by the party—his anger made perfect sense. It was not the staged anger of a crafty tactician out to mollify the right, as those who heard his tirades can testify. It was quite sincere, and it marked the shift in the Soviet political process from Communist reform to populist revolution. A TV program aired frequently after Vremya during 1988 had epitomized the kind of television glasnost Gorbachev encouraged. It was called Spotlight of Perestroika, a name that accurately reflected the way it zeroed in on a single problem (no parts for combine harvesters, delays in rewriting history textbooks, breakdowns at Aeroflot), airing it to the public and grilling bureaucrats about why they hadn't fixed it. It made for good, lively TV and was a giant step from pre-Gorbachev Soviet TV. But Spotlight of Perestroika rarely raised the larger questions Vzglyad often asked about the system that permitted such problems to occur. It was a spotlight; Vzglyad was more like broad daylight, and in daylight the system appeared to be beyond saving.

When Gorbachev put the brakes on reform in the autumn of 1990, one of his first and most important targets was television. Mikhail Nenashev, who had hoped to turn around the "destructiveness" of Vzglyad, had trimmed and curbed where he could, but he turned out to be too soft to fly directly into the wind of public opinion. Gorbachev appointed Leonid Kravchenko as chairman of Gosteleradio and assigned him the task of getting television back under control.

Kravchenko was a revealing choice. Like Kryuchkov at the KGB, he was a reformer—as long as he was being judged against the grey background of the Brezhnev stagnation. As a newspaper editor in the pre-Gorbachev era, Kravchenko had received four official party "reprimands" and three "severe reprimands," and had survived two attempts to fire him. He was named first deputy chief of TV and radio in 1985 in a move Gorbachev clearly intended to loosen the grip of longtime broadcasting chief Sergei Lapin, who had not only banned but ordered the destruction of mildly daring films on Lenin in 1969. (They were secretly saved by one conscience-stricken TV employee and shown in January 1987.) Lapin left for vacation in 1985, leaving the newly appointed Kravchenko in charge. When he came back, according to Kravchenko, Lapin grilled the younger man: "Who permitted the broadcast of critical material in Vremya?" "Nobody—I myself," Kravchenko replied. "And nobody [i.e., from the Politburo] called?" "Nobody," Kravchenko affirmed. In that key post during Gorbachev's first three years in power, Kravchenko was hailed in the press as a fresh force, and he often gave interviews to explain the innovative new shows. He deserved at least part of the credit for the new shows that emerged from the youth programming division under Eduard Sagalayev. In other words, Kravchenko was an early patron of Vzglyad.

Then Kravchenko left TV for two years as head of Tass, the Soviet news agency. When he came back to Gosteleradio as chief in November 1990, two things had changed. One was Gorbachev: if in 1986 Gorbachev was trying to shake up TV, in 1990 he was trying to rein it in. The other was the relatively liberated state of television. Back in 1986 a lively discussion about the shortcomings of the Komsomol was considered a TV breakthrough. But by 1990 dedicated viewers of Vzglyad and many similar shows—smooth-talking Vladimir Molchanov's Before and After Midnight, Leningrad TV's hard-hitting Fifth Wheel, the excellent daily Moscow variety show called Good Evening, Moscow—had different values and standards. If there was to be a discussion about the Komsomol, it might be a debate about how and when the Communist youth organization should be disbanded or an exposé of financial shenanigans by Komsomol wheeler-dealers.

In 1990 Kravchenko said his job was "to carry out the will of the president." He referred often to "presidential television," less frequently to "state television," and not at all anymore to "party television." Kravchenko told an interviewer he had wanted to return to television as chief: "Today it's the most important post in the mass media. And in this post a leader can, if, of course, he understands what is happening in the country, do a great deal for the country and society. I don't overestimate my possibilities and don't take on the role of national savior, but television can and must restrain society from destruction from within, from ideological civil war." He swiftly made clear what he meant. With meat-cleaver actions slightly veiled by his fuzzy disclaimers, Kravchenko set out to put the television genie back in the bottle. To a regular television viewer, the impact of Kravchenko's arrival was unmistakable. Where before the First Program, the main Soviet TV channel, had been abuzz with political conflict and new ideas, suddenly there seemed to be only dancing girls. Sometimes it was scantily clad chorus lines backing up a Soviet pop singer; sometimes a folk troupe. But in place of parliamentary debate and investigative journalism now there seemed to be only light entertainment. Kravchenko said TV had become "overpoliticized," and he was just trying to make it more entertaining. Beginning in late 1989 Sagalayev had moved from the youth programming division to the news division and had begun to force Vremya to loosen up and tell more truth, as well as creating a serious, fairly objective Sunday night news show called Seven Days. Seven Days succumbed to the Politburo's anger in the face of bold reporting even before Kravchenko's appointment and was taken off the air. With his arrival, Vremya began to be forced back into its old straitjacket.

Sagalayev quit. "I understood that I couldn't fight any longer," he told me. "It was like talking to a wall. They started to prohibit everything—information from the Baltics, information from Transcaucasia, information on strikes—in general, information that was seen to harm the party, the government, the President.... I'd give them a plan for Vremya every day, they'd look it over, consult the Central Committee, and they'd say 'This we don't need, this we don't need, this we don't need.' An accident or natural disaster—we don't need it. A strike—don't need it. Somewhere they fired the party first secretary? Don't need it. Why? They told me we shouldn't incite passions. They often used that image of Gorbachev's—'up to our knees in gasoline.' But, I said, it was not only information that could be the match [to set off an explosion]—the absence of information, too, could be such a match."

Then Kravchenko found excuses to take on the big guns of the new television. On December 20, 1990, a month after Kravchenko's takeover of Soviet TV, reformist Foreign Minister Eduard Shevardnadze suddenly resigned, warning alarmingly of "dictatorship on the offensive." Vzglyad tried for two weeks running to air interviews with Shevardnadze and his advisers; Kravchenko banned the show both times. Once it was replaced by a primitive propaganda documentary called "The Face of Extremism" and made—as I found out later—by the KGB. It associated ethnic violence in Transcaucasia and Central Asia with the nonviolent independence movements in the Baltic republics in a crude attempt to compromise the latter. Negotiations between Kravchenko and the Vzglyad team dragged on, and the show remained off the air.

Then came a watershed event in the rocky progress of Soviet reform. In the early-morning darkness of Sunday, January 13, 1991, Soviet troops smashed through crowds of peaceful demonstrators and seized Lithuanian television facilities in Vilnius, leaving fourteen people dead and dozens injured. Gorbachev claimed not to have known about the attack in advance—a claim never proven or disproven. But he never disowned the assault, blamed Lithuanian leaders for the bloodshed, and spoke in chillingly dismissive tones about its significance. In the ensuing months, despite the disinformation that came from the Kremlin, the army, and the KGB, aggressive

Soviet and foreign reporters would show that the assault had been led by the KGB's Group Alpha, a highly trained squad of commandos who took orders only from the Lubyanka. Clearly a signal was being sent by the originators of Communist reform, who, after all, had set out in the mid-1980s to strengthen socialism and the empire: We will not stand for the breakup of the union, the KGB leadership was saying, and we will use force to stop it. Yet the KGB could have attacked the headquarters of the Sajudis independence movement, the Lithuanian parliament, or some other symbol of Lithuanian separatism. Acting out of deep Russian-Soviet political instincts, it targeted the enemy's most important information source. As when Yuri Vlasov had unleashed his attack on the security police two years before, the greatest institutions on the two sides of the information war, TV and the KGB, squared off.

In the ensuing days the attack was rationalized from Moscow as necessary to stop "anti-Soviet propaganda" broadcast by the independence-minded Lithuanian authorities—a remarkable throwback to the days when Article 70 had sent Andrei Mironov and hundreds like him to the labor camps. Of course, the KGB could have interrupted Lithuanian TV broadcasting with a pair of clippers to cut the power. Doing the job with tanks, Kalashnikovs, and concussion grenades—and before the eyes and cameras of the Soviet and foreign media—was the KGB's way of making a public statement.

The Vilnius killings sparked ferocious criticism from the liberal press; *Moscow News* denounced the violence in a black-bordered front-page commentary as "CRIMINAL," the "last-ditch stand" of "a regime in its death throes." "We appeal to reporters and journalists: If you lack courage or opportunity to tell the truth, at least abstain from telling lies!" the newspaper's editorial board declared, echoing Solzhenitsyn's famous essay "Live Not by Lies." Infuriated by the coverage, Gorbachev actually proposed to parliament that the landmark press law passed five months earlier be suspended for a time to permit a legal return to preliminary censorship. "In connection with the period we're in, a period of important decisions, we need constructive dialogue and cooperation," Gorbachev said. "We could take a decision to suspend the press law for these months." Liberal deputies protested, and Gorbachev backed off, substituting a milder measure calling on the parliament to consider ways of ensuring "the objectivity of the press." But the contrast between his cool reaction to the KGB's killing in Lithuania and his fury at the press coverage was unforgettable.

Meanwhile television coverage of the Vilnius tragedy and its aftermath led to a showdown between Kravchenko and the sixteen-month-old news show Television News Service, which Sagalayev had created as a livelier alternative to Vremya. In the days of tension before the KGB attack, the young, hip anchors of Television News Service, known by its Russian initials as TSN, repeatedly refuted Vremya's reports from the Baltic republics. Vremya, following party orders, routinely misstated facts and gave a drastically distorted picture of events in Lithuania, portraying the republic as on the brink of interethnic violence. After the January killings TSN's presenters, who were already celebrities in Russia, clashed head-on with Kravchenko and his subordinates, who ordered them to read the patently false official version of events in Vilnius. Once Tatyana Mitkova, a feisty TSN anchor, ordered to read a false account of events in Lithuania, gave the text to a blank-faced young man and had him read it on the air. Then, still live on camera, she announced tartly that she was not permitted to give viewers any more information on the subject. Another anchor, Sergei Dorenko, read a contradictory and improbable official account in an exaggerated, sarcastic tone, underscoring its absurdities. For two months the tense standoff between TSN and Kravchenko continued. In mid-March the TSN anchors were purged, replaced by colorless news readers who rarely ventured beyond the news as defined by Vremya. An avalanche of protest telegrams arrived at television headquarters next to the giant hypodermic needle in Ostankino, but Kravchenko was unperturbed. He was in charge of "presidential television," and the president was not displeased.

Kravchenko had harassed or embarrassed off the screen some of the biggest names in Soviet TV: Vladimir Pozner, whose fluent, New York–accented English was familiar to American TV viewers; Vladimir Molchanov, whose Before and After Midnight rivaled Vzglyad in popular appeal; and a number of film directors and other leading cultural figures who vowed publicly not to appear on television as long as Kravchenko was in charge. Meanwhile Kravchenko had promoted a shocking new series of broadcasts by the eccentric TV personality Alexander Nevzorov, whose nightly Leningrad show, 600 Seconds, had won a large following with anti-Communist commentary and exposés of privilege and corruption. In the Vilnius killings Nevzorov saw heroism by Russian soldiers defending the empire against Lithuanian separatists. Now he produced a splashy series of programs called *Nashi* (Ours), aimed at convincing Russians that the Baltic nationalists were dangerous fanatics who had to be stopped. With the heroic strains of Wagner in the background and shots of Nevzorov himself, armed with an automatic rifle, strutting among the soldiers, the shows offered a version of the Baltic events even more egregiously distorted than Vremya's account. Nevzorov, given plenty of air time by Kravchenko, pioneered a new strain of neofascist Russian imperialism. He offered a rationale for preserving the empire that did not depend on Communist party ideology.

Since the fall of 1990, under heavy pressure from the KGB, the military, and the bosses of industry, Gorbachev had retreated from radical reform. He had rejected a shock-therapy economic program. He had supported military intimidation against the Baltic independence movements. And he had installed Kravchenko, who, within four months of taking over Gosteleradio, had managed to reverse four years of uneven but unmistakable progress toward accurate, fair, and hard-hitting coverage of news and politics by Soviet television and radio. There was, it should be emphasized, no question that Kravchenko was carrying out Gorbachev's instructions; the Soviet president clearly had decided that glasnost, which he had initiated, had to be curbed. Undoubtedly with encouragement from Kryuchkov and others in the leadership, Gorbachev had come to understand that the liberated television of Vzglyad and shows like it was no longer an instrument of Communist reform. TV was now an engine of populist revolution. Television was not renewing socialism, it was torching socialism; it was not criticizing the system, it was blowing it up. The fact that the leadership paid such attention to television at such a moment testifies to their appreciation of its power. In February, to consolidate Kravchenko's control over television, Gorbachev issued a decree transforming Gosteleradio from a government agency to a state-owned company—which made it unnecessary for Kravchenko to be confirmed by the parliament. The new chief of TV had become a symbol for the wrong side in the information war, for the threatened retreat into the old Soviet illusion.

Gorbachev's protection for Kravchenko could not reach everywhere. In April the Soviet Union of Journalists expelled Kravchenko and recalled him as a parliamentary deputy, since he had been nominated for his seat by the union. These moves underscored the fact that to the overwhelming majority of Soviet journalists, Kravchenko was a detestable figure. But they were symbolic gestures. Many journalists thought Kravchenko's manhandling of television showed that the clock could be turned back and the information battle lost.

Their pessimism was premature. A couple of years earlier, it was true, a crackdown at Ostankino could have been carried out swiftly, efficiently, and, most important of all, quietly. The chains of Communist party discipline that held all the media in thrall could have been pulled tight, the limits of televised discourse shrunk, and that would have been that. But many of the most popular TV journalists had followed Boris Yeltsin in quitting the Communist party in 1990. Many of those who nominally remained Communists paid scant attention to the party's ideological watchdogs. Moreover, by virtue of their success, shows such as Vzglyad had a huge popular following; its absence was immediately a political issue and its hosts political martyrs. The television heroes fought back, and the Kravchenko regime never got control of all the channels all the time. In particular the Leningrad channel, which could be seen by about 75 million people, was vigorously defended by the reformist mayor Anatoly Sobchak, and never capitulated. Its most popular program was Fifth Wheel, a Vzglyad-style news and talk show hosted by the crusading Leningrad journalist Bella Kurkova. Like her colleagues from Vzglyad and *Argumenti i Fakti*, Kurkova had been elected to the Russian parliament. She had aired shocking KGB film—obtained by Sobchak for a parliamentary inquiry—of Soviet troops attacking Georgian demonstrators in Tbilisi in 1989. Now, when Kravchenko banned accurate reporting on the Vilnius violence from other channels, Kurkova showed graphic footage of the assault on the crowds outside the Lithuanian TV facilities. A week later, when other Soviet troops attacked Latvian police headquarters in Riga, Kurkova ran film of that incident as well. One night she turned over her entire air time to Vzglyad, permitting the show to evade Kravchenko's ban. The Vzglyad team, masters of public relations, taped the show in host Alexander Politkovsky's kitchen—implying that the truth could now be told, as had been proverbial in Brezhnev's day, only in the privacy of one's kitchen. They kept filming at a furious pace, in fact, producing Vzglyad from Underground and making it available for showing by progressive local and republican TV outlets that were willing to ignore Moscow's orders, in commercial video salons, and on the cable TV systems that were fast multiplying around the country.

There was, of course, something a little melodramatic about all this. Vzglyad from Underground was not really underground; it was merely deprived of the state-subsidized broadcasting network that had given it easy access to an audience in excess of 150 million. With a phone call from Gorbachev to Kryuchkov, the Vzglyad heroes could have been deprived, if not of their freedom, at least of their video cameras and their videotapes. But Gorbachev was engaged in a difficult balancing act as he tried simultaneously to preserve the empire and preserve reform. The half-crackdown carried out on TV, like the half-reforms tried out on the economy, were characteristic of Communist reformers such as Gorbachev, Kryuchkov, and Kravchenko.

Kravchenko's—and Gorbachev's—decisive retreat in the battle for television came on May 13, 1991, at 8 p.m., when a cartoon *troika*, the traditional three-horse Russian carriage, galloped across the screen of the Second Program to announce *Vesti*, the new news program of Russian television. Though it drew little notice in the West, it was a critical breakthrough in the information war raging in Moscow.

For months, as Gorbachev shifted to reaction and retreat, Boris Yeltsin, as leader of the Russian Federation parliament, had put himself forward as the new hope of reform. When Gorbachev rejected a radical economic program, Yeltsin pledged that Russia would implement it unilaterally. When the troops attacked in Vilnius, Yeltsin flew overnight to Tallinn, the Estonian capital, and signed a mutual defense pact putting Russia's wealth and might on the line in defense of the tiny Baltic republics' sovereignty. By portraying Russia, with more than half the Soviet population, as a victim of Soviet rule alongside Lithuania or Armenia or Ukraine, he drove a wedge between Soviet imperialism and Russian patriotism. He made it possible to be a Russian patriot and still favor independence for the Baltic republics. Finally, in March 1991 coal miners from Donetsk in Ukraine to Kuzbass in western Siberia and Vorkuta in the far north simultaneously went on strike, backing Yeltsin's program for Russian sovereignty and the anti-Communist reform coalition Democratic Russia. The strike demonstrated the democrats' raw economic power—the immense power of the work stoppage, which did not respond to threats of military or police force. The miners stuck by Yeltsin's program in the face of the Soviet government's bribes of sausage and vodka. Though thousands of miles apart and generally not well educated, they shared a surprisingly sophisticated anticommunism. Probably one of its sources was the television all the miners had been watching in 1988, 1989, and 1990.

Among the chief demands of Yeltsin and the Russian parliament since May 1990—and on some lists of the miners' demands—were television and radio facilities controlled by the Russian Federation and independent of the central government. Negotiations had taken place on and off. Gorbachev and Kravchenko had made promises and broken them, fearful of the consequences of sharing the most powerful information technology with their political adversary. But finally, in the wake of the coal strike, the forces on Yeltsin's side prevailed. "It was very, very hard," said Eduard Sagalayev. "The battle went on for many months. They didn't give [Russian TV] air time, they didn't give it equipment.... But the genie burst out of the bottle."

Now, that night of May 13, Russian TV debuted with a bang. The very first broadcast of Vesti, an old Russian word meaning news, showed its reporters and cameramen actually under fire from a Soviet army unit on the Armenian-Azerbaijani border. "They probably took you for guerrillas," an officer later said, shrugging his shoulders. The fast-paced aggressiveness of Russian TV news made a striking contrast to the ponderous obedience to authority of the Kravchenko-controlled Vremya. The first show also included a clip of Lithuanian President Vytautas Landsbergis, whom Gorbachev despised and who was rarely seen on Soviet TV, predicting that Lithuanian independence would triumph over Soviet military resistance. Breaking another story, Vesti reported that a high-level KGB agent had defected to Britain.

To Russian TV viewers it was quite clear that the new Russian broadcasting represented a huge political victory. For one thing, several young TV reporters who had been purged from Soviet screens by Kravchenko suddenly reappeared on Vesti. Moreover, Svetlana Sorokina, the Leningrad-TV news star anchoring the new show, interrupted her news reading to announce that she had been told Vesti was not being shown in parts of the Ukraine and in Stavropol, Gorbachev's old hometown, where it had been replaced by old films and shots of a local vacation resort. "That is hardly a misunderstanding," she commented acidly. "More likely, our battle for the right to be heard is just beginning." Introducing the weather at the end of the show, Sorokina remarked that it was probably the only information presented by Vesti that would coincide with Vremya.

After Vesti, Russian TV continued with more of the six hours of daily air time it had won. There was a tone of giddy triumph. An old woman sang a satirical song accusing Gorbachev of beginning by banning vodka and ending by banning food. Then Around Laughter, a popular comedy show that had defected to Russian TV after facing severe cuts from Kravchenko, depicted a mock auction of a video cassette containing all the bits censored from the program's earlier appearances on Soviet TV. Finally there was comedian Mikhail Zadornov, painting a portrait of the USSR in the year 2000, when food rationing has been canceled because people have eaten all the ration coupons and the Soviet leadership gets the Nobel Prize "for the destruction of socialism."

Indeed, Russian television's young radicals might have been taken for guerrillas not only by army units in Transcaucasia but by ideologues at the Central Committee in Moscow. The spirit represented by Yuri Vlasov's challenge to the KGB in 1989, by the fierce inconoclasm of Vzglyad in 1990, by the TSN anchors' resistance to censorship in 1991, was back on millions of television screens across Russia. Television's struggle for Soviet minds would go on.

7

A Normal Country: The Pop Culture Explosion

Discotheque: a form of collective leisure activity and
cultural-educational work predominantly among the *young*....
D. facilitates a broader involvement of young people in
artistic endeavors, the elevation of their internal culture, the
overcoming of the drinking tradition in social life, the
strengthening of the education of young men and women in
ideas, morals, and aesthetics, inoculating them with a certain
immunity against the penetration into their environment of
bourgeois ideas and morals.

> —definition from *Short Dictionary and*
> *Reference Book for the Agitator and*
> *Political Information Specialist*,
> revised edition, 1989

I simply don't get how we can fight the Communist party
under the leadership of the Communist party. And on top of
that, under the slogan "More socialism!" What? Still more!?
...And now I'll whisper, so that only those who agree with
me can hear. I don't get why perestroika is being carried out
by the same people who brought the country to the point
where it needs perestroika.

> —comedian Mikhail Zadornov, "I Don't
> Get It," 1990

On a half-dozen tables outside our Metro station, the booksellers of the new age spread their wares. Beginning in 1989 these

street-corner book sales had gradually grown ubiquitous. One day in June 1991 I stopped with my notebook to record what was on sale.

There was psychology: Freud's *Introduction to Psychoanalysis* and *The Interpretation of Dreams*. There was religion: *The Bible for Children*, *Foundations of Buddhism*, and *Aum—Synthesis of Mystical Teachings of East and West*. There was history and politics: *Speeches by Trotsky 1918–1923*, *The End of Beria* (on the arrest and execution of Stalin's secret police chief), *Essays on the Russian Revolution* (typical first sentence, from the Christian philosopher Nikolai Berdyaev in 1918: "Russia has suffered a terrible catastrophe").

There was business: three different Russian-language editions of Dale Carnegie's *How to Win Friends and Influence People*, *Effective Advertising*, *How to Invest Money: A Practical Guide to Stocks, Bonds, Dividends, Interest*, and *The Imperturbable Manager*. There was sex: *Sex in Human Love*, *Sex in the Life of Men*, *The End of Iron Bella* (paperback with bare-breasted woman on cover), and *A Sensitive Woman—The Head-spinning Tale of a Woman Who Lived for Sex*.

For anyone who had experienced the old, prudish, prohibitionist Soviet Union, it was a head-spinning list. These diverse titles, only a small fraction of everything on sale, had one thing in common: just four years earlier, two years after Gorbachev had come to power, none could have been purchased legally. All were still banned to protect the Soviet illusion from heretical or dangerous information. According to the official Soviet worldview, the Revolution was a momentous turn for the better in human history. Trotsky was a nonperson. Sex was pornography. Stocks and bonds were mere ornaments for the "general decline of capitalism" predicted by Marxist theory. Anyone printing or peddling such books would have risked an unpleasant encounter with the police or KGB, trouble at work, possibly a jail term. Watching browsers swarm around the book table, it was poignant to picture Andrei Mironov perhaps six years before, carrying along the same streets a backpack filled with illegal photocopies of some of the books now on open display.

But the book table boom was not merely a question of the end of censorship. Many previously unavailable books for sale outside the Tsvetnoy Boulevard Metro station that day were politically innocuous: historical romances, detective stories, science fiction, cookbooks, astrological treatises, foreign classics in translation, and even Russian classics. These had never been banned. But state publishing houses had been too busy printing big runs of party bosses' speeches and leaden novels by Writers' Union big shots to cater to popular demand. Until the late 1980s, to walk into Dom Knigi (House of Books) on Kalinin Prospekt and ask for *War and Peace* or *Crime and Punishment* was to brand yourself a naive foreigner or an ignorant country rube. The Soviet Union published more books than any country in the world—just as it led the world in shoe production. But what it produced was not what people wanted.

Now market forces had taken over publishing like no other industry. Books could be sold for whatever people were willing to pay. Everyone with a printing press was churning out books to please the public, not the bosses. There were no accurate bestseller lists in the USSR, but the weekly *Knizhnoye Obozreniye* (Book Survey) invited people each year to "vote" by mail for their favorites. The results offered a rough sketch of public taste, an interesting mix of political engagement and pure escapism. The top ten books for 1989 and 1990, nearly all of which had sold more than a million copies, included several works just freed from censorship—Solzhenitsyn's *Gulag Archipelago* and *The First Circle*, Pasternak's *Doctor Zhivago*, Vasily Grossman's *Life and Fate*, and balladeer Vladimir Vysotsky's *Poetry and Prose*. But also on the list were such foreign classics as Alexandre Dumas's *The Count of Monte Cristo* and *Three Musketeers*, Emily Bronte's *Jane Eyre*, and Margaret Mitchell's *Gone with the Wind*.

This explosion of the printed word was a revolution, and it was a reflection of the revolution that was taking place in people's minds. Before, people had walked out of the Metro station and seen perhaps a banner saying "The Party and the People Are One," or "*Pravda*" (Truth). Those were falsehoods—they were not one, and it was rarely the truth. But just as important, they were monodeclarations, the monolithic state pretending to speak for everyone. Now Marx's dictum that under communism the state would wither away appeared to be working in reverse: as Communist ideology shriveled, so did the totalitarian state. It was butting out of people's lives, no longer telling them what to think, where to work, whom to vote for, whom to hate. At the book tables, people stepped forward to express their interests, which might be Buddhism or borscht or the bond market, but which were not dictated by the state. One guy went for Trotsky, circa 1921; another went for Iron Bella, circa 1991. The monopoly crumbled. Now when people came out of the Metro they saw a picture as variegated as they were.

Western reporting on the opening of the Soviet Union naturally emphasized the sober topics of economic and political change. One might have gotten the impression that whenever they weren't waiting in line Russians were marching in political demonstrations, watching documentary films on Stalinism, or perusing journals for the nuances of the plan to support the ruble. In fact the relaxation of government controls restored to the public arena not just the momentous but the trivial, not just the political but the spiritual— not only purged Bolsheviks and exiled dissidents but pop music idols, movie starlets, evangelical preachers, quack healers, and fanatics of every stripe. A new popular culture was born, and people who were not caught up directly in politics, whether their interest was Orthodox liturgy, rock music, or sexual techniques, became beneficiaries of glasnost. True, some bemoaned the immorality or bigotry or banality of some of what was on sale, but for once the state was not to be blamed. It was no longer "they" who were at fault; it was, more or less, "we." The answer to those who took offense was a Russian proverb Gogol chose as epigraph to "The Inspector General," his satire on provincial life: Don't blame the looking glass if the mug is crooked.

The sidewalk information market around Moscow's Metro stations was such a looking glass, a bazaar of facts, ideas, and opinions of astonishing range and diversity. Alongside the book tables were newspaper stands where the selection bore little resemblance to that of a few years earlier. The press had moved far beyond the exposés of Stalinism and the careful criticisms sponsored by the Communist reformers that had thrilled readers in 1987 and 1988. *Komsomolskaya Pravda*, once the squeaky-clean voice of Com-

munist youth, had become an aggressively anti-Communist paper—
what else can one say of its publication, in a special supplement in
September 1990, of Solzhenitsyn's ruminations on *Rebuilding Russia?*
Or at the other political extreme, take *Voyenno-istorichesky Zhurnal*
(the Journal of Military History), once a staid voice of the army's
general staff, now a far-right publication that had finally earned an
official slap on the hand by printing excerpts from Hitler's *Mein
Kampf.*

And these were established, official publications. New newspapers
and magazines, including once-samizdat publications gone legal,
multiplied like fruit flies. I purchased new newspapers for a while in
1991 and quickly collected a two-foot-high stack of perhaps fifty
different titles. Few had any advertising; they averaged perhaps eight
tabloid pages apiece. The papers ranged from serious, reliable
newspapers with substantial staffs selling tens of thousands of copies
to blurry two-page rags peddling extremism, sex, or scandal that
often lasted no more than an issue or two. The largest category was
papers representing new, non-Communist political parties and other
new public organizations. Their breadth and number may be
suggested by the following selection of translated titles and sponsor-
ing organizations: *Democratic Russia* (pro-Yeltsin reformist coalition),
The Alternative (Russian Social-Democratic Party), *Mister People*
(Republican Party), *Free Word* (Democratic Union—typical headline:
"Is Gorbachev a Bribetaker? Investigation Continues"), *Prologue*
(Federation of Independent Trade Unions of Russia), *Nevsky Courier*
(Leningrad People's Front), *Civic Dignity* (Constitutional Demo-
cratic Party—proud front-page headline: "The Gorbachev Team
Already Doesn't Like Our Newspaper"), *The Cry of Yaroslavl* (a
military reform group called "Parents of Soldiers"), *Morning of
Russia* (Revolutionary-Liberal Faction of the Democratic Union),
Charity (Soviet Charity and Health Fund), *Under One's Breath*
(Moscow Organization of the Democratic Union), *Variants* (the
Public Commonwealth Foundation), *Christian Politics* (Russian Chris-
tian-Democratic Party), *Lightning* (Communist Initiative), *Freedom*
(Moscow chapter of Memorial—"All profits go to survivors of the
Gulag"), *Crossing* (veterans of the Afghan War), *Democratic News-
paper* (Democratic Party of Russia).

Then there were nonparty, aggressively independent political papers: *The Independent Newspaper* (the best of the new crop), *Our Cause, Hour of Bravery, Russian Rebirth, Civic Referendum*, and more. There were religious newspapers for half a dozen faiths, environmental publications, papers for hobbyists ranging from automobile enthusiasts (*The Horn*) to animal lovers (*The Call*). There were periodicals devoted to ESP and UFOs (*Anomalies*, published by strange bedfellows: a club called "Ecology of the Unknown" and Tass). There were soft-porn magazines, how-to sex manuals, and collections of singles ads.

Far from everything on sale was cause for rejoicing at the fresh wind of press freedom. A whole class of crude newspapers fell into the extreme-Russian-nationalist, anti-Semitic category: *Pulse of Tushino* (a Moscow district), *Russian Battle-Cry, Sources*, and others. Their material ranged from the merely offensive to the truly terrifying. Among the latter was the issue of *Russian Battle-Cry* that appeared during the Persian Gulf War, illustrated with the smiling face of Saddam Hussein and the caption "Thanks to Iraq for the bombing of Israel—That's the way to treat those yids!" The same issue listed names and addresses of witnesses who had testified against Konstantin Smirnov-Ostashvili, a neofascist leader convicted of inciting ethnic hatred. The editor of *Russian Battle-Cry* in some issues was listed as P. O. Gromov—in other words, *pogromov*, a form of the Russian word pogroms.

But on a table a few steps from the piles of *Russian Battle-Cry* could be found another new paper: *The Jewish Newspaper*, reporting on a World Zionist Organization leader's Soviet TV appearance, offering information about Moscow's first Jewish school, and listing a classified ad for a twenty-two-volume nineteenth-century Talmud. On sale nearby was an explanatory brochure called "Jewish Traditions," aimed at the thousands of Soviet Jews who had lost touch with their religion. Now *this* was shocking. For while the Brezhnev period had seen the official publication of flagrantly anti-Jewish books and articles, always in the guise of "anti-Zionist" tracts, it had tolerated nothing remotely like the new Jewish publications.

Every interest group curbed under the old order took advantage of the new freedom to publish. Soviet Hare Krishna devotees, harshly persecuted by the authorities until about 1987, became some of the most prolific publishers. By 1989 chanting, tambourine-shaking Krishnaites were a familiar sight on Moscow's Arbat and Leningrad's Nevsky Prospekt. By early 1990 displays of their books, pamphlets, and posters were common on city streets. Over the next two years, by their own count, Krishna believers sold five million books in Russia and the other Soviet republics.

Even in the least likely, least controversial of places the information revolution left its mark. Early one Saturday morning in 1991 I stopped and chatted with a thirty-six-year-old mustachioed man named Pavel, who had set up his sales display of literature for dog fanciers near the entrance to Moscow's sprawling weekend pet market, known in Russian as Ptichy Rynok, the Bird Market. It was a jam-packed, squirming, chirping, barking city-within-a-city where you could sell or buy anything with four legs, two wings, or fins, from a newborn chick for a few kopecks to a champion show dog for thousands of rubles. Pavel's story was a classic piece of Soviet economic lore, one to leave an American shaking his head in wonderment: He was a cardiologist who had quit medicine the previous year because he wasn't making enough money to support his wife and three children. A dog lover, he'd had difficulty finding how-to material on canine matters and figured there might be a market. So he started his own business publishing and peddling instructional books and brochures on dogs. Soon Pavel, who feared his last name might tip off extortionists or tax collectors, was earning several times his old salary as a doctor. People mobbed his display to buy publications with names like "The Collie" and "Cutting and Trimming the Poodle," dog postcards, and dog calendars. Canine reference books, of course, had never been banned. State publishing houses simply had never bothered to meet the demand.

The new popular culture exploded like a volcano in the once-monotonous Soviet landscape, an important part of what people yearned for when they said they wanted "a normal country." The lava that burst free of the strictures of party and KGB after 1988 had been forming underground for many years, a product of urbanization, education, leisure time, and the influence of Western, especially American, fashion. For better or worse, made-in-America mass culture had at least the same appeal in Moscow and Sverdlovsk and Yerevan as it had in Paris and Copenhagen and Bangkok.

Even before Stalin's death the allure of America was strong among sophisticated young Russians. The emigré novelist Vasily Aksyonov describes a 1952 Moscow party where the featured attraction was an American phonograph, "the kind that let you stack twelve records at a time. And what records! Back in Kazan [Aksyonov's provincial hometown] we spent hours fiddling with the dials on our bulky wireless receivers for even a snatch of jazz, and here it was in all its glory... Bing Crosby, Nat King Cole, Louis Armstrong, Peggy Lee, Woody Herman.... One girl I danced with asked me the most terrifying question: 'Don't you just love the States?' I mumbled something vague. How could I openly admit to loving America when from just about every issue of *Pravda* or *Izvestiya* Uncle Sam bared his ugly teeth at us and stretched out his long skinny fingers (drenched in the blood of the freedom-loving peoples of the world) for new victims." In the next three decades this pro-American bias in pop culture spread beyond the privileged "golden youth" of Moscow and Leningrad to much broader segments of the Soviet public. But it remained illegitimate and threatening in the eyes of the leadership, whose domino theory proposed that Jimi Hendrix would lead inexorably to Adam Smith.

In the mid-1980s rock music was still officially frowned upon, making slow headway onto radio, TV, and the imprints of Melodiya, the state recording monopoly. By decade's end, rock was ubiquitous. It was the dominant music on TV, whether on such variety shows as Vzglyad or late-night clips from MTV. Rock was the lion's share of radio music, including the only offering on hot new stations such as Ekho Moskvy (Echo of Moscow) and SNC (for Stas Namen Center, the conglomerate of Soviet rock entrepreneur Stas Namen, grandson of Politburo member of the Stalin and Khrushchev eras Anastas Mikoyan). Rock was standard fare at concerts in even the most backward towns. Lenin had defined communism, in a famous slogan that long glowed in neon on the Moscow River, as "Soviet power plus electrification of the whole country." By 1990, parodying the dying ideology, the poet Andrei Voznesensky was describing a new phenomenon: "the electric-guitar-ization of the whole country."

But this transformation had been prepared behind the scenes for a quarter-century, perhaps beginning as early as 1964, when a Vladimir Vysotsky performance at Moscow's cutting-edge Taganka Theater featured lyrics about "rok-n-roll," described approvingly as "scandalous music." Rock was firmly ignored by the official cultural establishment until about 1980, when the music's overwhelming popularity prompted authorities to invite a few bands to offer toned-down concerts and censored records.

"The huge majority of rock performers remained in the underground, preferring poverty to the encroachments of censorship," Soviet rock musician and writer Artemy Troitsky wrote in 1990 in his encyclopedia, *Rock Music in the USSR*. "Not having the slightest access to Melodiya, TV, and radio, rock groups created an illegal recording industry that was unique in its scale. Precisely in those years of 'the late stagnation,' the social and cultural role of rock was especially great and especially positive: these recordings [i.e., magnitizdat, home-copied cassettes] brought to millions of young people most rare and necessary words of truth and spirituality."

In the Gorbachev years the entire ready-made world of Soviet rock came out from underground. For a time it was on the cutting edge of glasnost. Troitsky argued that because of the conditions of censorship under which Soviet rock developed, its core was "the Word," lyrics, while the core of Western rock was "the Rhythm." Rock lyrics, openly or in the disguise of youth slang or allegory, carried seditious messages of skepticism and dissent to big audiences. Mikhail Borzykin of the Leningrad group Televizor (Television) shocked a 1986 rock festival with lyrics referring to a watcher from the party or KGB: "And there behind the column is the same guy / In the grey suit, with the concrete expression." In "Going Out of Control" Borzykin told a longer tale:

They look after us starting from kindergarten,
Kindhearted ladies, kindhearted men.
In our sensitive spots, point-blank, not looking,

They beat us like common cattle.
We grow up as an obedient herd—
Sing what they want, live how they want,
And from top to bottom with a poisoned glance
Look over the one who's beating us.
Go out of control,
Go out of control
And sing about what you see
And not what they allow.

It was the nature of rock to speak in metaphor, in vague broadsides against the system. But such lyrics frightened the cultural bureaucrats, who threatened to reimpose the old ban. Borzykin took to carrying quotations from Gorbachev's bolder speeches in his wallet, pulling them out and reading them in defense of his songs.

Already by early 1988 Troitsky could complain that rock was losing its near-monopoly on protest: "Amazing, but a fact: there are now at times in the central newspapers articles bolder and angrier than the songs of the radical rockers!" But even as it lost its political edge, Soviet rock was shown to be an astonishingly diverse and extensive music. Troitsky's 1990 encyclopedia—which I bought for six rubles on a Metro station book table—listed hundreds of groups in its nearly four hundred pages, identifying distinct styles that developed in cities from Ashkhabad (Turkmenia) and Tallinn (Estonia) to Gorky and Sverdlovsk. After years of playing concerts in the woods and passing home-taped cassettes hand-to-hand, the rock bands suddenly found themselves legit. On the tenth anniversary of John Lennon's murder that year, the Olympic Stadium complex not far from our apartment staged a big memorial rock concert and called it—in ironic reference to the oft-repeated Soviet propaganda that *"Lenin s nami,"* Lenin Is with Us—yes, "Lennon s nami," Lennon Is with Us. The blasphemous pun stirred not a ripple of protest.

Even as rock swept the entertainment scene, the harsh contemporary ballads of Vladimir Vysotsky, all but banned from the official recording industry before his death in 1980, became the biggest moneymakers for state-run Melodiya, now a profit-oriented enterprise. Vysotsky's face peered out from every music store's album display, with a seemingly insatiable public buying up millions of posthumous records made from tapes of Vysotsky concerts and private recording sessions. His biting sarcasm, targeting everything from anti-Semitism to bureaucracy, and his image as a teller of hard truths were now actually being marketed by the state.

Magnitizdat had gone commercial—and not only the musical magnitizdat of Vysotsky and other "bards," as such folksingers are known in Russian. The other category of underground cassette tapes, the satirical monologue, likewise gained access to the official media and found a far larger audience than ever before. Even before glasnost the top Russian *satiriki*, stand-up comedians, had a prominence and popularity beyond comparable performers in the United States. Like Vysotsky, who starred in official films and stage plays in the Brezhnev era, the top satiriki—Mikhail Zhvanetsky, Mikhail Zadornov, Gennady Khazanov, Alexander Ivanov—all had national reputations before Gorbachev took office. But their scripts were censored and their range limited. Like the satirical monthly *Krokodil*, they were confined to ridiculing effects and not causes—the absurdities of daily life but not the party or the ideology that often stood behind them. If they wanted to tackle politics or other taboo topics they could reach only the urban sophisticates who had access to the underground cassettes of magnitizdat.

As glasnost began to encourage greater boldness, Mikhail Zadornov began to experiment with bypassing the censor, though the rules still required an index number indicating that Glavlit had approved the script. Zadornov told me of his first performance in Kiev, which had long been ruled by particularly conservative party bosses. As the comedian began to take shots at communism, Soviet history, Gorbachev and Raisa, and so on, the grey-suited party watchers in the front row began to squirm with anxiety, he said. What would get them into deeper hot water? Allowing this outrage to go on—only to be called on the carpet by superiors demanding to know who had sanctioned such desecration? Or cutting it off—only to discover that Glavlit had signed off on it in the spirit of glasnost?

"I read and read, people are howling, and these guys don't know what to do with me," Zadornov said. "Kiev was long closed to humorists, as Japan was to Europeans. And all of a sudden some Russian humorist comes from Moscow and starts saying this stuff from the stage. They want to stop it, but they worry: What if it's permitted after all?

"So a guy comes from the city party committee: 'Do you have a permission number?' 'Yes, I do.' 'What is it?' '983.' So he takes off. Of course there is no number. But he's satisfied."

With glasnost the satiriki did not break new ground or reveal new information in the way that *Ogonyok* or Vzglyad did. But they brought a new, anti-Communist, or at least politically skeptical, worldview to a huge popular audience that was looking to be entertained, not informed. Their pieces on the meaninglessness of official propaganda, the brutality of the regime, the privileges of the ruling class, and the hopelessness of the planned economy wore away at official dogma.

"Capitalism differs from socialism very simply," Mikhail Zhvanetsky deadpanned in a 1989 monologue after taking a trip to Japan. "[Under capitalism,] the hotter the weather, the colder the beer. With us, with every increase in outside temperature, beer becomes warmer and warmer before disappearing completely at 75 degrees." In the spring of 1991, when a reactionary army general named Albert Makashov ran for the Russian presidency, Gennady Khazanov scavenged a general's uniform from someplace, went on stage and in the press, and announced his own "election platform": "Comrade officers! Vigilantly standing guard on the borders of our conquests, certain units have experienced a decline in discipline. Example. Ensign Soloveychik, returning home from his unit, utilized antitank mines in order to stop taxis, in connection with which eighteen vehicles were annihilated together with their drivers. I call your attention to the inadmissibility of such destruction of state property...." "Communism is a world view," Zadornov said in a monologue aimed at the Communist bureaucracy. "Not in a single country in the world where there's democracy is a worldview the basis for receiving a salary.... And there are eighteen million Communists being paid for their worldview in ministries, in departments, regional party committees, city party committees, and other such committees. Before the reduction in force, there were sixteen million."

At times the comedians' denigration of things Soviet was so savage and thoroughgoing that I wondered whether they risked wounding the patriotism of their audiences. Before five thousand people at Moscow's Olympic Stadium in the spring of 1991, Zadornov plucked the wings from the Soviet illusion in a program sarcastically titled, "Ah, How Good It Is to Live in the Land of the Soviets!" Even before he got warmed up, he was saying: "Humanity should be looked at as a system. We're the starting point of all coordinates— complete zero on both axes. This great mission was assigned to us by the cosmos. No other people could take it. Look around! Nothing to eat. Nothing to wear. Nothing to breathe. Nowhere to live." Pause: "And yet, we continue to reproduce." I found myself looking around in the darkened hall to see how Russians were reacting; I saw only smiles and detected no hostility. Most people no longer saw the system's failings as their failings.

Later in 1991 Zadornov told me he was leaving stage work to try his hand at plays and film scenarios. He described his work in strikingly utilitarian terms, as if it had been his personal mission to subvert the Soviet illusion. In effect he told me the old system was a dead horse, no longer worth beating. "I love the work, but I'm giving it up," he said. "Because everything that had to be said, I've said. The ordinary Soviet person has begun to play my game. He already sees the idiocy for himself. Anyone who doesn't see the idiocy doesn't want to see it. So I consider that at this stage my duty is done."

If the old certainties were being destroyed, some Russians were grasping for some fairly strange new ones. As Marx and Lenin fell from their pedestals, among those competing to take their places were the *ekstrasensi*, a Russian coinage from "extrasensory perception." They took up an old, superstitious thread in popular culture in Russia, where many people still fear to shake hands across a

threshold or return to their apartment for something they've forgotten—both invitations to bad luck. Folk cures, in a country where
antibiotics were often unavailable, enjoyed a wide following. My
Russian teacher insisted that I apply hot-pepper plasters—essentially
adhesive tape with cayenne pepper sprinkled on—to the base of each
thumb whenever I had a bad cold; my wife was treated by friends
by having garlic juice dripped into her nose. And that was just the
down-to-earth stuff.

In the 1970s Brezhnev himself was rumored to have sought the
healing services of Dzhuna Davitashvili, an ethnic Assyrian from
Georgia whose miraculous powers included a flair for public relations. Her clinic off the Arbat still drew a steady stream of
customers in the early 1990s, and she also offered classes for
would-be healers. But the new age had new names—big names,
catapulted by the unrestrained media to a nationwide fame that had
been out of even Dzhuna's reach a decade earlier. Always before
there had been something politically incorrect about anything smack-
ing of faith or superstition, and that toned down its attention from
the state media. Now the ekstrasensi competed with politicians, rock
musicians, and comedians for newspaper space and broadcast time.

The biggest of the new stars of parapsychology was Anatoly
Kashpirovsky, a psychotherapist from Kiev whose riveting gaze
became a frequent sight on Soviet television. His reputation took off
in 1988 when, in a nationally televised episode, he purportedly
anesthetized a woman without drugs during major surgery—by
talking to her over closed-circuit TV from another city. That
sensation prompted fifty thousand letters from people interested in
his powers. Soon Kashpirovsky was drawing thousands to his
road-show healing sessions and reaching millions via regular TV
broadcasts. The uninitiated onlooker saw the dark-haired Kashpirovsky at the front of an auditorium, speaking calmly and authoritatively to the audience, waving his hands significantly before him.
The most striking feature was Kashpirovsky's hypnotizing gaze.
"Man's a genius, you understand?" he told a television interviewer
in early 1989. "He has hidden possibilities, which I help him
uncover."

Kashpirovsky's major competitor was Alan Chumak, a former

journalist who claimed he had discovered his special powers after being dispatched by an editor to unmask another healer. Chumak not only could heal; he could "charge" substances with his special energy, giving them healing powers. Better yet, he could do it via television. Thousands of Muscovites placed jugs of water or jars of cold cream in front of their TV sets to be "telecharged" by the obliging Chumak and used in the ensuing months to ward off illness, fatigue, and bad luck. Once Chumak "charged" an entire issue of the evening Moscow paper; hard-core believers shredded entire pages and ate them. For a while Chumak appeared on Moscow television briefly every morning, healing viewers according to an announced schedule: headaches on Monday, stomachaches on Tuesday, arthritis on Wednesday, and so on.

The attention and profit that accrued to the ekstrasensi spawned many imitators. An Estonian psychic named Koidu Mikael won local fame for leading police to the perpetrators of several crimes. *Komsomolskaya Pravda* discovered a twelve-year-old named Leila who could read minds. A Tbilisi healer named Lyusa Dzhincharadze, written up in February 1989 in the teachers' newspaper *Uchitelskaya Gazeta,* had to appeal to the paper's readers in March to stop visiting her; huge lines formed in front of her house every day. It became commonplace to turn on the television and see people demonstrating strange powers. Late one night I remember seeing an entire magnetic family, to whose skin nails, spoons, and even a clothes iron would cling, defying gravity.

The parapsychology boom was a spontaneous, populist phenomenon, but the state did nothing to discourage it. Occasionally it even lent a hand. One day in May 1989, at the Soviet Foreign Ministry press center where typical briefing fare was long-winded statements clarifying the Soviet position on Angola, correspondents were introduced to a clean-cut twenty-eight-year-old in a business suit who looked like an earnest junior diplomat.

Nikolai Levashov modestly explained that while he knew nothing about international relations, he did have some unusual abilities. He could cure many diseases—by long-distance telephone, if necessary—aided by his ability to see through flesh and to a patient's internal organs. He and his colleagues were using mind-power to cleanse the polluted air of several Soviet cities. He regularly communicated with various civilizations scattered here and there around the universe, and he had begun mental chats with dolphins. "You know what they asked the first time I talked with them?" Levashov asked, with a straight face. "They asked, 'Why has it taken you so long to make contact?'"

Levashov and some of his colleagues, including Alan Chumak, had come to the press center to promote a planned Folk Medicine City, where the gifts of Soviet psychics could be shared and studied. Chumak was selling video and audio tapes designed to awaken special powers in ordinary people. He played for our edification part of an audio cassette which to the naked ear sounded blank. Chumak explained that to avoid language problems with the multilingual press corps, he had chosen a "silent" patch of tape, but one that nevertheless carried great power. When it was over, he asked, "Did you feel that?" A few of those present answered, yes, they thought they had.

In the fall of 1990 the giant white-marble Palace of Youth, exhibition headquarters for the onetime scientific Communists of the Komsomol, featured a big display of photographs of UFOs, aliens of various descriptions, the Abominable Snowman, and other unusual phenomena which, it is safe to say, never before had received such attention from the Young Communist League. It drew sizable crowds, but far more visitors came to see another, larger exhibit arrayed in a half-dozen rooms on the same floor. It was entitled "The Last Years of the Romanovs: A Family Chronicle."

It was a fascinating hodgepodge of royal memorabilia, family photographs, and personal correspondence, amounting to a fairly complete portrait of the lives of Nicholas and Alexandra in the years leading up to his abdication in the February Revolution of 1917. Among the items drawing the most attention were the menus, printed in French, of royal breakfasts, luncheons, and dinners. I was amazed that people who spent most of their free time trudging from shop to shop to line up for basic foodstuffs would want to spend what was left salivating over eighty-year-old tsarist feasts. But the people I asked responded with a smile, a shrug, and the familiar refrain, "We didn't know anything about all this." Soviet schoolbooks long had made cartoon characters of the Romanovs, reactionary foils for heroic Bolshevik revolutionaries. Now people were starved for facts about them, searching for alternatives to Lenin and Stalin, eager to find a history and heritage to supplant the discredited Communist era. As in many Western societies, where tabloids aimed at those of modest means detail the lavish life-styles of the stars, so Muscovites struggling to get by were caught up in the romance of the Romanovs' fabulous and tragic lives. Young entrepreneurs in the Pushkin Square Metro station did a steady business in black-and-white photographs of the Romanovs and other members of the nobility.

An entire room at the Palace of Youth exhibit was reserved for the deaths of Nicholas and Alexandra and their five children at the hands of a Bolshevik execution squad on July 16, 1918. A portrait of each member of the royal family hung, framed behind shattered glass. Documents displayed nearby described the execution—including how the tsar's daughters had been particularly hard to kill, protected as they were by diamonds hidden in their corsets. Many visitors departed shaken by the brutality of the Bolshevik regime. Some left memorial carnations at the base of the dramatically lighted wall.

Eduard Radzinsky, a popular Moscow playwright, had helped spur the enormous interest in the Romanovs and their death with a series of publications in *Ogonyok*. He was involved in one of at least four films being made about the execution, and he was working on a popular book about Nicholas II, since published in English to considerable acclaim. In a fascinating detective story, Radzinsky had just about proven that Lenin personally approved the killing of the royal family; official Soviet historians, while justifying the executions as a tactical necessity during the Civil War, had distanced Lenin from the bloody act. For Radzinsky the execution was the prototypical act of violence that set the direction of the new regime.

"It was the fanatical idea, the favorite Bolshevik idea that blood unites," Radzinsky, a man of intense energy and humor, told me in an interview in his north Moscow study. " 'The cause is secure when blood is shed for it,' the revolutionary poet Nekrasov wrote." Though he had helped start it all, Radzinsky found himself a little taken aback by the idealization of the last tsar and the cries for vengeance against the Bolsheviks and their heirs. "We must understand that it was a murder—but not demand revenge," Radzinsky said. "We don't need an all-round settling of scores. We need repentance."

Nicholas II was the centerpiece when *Sobesednik*, the lively weekly tabloid supplement to *Komsomolskaya Pravda* and a keen observer of popular culture, set out in March 1990 to portray "popular idols" of the era. It was a whimsical offering—"Love them, clip them out, paste them up!" advised the editors—but it was nonetheless a revealing reflection of the diversity of unofficial heroes. The last tsar stood with curled mustache and splendid regalia, identified with deliberate irony in Soviet style as "Romanov N. II." There were two pop-music superstars, Alla Pugacheva and Zhenya Belousov. From politics there were two antipodes: a Leningrad teacher named Nina Andreyeva, who had become the heroine of neo-Stalinists for her published blast at reform in the newspaper *Sovietskaya Rossiya* in 1988, and Boris Yeltsin, the reformers' hope. Gazing from the page with his patented stare was Anatoly Kashpirovsky, the psychic healer. Sitting glumly on a rock ledge with the Vermont woods in the background was Alexander Solzhenitsyn. And finally there were two movie stars—Sylvester Stallone, a huge hit with Soviet audiences, and Natasha Negoda, raising her arms above her head just high enough so that her too-short T-shirt allows a glimpse of her right breast.

Negoda was a talented actress, but in 1988 that fact was in danger of getting lost in her historic role as the First Sexpot of Soviet cinema. In an era when taboos were being broken in every sphere of life, sex was no exception. It fell to Negoda, in a devastatingly bleak film called *Malenkaya Vera*, to play the first explicit sex scene on Soviet film. Made by Valentin Pichul and Maria Khmelik, a husband-and-wife team in their late twenties, the film is set in the town of Zhdanov, an industrial center on the Azov Sea named for the henchman Stalin assigned to oversee culture. The opening shot sets the tone of the movie: it is a long, slow pan of the city's horizon, a look at man-made hell, with choking smog, dilapidated buildings, and no promise of redemption.

Negoda plays the title role as Little Vera, but since *vera* in Russian means faith, the name of the film is a metaphysical statement as well. Vera is a rebellious teenager whose slender ideals are reflected in the Western pop posters on her wall and who inhabits a world of rock dances, gang fights, drinking, drugs, and easy sex. But the film's sympathy is entirely with the unlovable Vera, because we see what she is fleeing: the tension and violence of the crowded family apartment, where her truck-driver father regularly obliterates himself with *samogon*, moonshine, leaving Vera to undress him and put him to bed. When I talked with Russians of various generations about *Malenkaya Vera*, I heard one phrase again and again: *Eto nasha deistvitelnost*—That's our reality. It was harsh medicine, but many people were eager to swallow it after the cloying taste of officially sweetened portrayals of Soviet life. When it came out in 1988 local officials managed to block showings in many places, including downtown Moscow. But the film broke Soviet box-office records anyway, drawing fifty million viewers in the first three months after its release.

That staggering popularity cannot be explained only by Soviet viewers' appetite for cinema that confronted the darkest moments of their own lives. It obviously owed a great deal to the novelty of the sex scene, roughly what one would expect from a typical R-rated American picture, played between Vera and her lover Sergei in his room in a workers' dormitory. Negoda subsequently played the sex-kitten role to the hilt, posing for Soviet pinup posters and for *Playboy*, where she was pictured reading a copy of *Literaturnaya Gazeta*. The Soviet writers' newspaper printed a note of appreciation for the free publicity.

The territory that Negoda had been the first to explore was terra incognita for most of the Soviet public. Among the early Bolsheviks were a few who fervently advocated free love, asserting that satisfying sexual desire should be no more complicated than drinking a glass of water. But the middlebrow Lenin was scandalized by such talk, which he authoritatively branded as "bourgeois" and not properly "proletarian." Stalin, as in other matters, went further; he was disturbed by the nudes of classical sculpture and raged at his daughter when she wore too short a skirt. In later years Western prurience was seen as a threat to Soviet morals, and not only *Playboy* but even the *Sports Illustrated* swimsuit issue was confiscated from foreign tourists by vigilant customs officers, who presumably had the biggest personal collections of skin magazines in the country. Sex education in school and sex instruction manuals for adults were rare to nonexistent, as was birth control—which gave the USSR a legal abortion rate nearly four times that of the United States. Comedians insisted that, just as there was no poverty or unemployment, there was no sex in the Soviet Union.

All that changed with eye-popping speed in the late 1980s. Negoda's barrier-breaking sex scene set off an escalating incursion of nudity and sex into the Soviet media. Editors figured, hey, this too is glasnost, and as they began to have to pay more attention to profitability, they knew a bared body never hurt newsstand sales. By 1990 the amount of nudity on Soviet television and in general-audience newspapers and magazines outstripped not only the puritanical U.S. media but the less inhibited European media as well. What was striking to a foreigner was the general access to explicit material. Any U.S. newsstand had magazines that went beyond anything on a Soviet newsstand, but they were usually wrapped in plastic or hidden away out of reach of younger customers. Rarely could a bare breast be glimpsed in, say, *Newsweek* or the *Washington Post* or on prime-time TV. But by 1989 increasingly explicit postcards of nude women were on open display beside snapshots of the Kremlin or St. Basil's Cathedral at many newsstands. At a stand around the corner from KGB headquarters in early 1990, below a poster of a woman wearing only an ammunition belt, was a photocopied sex guide called "Guide to the Forbidden." Beside it was an imaginative placard displaying silhouetted couples making love, captioned "365 Positions for 365 Days."

By 1990 it was no longer surprising to see nudity on the pages of such solid periodicals as *Sobesednik* or the Moscow youth paper *Moskovsky Komsolets*. The Russian-language Riga paper *Sovietskaya Molodyozh* held a "Miss Erotic Photo" contest and splashed the contestants' entries across two pages. Sex scenes in movies went swiftly from being outlawed to being mandatory, as Russians lined up for films such as *Interdevochki*, a potboiler about prostitutes working the foreign-currency hotels. My filmmaker friend Sasha Nagovitsyn complained that when he proposed a serious film, based on a classic short story, the bosses at his Sverdlovsk film studio rejected it and encouraged him to make "an adventure film, with as many sex acts as possible." Television rarely cut the nude scenes from films, and nudity and suggestive dancing on TV became commonplace.

Not surprisingly, many older people were horrified by the sudden demise of official prudery, and even some sophisticated younger people thought explicit material should be limited to certain publications or TV channels to which children would not have access. Olga Dmitrieva, the editor in charge of *Komsomolskaya Pravda*'s quaintly named Morals and Law department, took this view, protesting in 1990 at an editorial board meeting after a full-length back view of a naked woman graced the back cover of *Sobesednik*. Dmitrieva, the thirty-five-year-old mother of a young son, sought no return to a total ban, arguing that the boom in explicit photos was itself a reaction to the ban: "The forbidden fruit is sweet, and this has been forbidden forever here." But she said that about a third of the one hundred letters a day received by her department expressed concern about the proliferation of sex and nudity in the media. "It's an explosion of letters in response to an explosion of erotica," she said. "Two years ago there wasn't a hint of this in our mail." In the newspaper *Rabochaya Tribuna* (Workers' Tribune) a police officer from the Urals declared, "Let's call a spade a spade: what's taking place is the massive corruption of our children." But, like conservatives' diatribes against rock music, such denunciations had little discernible effect. It seemed likely to be some time before the pendulum swung back the other way.

If the state tolerated the Soviet sexual revolution, the Komsomol energetically promoted it. Down the street from our apartment building, in the summer of 1989, there opened a "video salon" by the name of Lastochka, Russian for swallow, the bird. Such video halls were opening everywhere, at airports, train stations, youth centers, and on the street, in response to the demand for foreign video showings and the shortage of VCRs or the money to buy them for home use. Lastochka was a humble affair, consisting of a basement room with a bunch of folding chairs and, in the front, a big TV wired to a Hitachi VCR. The fare offered at first was mostly Bruce Lee–type martial arts films, leavened with the occasional Stallone or Schwarzenegger feature or a horror movie.

Then the Lastochka entrepreneurs, a group of young Georgians, comprehended a central tenet of Western marketing: violence sells, but sex sells better. They began adding, as a late-late show on the crudely typed schedule pasted each morning to the wall outside the entrance, an imported film marked in parentheses as "Erotika." They braced for a reprimand from the police or the district's Communist party bosses. None came. So gradually the erotic films migrated from their position at the end of the evening, getting earlier and earlier, until one day all the films were labeled "Erotika." Lastochka became an adults-only movie theater, offering for one ruble or 1.50 timeless features with names like *Swedish Wife-Swappers Club* and *Discoveries of a Driving Instructor.* The personable manager, a thirty-year-old Georgian named Zurab Todua, told me with a straight face that he was only trying to comply with Gorbachev's philosophy of putting the people first. "That's what the public wanted," he said. "I guess we're learning democracy." He also insisted on a clear distinction between "erotica" and "pornography," saying he would never dream of showing the latter. Whatever the films were called, the long all-male lines for every show suggested Lastochka was making a small fortune—and it was making it on behalf of the All-Union Leninist Communist Alliance of Youth, commonly known as the Komsomol. For Lastochka was administratively and financially a branch of the district Komsomol youth center. The sponsorship was particularly ironic in view of the notice at the bottom of the daily schedule: "Under 21 not admitted."

In fact the Komsomol was the behind-the-scenes proprietor of many of the new video salons. The Komsomol's commitment to ideology and its membership had both begun a pronounced slide in the second half of the 1980s, as membership appeared no longer to be a prerequisite for a successful career. Many of those who stayed in turned their attention to entrepreneurship, taking advantage of the huge organization's facilities, connections, and capital to make more money. Many of the street book tables were operated by the Komsomol under the flimsy guise of a lending library where a person could borrow a book for, say, twenty kopecks an hour—a noble socialist service. In order to ensure the book's return, however, the library required a deposit of ten or fifteen or twenty-five rubles, depending on the book. So the deposits became the prices, and the operations became for-profit street bookstores. With the video salons there was rarely any pretense of public service, though undoubtedly such operations turned up in reports as contributions to what in Sovietese was called *sotskultbyt*, a coinage combining the words for "social-cultural daily activity." In fact they were unabashed, unideo-logical, unreconstructed money machines, designed with no higher purpose than to keep their operators supplied with cars, co-op apartments, restaurant meals, and lavish vacations.

Video was a new, decentralized information technology whose popularity took off, catching the cultural overseers in the KGB and the party off guard. The Soviet VCR industry was slow to respond to demand, and its product was notoriously unreliable. But with the state price of a Soviet VCR at twelve hundred rubles in 1988, the street price of a foreign VCR hovered around five thousand rubles— equivalent to a substantial annual salary. As travel restrictions eased beginning in 1987, many people fortunate enough to be able to travel to the United States or Western Europe scraped together a few hundred dollars from friends or relatives abroad in order to buy a VCR, boom box, computer, or fax machine to bring back and sell. The resulting proceeds more than compensated the travelers for the steep price of air fare (often including an extra thousand rubles to bribe Aeroflot ticket tsars) and other costs. On any Pan Am or

Aeroflot New York–Moscow flight during the travel boom—which slowed considerably after Aeroflot began requiring hard currency for tickets in 1991—many of the Soviet passengers were burdened with cardboard boxes carrying new electronic equipment. Some takeoffs were even delayed when airline safety officials required that the treasured carryons be stowed in the hold.

VCRs and other consumer electronics, like many other imported items, also entered the country with truck drivers on European runs and sailors returning from Asian voyages. Another source was barter deals: a steel plant, for instance, would trade a few tons of steel plate for a shipment of VCRs or other hard-to-get items, which would then be sold to employees for a modest ruble price. In the non-Russian republics, especially the Baltic republics, Armenia, and Ukraine, nationalist groups often received gifts of information technology from the ethnic diaspora. Armenian activists in Moscow gathered outside an Armenian church each Sunday in 1988 to show videotapes of demonstrations in Yerevan. Once in 1989, Endel Lippmaa, a key Estonian envoy in tense negotiations with the Kremlin, told me that if I needed to reach him when he wasn't around, I should simply fax a note to his portable fax machine in his room at the Hotel Rossiya. Sheepishly I admitted that my bureau did not yet have a fax machine. When I installed one a few months later, it operated around the clock, spewing out political communiqués from nationalist groups and infant political parties, advertisements, and news from the new information services Interfax and Baltfax. Electronic equipment seeped into the Soviet Union the way water seeps into a leaky boat, and though for obvious reasons no reliable statistics were available, by the early 1990s there was a lot of it around.

I encountered the video boom most memorably in early 1990 in the oil town of Nizhnevartovsk, a West Siberian city of a quarter-million people who pumped more oil each year than Kuwait. They didn't live like Kuwaitis, however—a fact of which they became acutely aware as glasnost brought them word of what oil wealth had wrought in other countries. When I visited, about 10 percent of the population was still living in the leaky wooden shacks and old rail cars thrown up in the late 1960s as temporary housing following the

1965 discovery of Samotlor, an ocean of oil beneath the tundra. The *balki*, as the shacks were known in local slang, had no plumbing, and the would-be oil sheiks of Nizhnevartovsk scooped their water from open barrels on the street that were filled periodically from a city truck. In the long Siberian winter they had first to smash the ice on top before they could draw water for drinking, cooking, or washing. In the spring thaw the snowdrifts that could reach the roofs of the shacks often leaked into the living space. In the summer there was a battle to keep mosquitoes out.

It was miserable, but I had seen and written about housing as bad, or nearly as bad, in impoverished pockets of the rural U.S. What was stunning in the balki was something else, something incongruous—shiny Sharp TVs and Phillips VCRs and Sony stereos, electronics to make many a sophisticated Muscovite envious. Most came from the black market and had been purchased with the big salaries that had drawn the oil workers to Siberia in the first place—often two or three times what the same jobs would bring in the Big Earth, as the Siberians called European Russia. What suddenly dawned on me, as I looked around the balki, is that these people were not poor. They were rich. The state-controlled economy gave them no way to use their wealth to improve their housing. So with plenty of money, little to spend it on, and few outside leisure activities in the dark winter months, many had naturally sunk their savings into a VCR.

One was Nikolai Denisov, a remarkable thirty-nine-year-old Russian who had grown up in Baku, Azerbaijan, another oil boomtown that now was long past its peak. He described himself as a "simple working man," spent his days hauling around heavy steel pipes, and had a crushed finger and a crushed toe to prove it. As he hosted a long dinner, he gave a first toast that was pure Nizhnevartovsk: "To our health, because we'll buy everything else." Later he got out his guitar and sang Stalin-era Gulag songs, some learned from elderly neighbors who had stayed in Siberia after their terms of exile expired. Denisov devoted his time off to tending a remarkable collection of art and artifacts from the many remote corners of the Soviet Union, to reading a wide variety of books and journals, and to his VCR.

Denisov had tapped into the unofficial Soviet network of video-tape lenders and traders that was supplied by an invisible army of smugglers and tape-copiers. Blithely ignoring copyright restrictions, entrepreneurs bought videocassettes of foreign films from tourists and traveling Soviet citizens, paid language students to record a crude one-voice dubbing in Russian, and churned out copies for the market. These tapes circulated around the country and fed the burgeoning demand for fresh movies. In this way Denisov claimed to have viewed four thousand American movies, sometimes staying up all night to treat himself to a quadruple feature. He could rattle off the names of actors and directors and quote dialogue verbatim. Listening to him—"Robert Redford, he's great, did you see the baseball one, *The Natural?*"—it was hard to remember he was a working-class Soviet citizen on a little-populated island in the vast Siberian sea, thousands of miles from anyplace.

A year later, in the spring of 1991, I found myself sitting in the office of one of the leading bankers in the mountain city of Vladikavkaz, capital of North Ossetia. I was there to report on the combined devastation in neighboring South Ossetia of civil war and a powerful earthquake. But as often happened on trips to the south, where hospitality was an art form, every handshake developed into lunch and every interview into a drinking bout. So there we were, two bankers and two government officials and me, eating greasy meat-filled tarts called *chebureki* and toasting one another with *araka*, a powerful local moonshine.

For entertainment the banker was working the VCR with his remote control, dipping into his extensive office collection of American movies and settling on *Lethal Weapon*. We chatted over the Russian voiceover of the soundtrack, and it was hard to follow the plot—partly because whenever there was not either sex or violence on the screen, the banker hit fast forward. This way we ran through a film pretty quickly and could move on to more American movies. As we watched the hero blast away with his M-16, hop into bed with some sultry beauty, or dive from his car as it plunged off a cliff, my companions pelted me with the usual questions about the United States. What's your salary? How big is your house? What kind of car do you drive? As the VCR jabbered on, all these guys—three of the four of them still, apologetically, Communist party members—began talking about visiting the U.S. or moving there. It turned out they were looking beyond the violence, sleaze, and corruption of the plot at sleek cars, designer apartments, glittering high rises, and well-stocked stores. Whatever happened up front, the background was the promised land.

Several million people among those without the means or luck to buy a videorecorder of their own still could enjoy Stallone, Schwarzenegger and company in the privacy of their homes, thanks to another grassroots technology that swept the country without any assistance from the state. At the end of the 1980s cable television multiplied relentlessly as thousands of entrepreneurs with a VCR and a reel of wire proceeded to wire their apartment buildings, then the neighbors' building, then the neighbors' neighbors' building. Sometimes it was free or supported by donations; occasionally an electronic whiz managed to scramble the signal and rent decoders for a modest monthly fee. Most cable systems were tiny, but others grew fast. By 1991 the entire Ukrainian city of Zaporozhye, with a population of nearly one million, was wired. In this country where for so long information technology had been jealously guarded by the regime, cable spread according to no bureaucrat's decision and without being included in any five-year plan.

The beginning, as nearly as anyone could tell, came in the Youth Housing Complex in Sverdlovsk, an apartment complex built and managed by its young residents. Leaders of the Youth Housing Complex, or MZhK, had dreamed up the cable idea in 1985 when hobby clubs in the complex outgrew the activity rooms; if the instructions for rug-hooking or the Spanish class could be broadcast on closed-circuit TV, anyone in the MZhK could tune in. "We wanted to create an atmosphere for learning and communication," Alexander Mikh, one of the system's originators, told me. Using a three-thousand-ruble Komsomol prize awarded to the organizers of the housing complex, they bought one of the first Soviet-made VCRs direct from the factory in Voronezh. Their "studio" used black-and-white reel-to-reel videotape and a camera with no sound, Mikh said.

A few months later, party watchdogs came by: "They said, 'Who are you to take the media into your hands?'" Mikh recalled. The MZhK leaders agreed to form a "Council of Communists" from party members in the complex to oversee the cable programming and apply informal censorship. At first, he said, about half the proposed programs were banned, including two shows of Vysotsky singing his own songs. After a petition in defense of Yeltsin was read on the air during the uproar following his ouster from the Politburo in 1987, the KGB sought to close the cable system using surrogates, Mikh explained. Suddenly fire inspectors showed up, pronounced the "studio" at risk of an electrical fire, and ordered it closed until a third-floor fire escape could be constructed. "I added up all our equipment, and it came out about the same [amperage] as a clothes iron," Mikh said. Next the KGB sent a finance inspector to prohibit the collection of the two-rubles-per-month subscription fee. Then came the local police fraud squad, probing for hints of financial impropriety.

But gradually, as the official media loosened up, cable censorship ceased. When I visited in June 1991 the cable system had expanded beyond the MZhK proper and was reaching 28,000 people. Its fare was mainly entertainment—someone had rigged a satellite dish to show the rock videos of the European Super Channel when the studio wasn't operating. Locally broadcast material was dominated, in response to popular demand, by American movies—*Die Hard* and *Big Foot and the Hendersons* were a typical night's offering. There were classified ads ("Will exchange two Zhiguli tires for soft children's furniture") and public-service announcements ("Found near bus stop: rationing coupons for June with set of keys"). But there was also politics. The cable channel regularly showed meetings of the local soviet and at city election time broadcast candidate profiles and live debates.

The new pop information culture of detective novels, rock cassettes, American videos, and the rest fed a dramatic blossoming of petty commerce. Starting in 1989 the face and feel of every Soviet city was changed by the proliferation of kiosks selling myriad products that once had been available exclusively on the black market. The kiosks made a striking contrast with empty state stores, jammed as they were not only with printed matter and cassettes but T-shirts with Western slogans, Czech shoes, American cigarettes, Danish beer, French perfume, Italian cookies, Taiwanese car radios, and trinkets of every description. The prices were free to reflect supply and demand, which in Soviet conditions meant prices were out of sight. Most people could only gawk at twenty-ruble packs of cigarettes or thousand-ruble shoes. But the street markets had psychological significance: for the first time, all kinds of coveted imported items could be bought legally and for rubles. The restrictions on their purchase were now economic, not political.

The strange new world of the kiosks, which left many a babushka shaking her head in dismay, was ruled by apolitical young people obsessed with *beezness*, in Russian a far less dignified word than in English. One summer day in 1991 I stopped by such a stand, just behind the U.S. embassy complex in central Moscow, and chatted with its three teenage proprietors: Sergei and Sasha, both nineteen, and Lyuba, sixteen. The usual display of imported stuff cluttered the counter inside the glassed-in booth where all business was transacted through a little open window. Hanging above, dominating the display, was a huge German flag, priced at eighty rubles. The generation that had fought the Great Patriotic War might see the flag as a casual insult, but these young people weren't out to offend anyone; they were interested in profit, not political symbolism.

It was hot for Moscow, and Sergei was wearing only a pair of denim shorts, sipping a Russian beer, and smoking a Winston. The three had the jaded insouciance of hip, urban young people the world over. They professed not to care about politics, though Yeltsin's name stirred a glimmer of approval. Mention of the Communist party and Communist ideology drew pitying smirks, as if I had asked about an obscure sect that worshiped trees.

What caught their imagination was "the good life," what young Russians called *kife*, a flexible slang word used literally to mean a wave of alcohol- or drug-induced euphoria but also a metaphor for pleasures in general, for a lucky break or a good time. Buying cheap and selling dear, they were earning thousands of rubles a month and spending it in pursuit of kife. Sergei expressed pity for his parents, still working as "slaves" in a Moscow factory for three-hundred-odd rubles a month. "Hardly a day passes when I don't spend more than a hundred rubles," Sergei bragged. "To have a good life, you need lots of money," Sasha declared.

These cynical hypermaterialists might have been invented by Communist ideologues as a warning of what might become of youth in a market economy. But the kioskers were fashion leaders for the young, and they represented a substantial class of young people who seemed strangely unmoved by the political transformation that had so astounded their elders as well as the West. The big Moscow rallies of 1989–1991 attracted strikingly few young people, to the consternation of many middle-aged activists. An attempt at a political hunger strike by Moscow State University students in 1990 drew a handful of participants and fizzled out after a couple of days in the rain. The leaders of the democratic movement were disproportionately in late middle age, members of the generation of *shestidesyatniki*—the "sixty-ers" whose hopes for reform had first been kindled during the Khrushchev thaw.

But the end of information control had meant easier breathing for millions of people whose interest in politics was germinal or non-existent. One key answer to the question, Where are the young people?—was the new pop culture. Many young people skipped demonstrations because they were busy listening to rock music or watching bad American movies. Those may not have seemed very socially useful pastimes at a political crossroads. But for all its tawdriness, the pop-culture explosion had given young people a stake in reform. Eventually that would prove to be important.

8

Letting Go of the Leninist Faith

Some day a psychologist or poet will do justice to the drama of doubt in the minds of these political believers. Few individuals ever surrendered their belief in God with more agony, soul-searching, and inner resistance than these latter-day apostles of revolutionary brotherhood surrendered their belief in the monolithic validity of the monolithic Soviet system.

> —Sidney Hook, on the disillusionment of Western Communists visiting the USSR in the 1920s and 1930s

Attractive Moscow woman, height 165 centimeters, higher musical education, never married, constantly improving herself in every way, seeking man up to 33 years old with goal of starting family. Those not sharing the political views of Yeltsin need not apply.

> —personal ad in *Vechernyaya Moskva*, Moscow's evening newspaper, May 15, 1991

On January 13, 1991, within hours of KGB and army troops' assault on Lithuanian television facilities, a few thousand people gathered in a spontaneous protest on Manege Square, outside the

Kremlin, as a coarse snow fell. Anxiety as well as anger was in the air; some feared the Vilnius tactics might now be tried on Moscow demonstrators. Chanting "Today Lithuania, tomorrow Moscow" and "Butchers out of the Kremlin," the fur-hatted crowd marched past the heavily guarded Lubyanka to Communist party headquarters a few blocks away, where they were halted by rows of riot troops. A few people taunted or argued with the soldiers, but for most Muscovites, who were astonishingly peaceful at such rallies, the point of their presence was enough.

I climbed onto a low wall to read the hand-lettered signs and estimate the size of the crowd. Beside me two middle-aged men, clearly well educated, talked animatedly about the events in Vilnius and the likelihood that reactionary violence would reach Russia.

Then one man asked the other: *"Kogda ty znal?"*—When did you know? The stress was on the word *know*.

"Oh, I guess I'd had my suspicions for a long time," the second man answered. "But I really knew only about two years ago."

By that moment of passionate disillusionment, in the shorthand of Soviet opposition politics, the verb *to know* carried the weight of all the revelations of the past five years. When did you *know*? meant: When did you know that the number of innocent people slaughtered in the Stalinist terror numbered in the millions? When did you learn that the roots of the Stalinist terror could be traced to Lenin's Red Terror of 1918? When did you know that the average American worker had a material life-style that the average Soviet worker could not imagine? When did you understand that Solzhenitsyn was not a traitor and Sakharov not a fool? When did you realize that many of the failures and catastrophes of Soviet life had a common cause? When did you understand that Soviet official ideology was not just flawed by little lies but built on a foundation of untruth? In short, when did you know that the system was beyond reform?

Later I began to ask demonstrators in the seething crowd when and why they had lost their faith in the system. They dated their real change of heart not to the 1960s or the 1970s or even a decade earlier. They spoke of the immediate past. "There was a great deal we didn't know," said one woman. What didn't you know? I asked. "We didn't know anything!" said a man's voice. "They lied to us, starting in 1917, and they're still lying to us!" said a woman.

Another man grabbed my shoulder to get my attention. "I'm fifty-three years old," he said. "I'm Ukrainian. And I didn't know anything about the famine in 1933. I'm ashamed about that! That's what we mean—we didn't know anything."

This was the politics of Communist paradise lost, of Leninist faith shattered by the steady blows landed by the press and television since 1987. Moscow demonstrators were the activist fringe, of course, but by 1991 their views were widely shared.

Soviet opinion polls began to multiply in the late 1980s, after the Stalin-era ban on sociology was finally lifted. In the absence of polls the party leadership traditionally had gauged public opinion by means of letters and telegrams—letters and telegrams which had been organized by the party to support its policies. It was a perfect circle into which reality was not permitted to intrude.

The polls of the perestroika period are frustratingly flawed and incomplete. Telephone surveys were automatically skewed in a country where private phones remained a privilege, and the earliest respondents probably doubted the polltakers' assurances of anonymity. Until 1989 or even 1990 few pollsters dared even to ask fundamental questions about Lenin, party, and Revolution, presumably for fear of what they might find out. Thus there is no real pre-glasnost baseline from which to measure the decline of the socialist faith. But certainly until the later 1980s most Soviet citizens either believed in the system or had not raised the question of belief or unbelief. They were, in a phrase nearly as common in Russian as in English, the *molchalivoye bolshinstvo*, the silent majority. They might have been cynical about party leaders or petty bureaucrats. But they believed in the system in some vaguer, deeper way—in Lenin, in socialism, in the precious symbols handed over to them in their childhood as Octobrists and Pioneers. In the same way an American might say that the president is an idiot and Congress a bunch of crooks but still believe in "the American way" and advocate jail for flag-burners.

By 1991 polls showed that a majority of Soviet citizens and a substantial majority of urbanites had lost that basic faith in the system. They no longer thought it could be fixed. They might be confused about what they wanted—the word "capitalism" still scared most people—but they knew what they didn't want. What united them was their disillusionment.

The premier polling organization to emerge in the Gorbachev period, the All-Union Center for the Study of Public Opinion, provided me with a compilation of its results between 1989 and 1991 on broad ideological questions. Its polls, among the most professional in the Soviet Union, generally covered between one thousand and three thousand respondents chosen from all republics to reflect the demographics of the total Soviet population. They record a rapid decline in faith in "communism" and the Communist party, a slower erosion of belief in "socialism," and a growing uncertainty over alternatives. Some examples:

—In December 1989 those saying the Communist party "deserved complete trust" still barely outnumbered those saying the party "absolutely did not deserve trust," 27 percent to 24 percent. By June 1991 doubters outnumbered trusters, 55 percent to 7 percent.

—In January 1991, asked whether it was possible at all to "build communism," 69 percent said no, just 13 percent said yes. In March, 45 percent of respondents said they had a negative attitude to "communism"; 19 percent were positive, with 36 percent undecided.

—In February 1991, a month after the Vilnius violence, 72 percent said their faith in the Communist party had diminished "in recent months"; 8 percent said it had grown.

—In July 1991, 69 percent agreed that the party had "completely discredited itself." Just 10 percent said it had not.

The death of the Soviet illusion, for most people, took place between 1987 and 1991—an astonishingly rapid demise by historical standards, though to those of us watching by the bedside it sometimes seemed an agonizingly drawn-out illness. It was nearly equivalent to the death of a religion, and there are no real historical precedents. Perhaps the closest analogies would be with countries that have just lost a major war, such as Germany and Japan after 1945, when an expansionist, militarist, superior national self-image had been smashed. But the Soviet world-picture had been wrecked not by tanks and bombs but by facts and opinions, by the release of information bottled up for decades. The loss of faith was at once a national experience shared by millions of people caught up in a collective discussion about themselves, and a deeply personal experience with myriad variations.

Writing in 1950, the American philosopher Sidney Hook was able to list sixteen prominent American and European writers, including W. H. Auden, George Orwell, Arthur Koestler, and John Dos Passos, who had produced a substantial "literature of disillusionment" with Communist ideology. It is striking in retrospect that some of the events that contemporaneously alienated many foreign Communists and fellow travelers—the purge trials, the Hitler-Stalin pact, the Doctors' Plot (the blatantly trumped-up charge in 1953 that prominent Jewish physicians had planned political murders), the exile of Solzhenitsyn—contributed mightily to the disillusionment of Soviet citizens at the end of the 1980s, when those same events were replayed in the liberated Soviet media.

In his memoirs Andrei Sakharov wrote movingly of how, as a young scientist who had helped build the Soviet hydrogen bomb, "I needed, as anyone might in my circumstances, to create an illusory world, to justify myself. I soon banished Stalin from that world. ...But the state, the nation, and the ideals of communism remained intact for me. It was years before I fully understood the degree to which deceit, exploitation, and outright fraud were involved in those notions, and how much they deviated from reality. In the face of all I had seen, I still believed that the Soviet state represented a breakthrough into the future, a prototype (though not as yet a fully realized one) for all other countries to imitate. That shows the hypnotic power of mass ideology."

For all the Soviet believers in the "illusory world" Sakharov describes, the flash flood of information at the end of the 1980s was as traumatic as it was enthralling. To some older people especially, the old myths had been very beautiful, the old slogans deeply moving, interwoven as they were with memories of sacrifice and of victory in World War II. They had grown up in the conviction that communism, not just viable but superior to other social systems, was destined to triumph in every land. To embrace the opposite belief now was to drink bitter medicine.

A young avant-garde artist friend of mine in Moscow, Artur Glechyan, captured the trauma of disillusion in a collage he entitled

"Major Surgery." It is a towering canvas with blood stains every-where. A syringe and some scalpels are attached, but so are a long kitchen knife and a meat cleaver, suggesting that this surgery may be brutal. In the middle of the frame is affixed the kind of cloth used by surgeons to drape a patient's body. The cloth is held back by eight surgical clamps to reveal the site of the gaping incision and inside, the tumor: it is a plaque that Artur had scavenged from someplace, bearing at the top the visage of Lenin and the heading: "The Moral Code of the Builder of Communism." Enough of the code is visible to give an idea: "Loyalty to the cause of Communism, love for the socialist fatherland and the countries of socialism...." It is a sledgehammer of an artistic statement, but one that captures the pain and danger of stripping a society of long-cherished beliefs.

In 1989 in the city of Obninsk, a center of nuclear research a couple of hours from Moscow, I asked the party boss, a tough, proud man of fifty-nine named Alfred Kamayev, about the huge neon slogan that remained along the roofline of one building: "Glory to the Communist Party of the USSR!" Such primitive displays had been dismantled in Moscow by then, and Kamayev's answer was a little defensive. "We've removed a lot of them, but we decided to leave that one," he said. "It looks so beautiful at night, glowing red," he added, sweeping his hand across the sky with a sad, nostalgic smile.

In 1988 the labor newspaper *Trud* had picked out for analysis a letter from one of the many elderly Soviet citizens bewildered and shaken by the first wave of glasnost:

"What times are we living in?" wrote P. I. Sokolov from Kiev, describing himself as a war and labor veteran. "I'm seventy years old, an active participant in collectivization and de-kulakization and in the Great Patriotic War. For me and for many veterans it's painful to see what's happening at the present moment in time. It's simply incomprehensible. Day and night there are train wrecks, ship collisions, airplane crashes, airplane hijackings, crimes of every variety, antistate activity, strikes. Why this is taking place is impossi-ble to understand.

"Or take this—it's an accepted practice with us that every leader is a Communist. And now it turns out that this leader is a bribetaker, this one is a careerist, or a bureaucrat or an embezzler!!!! Shcholokov, Rashidov, Kunayev, Medunov, and others [all top officials accused of corruption]—who can we trust now???

"For those of us who fought on the front, the name of Stalin was the highest name of all, and we attacked, as the slogan went, 'For the Fatherland, For Stalin!' Now they're attacking him and forgiving, pardoning, and rehabilitating everybody, even though fifty years have passed.

"Why do we have to stir all this up? How are we supposed to understand it all? Explain, please."

To a Western reader jaded by the mayhem and catastrophe that fill the newspapers every day, Sokolov's *cri de coeur* may sound primitive and naive. But his point of view was widespread. *Trud*'s patient answer, called "Bitter Truth or Sweet Illusions," is fascinating. It's not so, the paper delicately informs Sokolov, that more trains and planes suddenly are crashing: "It's just that previous disasters were hidden from us." "For long years we were surrounded by propagandistic myths," the newspaper says. "The party has uncovered the reasons for stagnation, for all kinds of deformations, and aimed perestroika at changing the situation in all parts of our life, to create a healthier atmosphere." Having recited a selection of the great figures eliminated by Stalin, *Trud* declares: "What great strength a people must possess not to be broken and not to lose faith! That's why we say now that all the later generations have an unpaid debt to you—veterans of the party, war, and labor, who fought, in spite of everything, for the cause of socialism. That applies to the leaders of the army who in the years of the cult [Stalin] and the years of stagnation [Brezhnev] preserved their loyalty to party principles." What's happening now, *Trud* assures Sokolov, is a "continuation of the revolution." That means "we won't limit ourselves to the shameful repainting of the façade, but we will decisively destroy what is alien, clear away the ruins, and confirm genuine Leninist values in all spheres. There is only one way to do this: tell the people the full truth about the past and present."

In other words, the watchword of Communist reform: 2 plus 2 equals 5. In 1988 a newspaper ideologist still could refer a troubled reader back to the touchstones of party, Revolution, and Lenin without apology or further explanation. There was no questioning of whether it was a good idea to continue the Revolution; no inquiry into just what were "genuine Leninist values" or "party principles."

Gorbachev often emphasized that the party itself had launched perestroika and demanded glasnost, which was true enough, implying that people should therefore be grateful to the party. But if a swindler admits he has cheated you, your fury at being cheated may well exceed your gratitude for his confession.

In the great political-science laboratory that the streets of Soviet cities became, one could see the fury taking shape. On Pushkin Square, a favorite central Moscow venue for demonstrations, I watched a revealing ritual played out a half-dozen times in 1988 and 1989. The scenario was as follows: A political group, usually the uncompromising young radicals of Democratic Union, a tiny, self-styled opposition party, would announce an upcoming rally. The authorities would ban it, reroute traffic from the capital's busiest streets, and mount a hugely overblown defense: hundreds of riot troops, water cannons, buses to cart off arrestees. Only a ragtag handful of young people would show up for the rally. But they would be surrounded by several thousand people—mostly passersby curious about the commotion.

Then the drama would begin. A Democratic Union teenager would unfurl a political poster. A squad of riot troops would charge into the crowd, batons swinging, knocking people from their path, to grab the offender. If he didn't scramble away quickly enough, he would be dragged to the waiting bus and end up with the standard ten-day jail term.

What was remarkable was the reaction of the crowd. It was obvious to all that the police, not the demonstrators, were responsible for tangling traffic, closing Metro stations, and generally sowing chaos. Seeing the mismatch between the tiny number of young protesters and the army sent to quell them, the crowd would throw its sympathy to the underdogs. Initially neutral bystanders would soon be chanting their assessment of the security forces from the sidelines: "Fascists! Fascists! Fascists!" Within an hour or two the riot troops would have managed to turn a minuscule display of radical views into a large, spontaneous protest against police and party. Babushkas would lecture baby-faced Ministry of Internal Affairs draftees the age of their grandchildren: "Young man! What in the world do you think you're doing? Haven't you got anything better to do? You should be ashamed of yourselves! Young man, I'm talking to you!" Men in suits would jump in to complain about the inanity of the massive police response. Students would taunt the troops with Gorbachev's policies: "You call this *demokratizatsia*?" Eventually the crowd would be alive with scorn for the system and its baton-swinging defenders.

Another glimpse of a changing worldview came as word spread that Sakharov had died, on the morning of December 15, 1989, and about two hundred people gathered in the snow outside his apartment building on the Garden Ring road. Several told me candidly that in the past they had accepted the stance of the official media that had once branded Sakharov an "imperialist agent" and called his 1975 Nobel Peace Prize an act of "political pornography." Then they had watched his rehabilitation and his performance as a parliamentary deputy—including his celebrated duels with Gorbachev, who more than once turned off Sakharov's microphone to stop his speeches. They had seen how the Communist reformers had adopted, one by one, the heretical ideas Sakharov had advanced in the 1960s and 1970s. And they had realized they had been duped.

"They said he was against our state, and I thought so too," a fifty-five-year-old engineer named Boris Bakkum told me as we waited for the body to be carried to a waiting ambulance. Then he offered the familiar refrain: "But now we know a great deal we didn't know before, and I've changed my opinion." A woman in a fur hat, holding red carnations in the falling snow, said simply, "He fought for the happiness of my grandchildren."

Sometimes a single fact stuck in a person's mind like a fishbone in his throat, impossible to ignore or explain. When Minsk, the capital of quiet Byelorussia, now Belarus, erupted in a wildcat strike in the spring of 1991, a young economist was one of the many who took a turn at the microphone to address the thousands of workers gathered in the capital's broad square. Among other things he informed the crowd that the average American worker earned about twelve dollars an hour. A couple of hours later, as I moved around the square interviewing workers, many of them repeated the figure, as if in shock. These were not the usual well-educated *intelligenti* who turned up for Moscow demonstrations; these were average, ordinary factory workers in a political backwater. If they earned three hundred rubles a month—roughly the black-market value of twelve dollars at the time—they were doing well. For many in the crowd, that sole, stark statistic brought a venerable set of myths about socialism and capitalism crashing to the ground.

Of course these workers might have refused to believe the economist's astonishing claim about American salaries. It was to Gorbachev's credit that they accepted it. When Gorbachev announced that two plus two was not, after all, six, he helped create the powerful skepticism with which people greeted his assurance that two plus two was, in fact, five. People were ready to suspend their prejudices and accept new facts. What changed minds was the cumulative, synergistic effect of a great deal of new information on a variety of subjects at once. It was not just Stalin's notations on the lists of those to be executed, but Lenin's declarations of the usefulness of terror. It was not only that spacious Moscow apartments were set aside for Central Committee bureaucrats, but that party officials in Vladivostok had cruised to Japan and brought back Toyotas for their families. It was not just that, as Vzglyad showed, an American construction worker could own a car and house; it was that he could shop in a supermarket that seemed to have more food on its shelves than all Moscow.

If the Soviet system was on trial, all this was evidence for the prosecution. In the summer of 1990 the writer and filmmaker Stanislav Govorukhin took up the regime-on-trial metaphor in a devastating documentary, *Tak Zhit Nelzya* (We Can't Live Like This). Starting out as an exposé of depraved criminals and the inadequacy of Soviet law enforcement, the film suddenly shifts gears, revealing a more comprehensive thesis: "Part II: Criminals in Power," the screen announces. Govorukhin offers in deadpan narration a nightmarish tour of Soviet absurdity and suffering, from a terrifyingly long Siberian vodka line in which old ladies and bemedaled war vets are trampled, to a Soviet hotel where only Soviet citizens and Soviet currency are not allowed. There is a ruined church in the Urals, closed by the regime, that people have turned into a filthy drinking spot. There is a group of red-kerchiefed Pioneers being taken around Moscow's grandiose Exhibit of Economic Achievements, contrasted to West German shop windows stuffed with economic achievements that no one feels the need specially to exhibit.

All this degradation and hypocrisy is laid at the feet not just of Stalin but of Lenin and the Revolution that made his rule possible. All the crimes great and small on Soviet territory are traced to the first great crime, the execution of Tsar Nicholas II and his family in 1918. Showing old documentary footage of the Nuremberg Trials, Govorukhin tells his viewers that the main defendant in Nuremberg was the Nazi party itself, "the inspiration and organizer of the crimes of Hitlerism, just as in any trial the major guilt falls on the organizer of the crime." Then he continues matter-of-factly: "Monstrous evil has been committed in our country—genocide, mass murder, artificial famine from which millions died, the destruction of the economy and culture, the corruption of the people.... Will there be a new Nuremberg Trial? Is one needed? We should not take the path of blind revenge, as Academician Sakharov said more than once. What is important is something else: a moral trial of the party is already underway. You can sympathize with honest Communists, of whom there are after all many in the party. But why should they carry on their shoulders the burden of the criminal history of the party? That burden will crush those carrying it. Let those be hunched beneath it who lack the mind and conscience irreversibly to condemn the past and repent before the long-suffering people."

Quite possibly Govorukhin's verb, *gorbyatsya*, or hunched, is a deliberate hint that Gorbachev, the party's leader, had refused fully to condemn the past and repent before the people. Be that as it may,

Govorukhin's shattering film, the diametrical opposite of seventy years of Soviet official propaganda, provoked no apparent criticism or skepticism in the two Moscow movie theaters where I went to watch it and judge viewers' reaction. But neither was there any of the euphoria of liberation that commonly could be felt a year or two earlier. People were focusing not on their restored right to know the truth but on that truth—a truth far more bitter than *Trud* had let on in 1988. A man behind me in the theater at one showing of *Tak Zhit Nelzya* said to his companion as the credits rolled, "After that, you want either to shoot yourself or to emigrate. There's nothing else left."

Daniil Granin belongs to a category of Soviet writers too honest to become servile mouthpieces for the regime but so determined to keep writing for a domestic audience that they could not break completely with the state and become dissidents or emigrés. Instead they skated along the sometimes thin ice at the edge of the Soviet literary pond, skirmishing and compromising with censors and editors, drawing official praise when their works coincided with someone's notion of political usefulness and bearing harsh criticism when they were seen to have strayed too far from Leninist scripture. They saw the faults of the regime, but they believed it to be reformable. Indeed, they believed, or persuaded themselves, that it was their duty to try to keep writing and publishing to steer the system toward greater freedom.

Trained as an engineer, Granin specialized in stories of conflict among scientists, whose clashes with the system over innovation or intellectual honesty offered an acceptably oblique way of examining the Soviet social order. As early as 1956 he came under official fire for a short story entitled "My Own Opinion," in which the narrator said: "Silence is the most convenient form of lying. It knows how to keep peace with the conscience; it craftily preserves your right to withhold your personal opinion on the grounds that someday you will have a chance to express it." Granin joined in the outcry of the Russian intelligentsia in 1965 when the dissident writers Sinyavsky and Daniel were tried. In 1969 he was the only member of the Soviet Writers' Union secretariat to vote against expelling Alexander Solzhenitsyn from that body. The next year he sent a telegram of protest when the dissident biologist Zhores Medvedev, whom Granin knew to be perfectly sane, was locked in a mental hospital. Those acts of undoubted courage caused temporary damage to his career, as he was stripped of certain official positions and saw some publications delayed, but he managed to maintain his status as a liberal, official author.

This status, and his longtime party membership, made him an ideal figure to endorse Gorbachev's plans for Communist reform. He did so, and made a major early contribution to glasnost in 1988 with *Zubr* (The Bison), a nonfiction story of the important Russian geneticist Nikolai Timofeyev-Resovsky, his refusal to return from Germany during the war, and his imprisonment by the NKVD while Soviet science was ruled by Stalin's and Khrushchev's charlatan pseudobiologist, Trofim Lysenko. During the first parliamentary election campaign of 1989 Granin was nominated by the students and faculty of his alma mater, Leningrad Polytechnic Institute. But then he was offered one of the party's quota of one hundred set-aside seats. He accepted, considering it awkward to refuse and figuring his decision would open up the contested seat to be won by another liberal-minded candidate. In June 1991 I went to see Granin in his Leningrad apartment, curious about the views of a liberal intellectual who had cast his lot with Communist reform.

A white-haired, stocky man of seventy-one, Granin greeted me with a gentle smile and a world-weary tone. As we talked, low sunlight streamed across his study. I could hear pans clattering as his wife worked in the kitchen and traffic and children's voices from the street below.

He told me he had joined the Communist party as a twenty-two-year-old soldier on the Leningrad front in the winter of 1942. The Germans had nearly reached the city, and he did not expect to survive. "I wanted somehow to show that I not only was fighting the Germans but that I was fighting against fascism, that I was for Soviet power, so I joined the party," he said. "I understood at the time that we were hardly likely to live; it was the coldest, hungriest part of the winter of '42." He paused and smiled very slightly: "Therefore I rather like that boy who joined the party then, and I would be very sorry to disillusion him."

"But nevertheless you'll have to disillusion him?" I asked.

"I'll probably have to. Somehow I just don't feel like telling him everything, like disappointing that fellow. It's a great tragedy for him, and for me too."

He spoke quietly and with palpable sadness, despite his storyteller's habitual cleverness. He said he was still a member of the party, waiting, he said, to find another one to join. "I still have some hope, albeit slender hope, that a party of a new type will be created, where I can take all that is left of my illusions."

Granin warmed to his subject and described the excitement with which he had greeted Gorbachev's early reforms. "You know, perestroika achieved a great deal in the spiritual life of the people. It took the gag off their mouths and let them start speaking, it cleansed their brains and let them start thinking, it permitted us to return to such concepts as charity, history, honor, worthiness. What Gorbachev declared at the beginning of the path, that universal human values have priority over political values—that was very important. A lot was done to make people straighten up, look around, and feel like human beings," he said. "And then began..." His voice trailed off.

He tried again. "You know," he said, "there's a Russian proverb: 'Don't awaken evil.' Nobody knew the scale of this 'evil.' Nobody knew what was going on in our country. When everyone began to wake up, some terrible things came to light. Things connected with the repressions, and with the KGB, and with our history, and with our economy, and with the statistics about our economy, and with the statistics about our military spending, and with our army, and with our party apparat.

"And the main thing that happened was this: We were deprived of the point of life." He leaned forward and looked directly at me and repeated: "We were deprived of the point of life."

What did he mean? "We had the idea that we were building the most advanced society in the world, the most progressive society, the most fair society. We were building socialism, and once we finished building socialism, we would begin to build communism. Everything would get better, better, and better. We would teach everybody else how to live. And that idea helped people bear adversity, and people didn't notice where they were—as a mountain climber can't tell whether he's nearing the summit. And it turned out there was no summit. It turned out that we were not climbing higher, we were climbing lower."

This was a brilliant portrayal of the demise of the Soviet illusion. But something bothered me: Granin had for three decades mixed with the Soviet literary "generals," as they were cynically called in Russia, rubbed shoulders with the political elite, and enjoyed the privilege of privileges: travel in the West. He had visited the United States five times, and the first time had been in the early 1970s. Had the information in the Soviet media over the last few years really been new to him?

"I never imagined the scale of our misfortune and collapse," he said. For example? "The party apparat. I saw that there were stupid people and careerists, but I didn't know to what degree the whole thing had rotted, how corrupt it was. I didn't know how militarized our society was." And when did he find out? Granin insisted that the real breakthrough in his own thinking had come only recently. "From the newspapers, television, reports, speeches—it was glasnost. We came a very long way in the first three or four years [of perestroika], and you can't help but be glad about that.... We had been living in complete ignorance about what was happening in the economy, in agriculture, in the army, in ideology, in the party, in all the other structures. I didn't know, for example, how much we were paying from our budget for the defense industry and the army. I've only now begun to find out. I didn't know how huge the bureaucracy was. We were living in a completely distorted world—the world our propaganda had built for us. You can't even imagine it now; that's what's happened—we ourselves now can't really imagine it. Young people these days come out with these statements: 'Why were you silent? Why did you start speaking only now?' Those questions attest to the fact that people have already changed."

Granted, I said, you did not know precisely what was being spent on the army—but you knew your government refused to say how much it was spending. Didn't you suspect the worst?

"They told us that we were protecting the peace, that we were the most peace-loving country in the world, that in our country everything was done for the people, for the people's sake, that we had the finest, free health-care system in the world—that's what they told us."

Not everyone believed the propaganda, I said. What had he thought of Solzhenitsyn and Sakharov and the other famous dissidents of the 1970s and early 1980s?

"I looked on them with enormous respect," Granin said unhesitatingly. "But for the most part, they were for us like characters in a silent film. They were saying something, but it didn't reach us. The sound didn't reach us, because they did not have the possibility of speaking out in the newspaper or on radio and TV—there was just the so-called samizdat. That sometimes reached us, but it was very incomplete. We heard that so-and-so had been arrested, that so-and-so had been put on trial, and we understood that these were heroic people."

While I found Granin emotionally persuasive, I found his account of his loss of faith contradictory. When such outright opponents of the system as Sakharov, Sinyavsky and Daniel, and even Solzhenitsyn spoke out, he protested and thought them heroic. Yet he still believed in the system that was persecuting them?

"No, you're oversimplifying. Perestroika is not an earthquake. It was not a catastrophe, not an earth tremor. It was rather a *result*. Why could perestroika come about? Because there had been dissidents. Because there had been samizdat. Because all of that had played a huge role. There had been journals like *Novy Mir*, there had been Tvardovsky [the liberal editor of *Novy Mir* in the early 1960s who published Solzhenitsyn's "One Day in the Life of Ivan Denisovich"], there had been opposition. And a large number of people had participated in that opposition—in different ways. Some, the most heroic people, as dissidents. But how much they had worked over my literary works, and what else didn't they do! They criticized, banned, all kinds of things. It was a process, a long process—but certain central values remained intact. We saw how

awful censorship was. We were outraged by the existence of censorship and saw how it mutilated literature, film, theater. We fought
censorship—but that doesn't mean the idea of socialism no longer
existed."

Granin tried another metaphor. "You understand that when you
go to court and see a divorce case, that's a *result*. And the path to the
divorce may have taken many years. That's the way it was for us
with socialism and the party and Soviet power. The divorce began
with perestroika. You know how torturous and difficult the breakup
of a marriage is. You're disappointed in your wife, then you pity her,
then you're reconciled, then it happens again, right? It is far from
simple."

Then he described for me some of the moments in the breakup of
this political and existential marriage, what he called "this extremely
contradictory story."

"We came home as victors after the war. We had destroyed
fascism. We believed that we had not only destroyed it in the
military sense but that we had destroyed it as a fallacious idea. It
was the triumph of our idea, you see." Then, he said, came the
vicious official attacks on the writers Anna Akhmatova and Mikhail Zoshchenko in 1946 and the concocted Doctors' Plot of 1953.
Then there were the dissident scandals of the 1960s and 1970s, the
forced exile of talented artists and writers. He stressed the gradual
nature of his disillusionment. I asked whether self-interest had
played a role—the fact that in a crass sense it was far more
profitable to believe in the Soviet illusion than not to believe. He
seemed slightly uncomfortable. "I'll say this: for a writer it was
especially difficult. Writers helped the dissidents, but writers became
dissidents themselves only with great difficulty, because it would
deprive them of the possibility of creative work. And that creative
work itself gave them the ability at least to say something."

This I took to be a confession, or as close as Granin chose to come
to one. I found our conversation extraordinarily thought-provoking
and paradoxical. On the one hand the revelations of glasnost were a
tragedy for him—and on the other hand they had "achieved a great
deal in the spiritual life of people," and "you can't help but be glad"
about them. He had lost his faith after learning a great deal he never

knew before from the press, radio, and TV after 1985—yet he had been shaken by events in 1946, 1952, 1965, 1969, 1970.... In the end I was left with a writer's potent images: the mountain climber who lacks perspective and does not know he is lost, the marriage that dissolves unnoticeably but inexorably over many years. I was left also with the paradox that liberation from the lies was a process of almost unbearable pain for people such as Granin, who had begun as a true believer, who had wanted to keep believing, and who had profited from his belief. As I parted with him that afternoon in Leningrad, Daniil Granin seemed to me a broken man.

Anatoly Malykhin paced his room on the seventh floor of the Hotel Rossiya like a caged animal, muttering orders to fellow coal miners, whose big arms and calloused hands marked them as interlopers here on the territory of Kremlin bureaucrats. It was March 1991, and this two-room suite was Moscow headquarters for the coal miners' strike, on which the fate of Soviet politics seemed to hinge.

"We've got to get a truck to Riga—the Latvians have food to donate to the strikers," he said. "Misha, you're going to Yakutia to talk to the gold miners. You have to be tough.... Someone should buy a copy of [the newspaper] *Kuranty*—they had a photographer here yesterday."

Malykhin was in his ninth day on a diet of mineral water and cigarettes, nourished only by his simmering anger at the regime he was determined to topple. Dipping into their rediscovered arsenal of street politics, the strike leaders had themselves declared a hunger strike, trying to turn up pressure on Gorbachev and his government to meet their immodest demands: resignation of the Soviet president and his government; dissolution of the Soviet parliament; and transfer of all political power to the elected leaders and parliaments of the republics.

"Our first demands were ridiculous—'Make our lives better,'" he told me. "Now we know it is necessary to change the system."

Puffing his filter Ava cigarette, still pacing, he went on. "We have to break the old system, the idiocy that's driven us to destitution for seventy-three years. Over the last two years we've understood that economic reform is impossible without a change in the institutions of power: the Communist party, the KGB, the military-industrial complex, these imperialist-monopolist ministries."

If I, as a foreign correspondent, had miraculously found you ten years ago, I said to Malykhin, and asked you what you thought about "the system," how would you have answered?

A smile broke through the intense look on Malykhin's face, topped with a nearly bald dome where there was a fast-disappearing patch of blond hair. He was struck by the absurdity of the idea.

"I would have been too scared to say anything," he said. "At best I would have repeated some official slogan. Maybe I would have said we were building communism.

"You see, it wasn't our affair. We were given our job to do, and we did it. They were the bosses. We were the idiots. It was slavery: Work diligently, love the boss, and listen to him. We weren't supposed to know anything."

Anatoly Malykhin's life story was about as different from Daniil Granin's as could be imagined, and Malykhin's fierce activism was the opposite of the writer's depressed resignation. In early 1991 Malykhin was thirty-four—not quite half Granin's age. Granin had spent most of his life in the rarefied literary circles of Leningrad and Moscow. Malykhin had spent most of his life in the grimy coal mines of western Siberia, where his father had worked for thirty-three years before his death in 1984. At sixteen Anatoly had quit school and started working construction in his hometown of Novokuznetsk. Then he had served his two years in the army, in Vladivostok in the Far East. "Then I came back home and went to work in the mine. In the Kuzbass [the west Siberian coal basin] we have only one career path," Malykhin told me.

Granin had joined the party as a fervent, idealistic believer. Malykhin had never thought of joining the party and nobody had thought to ask him. If he was a believer, he was a believer only by default. It had not occurred to him, as indeed it probably had not occurred to most ordinary working people before the late 1980s, that one could or should think about one's global attitude toward the system. He did his job and kept pigs and chickens on the side, struggling to make a decent life for himself, his wife, and their two children. The biggest victory of his life came when, by leaving the mine for two years to work construction, he managed in 1987 to get a big, four-room apartment, enabling the family to leave the chilly, one-room shack they had shared for years with his wife's grandmother. "Politics was totally alien to me," he said. His hobbies were photography and fishing.

All that changed abruptly on July 11, 1989. The biggest strike since the Revolution had been sparked by gripes over stores emptied of soap and sausage, and Malykhin's fellow workers at the Yesaul Coal Mine saw him as fair, smart, and tough, whatever his lack of polish and whatever he thought of himself. They elected him as their representative to the regional strike committee. Soviet theory had always taught that Soviet workers, whose employer was the workers' state, logically could not strike, since they would be striking against themselves. Soviet practice discouraged workers from challenging this theory—such as the infamous incident in the city of Novocherkassk in 1962, when troops shot down dozens of strikers, arrested the rest, executed nine ringleaders, and exiled many others to Siberia along with their families. (The facts about Novocherkassk, never mentioned in the press at the time, were first revealed by the media in 1990.)

The coal miners of Kuzbass flew in the face of this history in 1989. Sick of miserable housing conditions and dwindling supplies, which made their relatively big salaries fairly meaningless, they walked off the job. The workers spurned the despised official trade unions, which had always been a fig leaf for unimpeded decision-making by state managers. Instead they elected strike committees from the ranks of the suddenly politicized, charismatic young miners who were speaking up at spontaneous strike rallies. Quickly the strike committee leaders, who had such moral authority that few dared say "no" to them, moved into offices in government buildings and began to function almost as surrogate local governments. Local mine administrators and party officials, seeing little to be gained from a hard line and considerable potential in using the strike to squeeze money and supplies out of Moscow, endorsed the strikers' demands. Within days the miners were negotiating directly with the Politburo, winning wage and supply concessions from a Kremlin terrified by the prospect of a long strike. But the government made promises it couldn't keep. Nearly two years later, when miners' discontent sparked a renewed walkout, many of their leaders were no longer seeking promises from the regime. They wanted to oust it.

First among them was Anatoly Malykhin, who suddenly found himself propelled into big-time politics. The strike had uncovered in him a natural talent for leadership. He came across as coolheaded and articulate but without a trace of slickness or pretension, and he was at home with miners and Moscow politicians alike. Moreover, Moscow radicals' democratic, anti-Communist rhetoric meshed closely with his own, new political views. Once he had ignored the news and been completely indifferent to politics. The first strike had transformed him into a news junkie, soaking up the contents of *Ogonyok* and *Argumenti i Fakti*, transfixed by Vzglyad and TSN. He had read widely in the growing literature of anticommunism purchased from the sidewalk book tables. He told me with real pleasure of having spent 250 rubles, two weeks' wages, on a six-volume edition of the works of Solzhenitsyn. "A Soviet edition," he emphasized, "done by a new small enterprise in Leningrad." Malykhin had come to see the coal miners' future as bound up with the Kremlin politics that once had seemed distant and irrelevant. He knew all the players in Russian politics by name, face, and views and had consulted with many. He was acutely aware of the changes in television news coverage since Leonid Kravchenko's takeover of the previous autumn and cursed softly when the hotel TV displayed the newly sanitized version of the TSN news broadcast, on which he could be certain not to find accurate coverage of the strike. "It's Vremya No. 2 now," he griped.

While Malykhin had been strongly influenced by democratic activists from the Moscow intelligentsia, he was not parroting their ideas. He had made those ideas his own, assimilated them, woven them into his own experience. When I noted that there were plenty of discontent and strikes among coal miners living in the West, he unhesitatingly answered: "Their strikes are totally different. They're about local issues—usually wage demands. We're demanding freedom. If we're not victorious, it'll be back to the Gulag, and Solzhenitsyn will have to write another book." As long as the central bureaucracy existed, its octopus arms reaching to coal mines from the Ukraine to Vorkuta in the arctic North, mines could have no autonomy in setting wages and working conditions and selling their production, he said. As long as mines were state property—"belonging to no one"—inefficiency and waste would be the rule. From an unthinking cog in the Soviet wheel, an apathetic ordinary man, he had been transformed into a well-informed and passionate grassroots political leader. There could have been no more persuasive example of the power of the information exploding from newspapers, television, and publishing houses. One day in the spring of 1991 Malykhin addressed a rally of 100,000 people outside the Kremlin; the next he spoke to a session of the Supreme Soviet. He made a powerful impression in both settings.

In one of the savory ironies of Soviet reform, Communist party leader Gorbachev and his aides denounced the leaders of the mine strike and their political supporters as "neo-Bolsheviks," blasting them for trying the Leninist tactic of sowing economic chaos in order to bring down the government. Indeed, even to their allies the picture of these burly Siberians starving themselves at the Hotel Rossiya until the regime voluntarily relinquished all its power seemed to border on the absurd. But the truth was that by refusing to be bought off with a few boxcars filled with beef and television sets, and aligning themselves with Boris Yeltsin's Russia and the rest of the republics against Gorbachev and the central bureaucracy, the coal miners were tipping the political balance against the imperial "center," the once omnipotent Moscow ministries. The miners were showing the Soviet leaders that many workers wanted to junk communism, not reform it. They were demonstrating that strikes in key areas of the economy could quickly cripple production while leaving the government no realistic way to resist, since the crude military intimidation used in the Baltic republics would probably be both ineffective and dangerous against Russian coal miners.

So it was that, after dallying for several months in late 1990 and early 1991 with the KGB-military-industrial coalition in an attempt to halt the decentralization of power, Gorbachev reversed course in April and began serious negotiations with the republics toward a new Union Treaty. More than any other single factor, the miners' tough political stance was responsible for this turnabout. Thus would the transformation of the mind of Anatoly Malykhin and many like him be not a personal matter but of the greatest political consequence for the future of the Soviet Union.

But in March 1991 that still lay ahead. My last recollection from Malykhin's Rossiya room, littered with mineral-water bottles, was of somebody bringing in that day's copy of the newspaper *Kuranty*, the feisty tabloid published by the new, radical-dominated Moscow City Council. On the front page was a photograph of the hunger-striking miners—minus Malykhin, who had stepped out when the photographer dropped by.

"Malykhin died already," one of the miners deadpanned.

Anatoly Malykhin smiled and puffed on his cigarette.

The lives of Granin and Malykhin followed very different paths. But by the beginning of the 1990s their paths intersected with those of diverse millions of other citizens at one point: the death of the Soviet illusion. And precisely at that intersection stood a politician, rising as the regime fell by reaffirming the popular disillusionment but also offering a way out, a rallying point to prevent disenchantment from dissolving into chaos.

At first glance Boris Nikolayevich Yeltsin seemed by biography and temperament an unlikely candidate to become populist leader of the democratic forces moving against communism and against the Russian-dominated empire. He had been a dyed-in-the-wool party man, having spent ten years as the tough party boss in Sverdlovsk, a closed city in the Urals associated with heavy industry and the military-industrial complex. Under Brezhnev, as *Pravda* gleefully demonstrated in one of its many subsequent attacks on him, Yeltsin had come across in speeches as an enthusiastic yes-man. The celebrated instance was Yeltsin's performance at the 26th Communist

Party Congress in 1981: "The past five years have been another major milestone in the heroic annals of the Land of the Soviets! As the latest Party Congress demonstrates, the country today consists of the powerful productive forces that our society possesses, the real benefits that developed socialism provides for Soviet people, the peace and tranquility that protects them. And all this is the result of the wise collective reason, titanic labor, unbending will, and unsurpassed organizational talent of the Communist party and its combat headquarters—the Central Committee and the Politburo headed by Comrade Leonid Ilyich Brezhnev (Applause). . . ."

Yeltsin himself had disavowed that speech at the 27th Party Congress in 1986, saying that in 1981 he had lacked the "courage and political experience" to swim against the prevailing tide of cant and hypocrisy. But such a public confession was ambiguous. Was Yeltsin finally telling the truth? Or was he just trimming his sails to hew to the Gorbachev line, as before he had so closely followed the Brezhnev line? Was Yeltsin a refreshingly candid politician or a completely unprincipled opportunist?

Apart from his ambiguous political record, there was his style: gruff, coarse, unschooled, authoritarian to the core. Compared with, say, the polished cool of Gorbachev, with his Moscow State University law degree and charm that could tame Margaret Thatcher and Henry Kissinger, Yeltsin's rough-hewn bossiness seemed peculiarly unsuited to the new era. His degree was in construction engineering and came from the Ural Polytechnic Institute. He was a Russian who, unlike Gorbachev, wore his Russian-ness on his sleeve, a Russian nationalist at heart who had little experience with other nationalities.

Yeltsin's service as Moscow party chief from 1985 to 1987 seemed to some invigorating, to others full of sound and fury and cheap publicity stunts. Even in 1987, when Yeltsin lashed out at Yegor Ligachev and resigned under pressure, enduring the denunciations of his former colleagues, his martyrdom struck many people as flawed. A few months later, in early 1988, I remember a Western journalist with generally acute political judgment declaring that Yeltsin was "a dangerous man." It was not the last time Westerners would misinterpret and underestimate Yeltsin.

In retrospect it is clear that Yeltsin's solid and steadily growing status with the Soviet public came about not despite his past as a party man but because of it. Between April 1986, when he gave the self-critical speech, and June 1991, when he was elected president of Russia, becoming the first democratically elected leader in Russian history, Yeltsin underwent a complete political conversion in full view of the public. From party believer and cheerleader he passed to the Communist reform stage, vowing with Gorbachev to return to Leninism, renew socialism, and strengthen the union. Then, chastened by his ouster from the Kremlin's inside circle, he began to question the Soviet fundamentals of Leninism and socialism and to place them in side-by-side comparison with Western parliamentary democracy and capitalism. Finally, guided by his own Russian nationalism, he came to terms with the nationalisms of the Balts and other Soviet peoples, arguing that the Russians no less than the Estonians or the Georgians were victims of Soviet imperialism, and accepting the solution of sovereignty for all. Yeltsin's rough manners, directness of speech, peremptory manner with subordinates, even his escapades while under the apparent influence of vodka, turned out to be not political handicaps but reassurances for the public that this was a flesh-and-blood Russian who resembled them and would level with them.

Sometimes Yeltsin's unique status as a renegade former Communist boss was invaluable. When Vladimir Kryuchkov became the first KGB chief to appear before the newly elected parliament for confirmation in his post in 1989, it was Yeltsin who posed the toughest questions. As Sverdlovsk party boss Yeltsin had regularly received reports from the local KGB, so he spoke not from liberal dilettantism but from party experience.

Answering deputies' questions, Kryuchkov had blanched at a suggestion that the KGB used "secret informers" to spy on Soviet citizens, preferring to speak instead of "helpers" planted by the agency in factories and other organizations. Yeltsin replied: "In the first place, most of the major organizations have not 'helpers' but an actual network of agents from the state security bodies, and this causes great moral damage to our society, since they are not engaged in catching spies there but are simply engaged in, well, putting it mildly, let's say, gathering certain information. In my ten years as first secretary of Sverdlovsk Region party committee, I do not remember a single spy being caught with their assistance. But it is a thousands-strong army that constantly passes on information on what is happening in this or that work collective. In my opinion, this is quite intolerable for us in the period of democratization."

Again drawing on his own experience, Yeltsin referred to other deputies' complaints about big, new KGB buildings around the country. "Their buildings are built because the apparatus is growing," he said. "I know that for sure. It is growing at the center and in the provinces. And since that apparatus is growing, it is becoming a super-monopolistic organization, and moreover an organization that could sometimes bring its influence to bear one way or the other on the life of our society." He offered his skepticism about the supposed reforms taking place inside the KGB and proposed "a drastic reduction in the size of this organization at home." He singled out KGB infiltration of the church as a particularly insidious phenomenon.

The KGB remembered the tongue-lashing, not the last it got from Yeltsin. In May 1990, when Yeltsin was a candidate for chairman of the newly elected Russian parliament, fiercely opposed by Gorbachev and the Soviet bureaucracy, anonymous anti-Yeltsin leaflets appeared in big quantities in the foyer of the Great Kremlin Palace where the Russian Congress of People's Deputies was meeting. The leaflets were quite professionally done, juxtaposing contradictory statements made by Yeltsin at various times with the intention of exposing him as a fraud. But for many deputies the leaflet raised more questions about its authors than about Yeltsin: Who had supplies of such high-quality pure-white typing paper? (I had scoured the stores for office supplies and found only coarse, greenish paper.) Who had a top-quality photocopier? Most telling of all, who happened to have handy the verbatim texts of Yeltsin's speeches in Japan and his interviews with Radio Liberty? Who but the information-control agency itself? The fingerprints of the KGB were unmistakable.

Yeltsin's political portrait can be viewed most clearly if he is contrasted to two other reformist leaders, Sakharov and Gorbachev.

Sakharov had articulated his opposition to the Communist system publicly, and at great personal cost, years before Yeltsin. He had abandoned the Soviet illusion long before most Soviet citizens. For this he had their belated respect, but as a dissident he was a special case, by definition not one of them. Gorbachev, at the other end of the spectrum, never renounced communism, remained general secretary of the party, and stuck with the increasingly threadbare idea that nothing was irrevocably wrong with the ideology or the union. Whether by conviction or because of political constraints, Gorbachev shifted only slowly away from the original foundations of Communist reform. He seemed determined to cling to the Soviet illusion long after most of his compatriots had given it up; by 1990, certainly, his recurring references to "the people's socialist choice" sounded disingenuous.

Yeltsin's political strength lay in the fact that he had taken the same journey from believer to doubter that most people had taken, under the influence of the same media explosion, and at about the same time. In a sense he had been Gorbachev, and he had become Sakharov, all in public view. If a slicker politician might have seemed a mere opportunist, Yeltsin's growling look-you-in-the-eye style made his conversion convincing. And if any skeptics remained, the dunderhead party and its remaining loyal press organs, such as *Pravda* and *Sovietskaya Rossiya*, attacked Yeltsin so frequently and outrageously that his credentials as an antiestablishment, anti-Communist leader could not be doubted. (Perhaps no such publication ever topped the bareknuckle party weekly *Glasnost*, which in February 1991 carried an interview with an anonymous police official who offered the absurd claim that Yeltsin was the behind-the-scenes head of the "Chechen mafia," a criminal gang coming from a particular Caucasus ethnic group. Noting that "it's difficult to confirm anything for certain," the nameless policeman nonetheless declared, "You'll agree—to have at hand a nine-thousand-man armed guard who in their free time engage in robbery, murder and so on—that's the height of immorality.")

Yeltsin's strength in public opinion was that he had repented. He had not groveled and beaten his breast, but he had unmistakably and publicly regretted his past participation in the Communist system in a way that Gorbachev had not and could not. His message was simple: I believed A, and A turned out to be wrong, and now I believe B. This struck a chord with the great mass of Russians, who themselves had believed and then stopped believing.

One landmark in Yeltsin's public repentance was his fabled first trip to America in September 1989. Exaggerated accounts of his drunkenness overshadowed the real import of the trip. After his return Yeltsin deflected, with a characteristically deft comment, a grossly overblown article on his drinking, written by an imaginative Italian journalist and swiftly reprinted in *Pravda*. The article purported to list the precise quantity of liquor consumed by Yeltsin during his trip—"and here the Italian's imagination clearly failed him, since the amount he counted could bring down only a weak foreigner," Yeltsin wrote later. The point is that to most Russians watching the U.S. tour from afar, the drinking brouhaha was dwarfed in significance by the picture of a former Communist boss having the scales fall from his eyes as he toured the wonders of a market economy and a democracy.

Here is the Tass version of a Yeltsin press conference in New York that ran in a number of Soviet newspapers: "This is my first time in the U.S.A., and I must say—not because I am the guest and you are the hosts, but really sincerely—that the opinion hammered into us and me all our lives, by means that included the 'Short Course on the History of the Russian Communist Party (Bolshevik)' [Stalin's infamous distorted history], with regard to capitalism, America, Americans, and New York—has been turned around 180 degrees during this day and a half. It turns out that capitalism is not decaying and thus will not soon rot, as they told us all the time, but is flourishing. It turns out that Americans are not aggressive and unduly familiar but very affable, cheerful, and good-natured and generally know how to live and work...."

And so it went, one traditional Soviet myth after another stated for the record and dashed to the ground with a combination of sarcasm, bitterness, and glee. "The Statue of Liberty is not some monstrosity but a very attractive woman, well executed not by nature but by man. And when we flew past it twice, I felt I had become twice as free. It turns out that in the evening and at night you can quite freely eat in a restaurant, and it is not so expensive on the wages of the average American, and thousands of restaurants are open twenty-four hours a day...." A questioner asked whether he believed the Revolution of 1917 had been a mistake. No, he said—but: "But at the same time it has to be said that we have always given the idea priority over practical reality and built so-called 'slogan socialism,' which is sometimes called 'barracks socialism.'"

In an interview with PBS, later reported by Tass, he was asked whether the USSR would remain a Communist state. "Well, 'Communist' is a word which, in my view, needs generally to be understood simply as a dream or an idea which one can constantly cherish, but only cherish—it cannot be used. What is needed is some sort of a new model of socialism which would be constructed taking account not only of the experience of socialist countries but also the experience of the U.S.A., for instance, which has more than two hundred years' experience of bourgeois democracy." Do you still regard yourself as a Communist? he was asked. "Yes, I haven't been expelled from the party." But what about the idea of communism? the interviewer persisted. "It's a sort of dream beyond the clouds, so to speak." As to the indivisible union, Yeltsin said of Baltic states: "Let them decide for themselves whether to secede from the USSR or not." All of these answers were replayed in the Soviet press.

Later he would stand in a Houston supermarket and deadpan: "Even the Politburo doesn't have this much choice!"—a remark that at one fell swoop denounced Communist leaders' privileges, of which he had firsthand experience, and the failure of their system. He gave a revealing account of the supermarket visit a few months later in his autobiography, dictated to journalist Valentin Yumashev, called in Russian *Confession on an Assigned Topic* and translated into English as *Against the Grain*. The book was grabbed up by the new profit-making publishing ventures springing up everywhere and turned into an overnight best-seller. "When I looked at those shelves with hundreds, thousands of cans, boxes, and so on," Yeltsin said of his Houston stop, "for the first time I felt sick for us and for our country. To lead such a wealthy power into such beggary.... It's terrible."

Were it not for Yeltsin's image as a thoroughgoing Russian patriot, his U.S. tour might have rebounded against him: as it was, the Communist press portrayed him as a naive rube who had denigrated his own country to play up to his hosts. But Yeltsin's standing was already sufficient not to be shaken by party diatribes. He managed rather to lend credence and legitimacy to the view, alien to official Soviet and Slavophile tradition, that the West had crucial lessons for the Russian future. The political morality play of the ex-Politburo member simultaneously crushed and thrilled by the abundance of the American supermarket was unforgettable to the Soviet audience: here at once was bitter disillusionment with what existed and a tantalizing picture of what might be in the future.

In May 1990, when Yeltsin was standing for the post of chairman of the presidium of the Russian Federation Supreme Soviet—essentially the presidency of Russia—he and Gorbachev squared off in a revealing confrontation over just what "socialism" meant. In his address to the Russian Congress of People's Deputies on May 22, Yeltsin scrupulously avoided all hints of ideology, even to the point of referring to the RSFSR, the Russian Socialist Federative Soviet Republic, as "the Russian Republic." The next day Gorbachev, who was not a deputy and appeared by "invitation" of some Communist deputies, interrupted the Congress's proceedings with a long speech countering Yeltsin's views on Russian sovereignty and urging the deputies not to elect Yeltsin their chairman. Yeltsin's speech, Gorbachev said, "contains an attempt to separate Russia from socialism, something which is not mentioned once in Comrade Yeltsin's speech." Yeltsin, he charged, wanted "with one stroke of the pen, as it were, to invite us to say farewell to our socialist choice of 1917. Moreover, if you pay attention, judging by Comrade Yeltsin's speech, socialism hasn't even found a place in the title of the RSFSR. That is, there is no longer any socialism or Soviet power here.... I would say, to sum up this thesis, that for us Russians, as for all the people of our country, 'socialist choice,' 'power of the soviets' are not just empty phrases. These are our fundamental values, our points of reference. And so I do not know what reference points Comrade Yeltsin wishes to offer on this score. What, then—are we supposed to alter our political structure? That runs counter to our line of perestroika, which we have proposed to give socialism its second wind." Gorbachev was making perfectly clear his allegiance to the principles of Communist reform and his horror of alternative "reference points." Invoking the sacred word "socialism," he was pushing old ideological buttons, trying to make the Bolshevik word-magic work one more time.

Two days later, answering a Communist deputy's question about socialism, Yeltsin made his reply. "I consider that in our world there is neither the capitalism spoken of in the classic works [i.e., of Marx and Engels], nor is there the socialism of which they speak— although socialism has existed in various forms. There have been developed socialism [Brezhnev's term for the Soviet system], national socialism, Pol Pot socialism. There have been various interpretations of socialism. I do not believe in socialism for its own sake. I believe that the people of this country should live well, that the people should respect the leadership and supreme authorities of their country, of their republic, and that, vice versa, the supreme authorities of the republic should respect their people."

Yeltsin directly assaulted the Bolshevik linguistic tradition. "Socialism" could no longer be a totem before which all Soviet citizens must unthinkingly genuflect—or the consequences could be as meager as those achieved by Brezhnev or as horrible as those of Hitler or Pol Pot. Leaders should not scare people with the bogeyman of capitalism or hypnotize them with the mantra of socialism. People should "live well," period.

Exhausted by utopia, stripped of the Soviet illusion, many people were looking not for any mythical "glorious destiny" but for just this kind of down-to-earth language from their leaders. By praising the American economic system, by taking the side of the Balts in their fight for independence with Gorbachev and the Soviet government, Yeltsin risked offending Soviet patriots. But in practice he managed to pioneer a new, progressive form of Russian patriotism in which one could be a Russian patriot and still favor free markets and Estonian independence. The Russian Federation, he argued, was just another victim of Soviet imperialism—in many ways, indeed, its ultimate victim. "The issue of primary importance is the spiritual, national, and economic rebirth of Russia, which has been for long decades an appendage of the center and which in many respects has lost its independence," he said in 1990. There was an empire, Yeltsin reasoned, but it was in essence a Soviet empire, not a Russian one. At the center of this empire the Soviet bureaucracy thrived while the Russian people struggled for a decent life.

This view struck a chord with ordinary Russians, who were tired of being accused of imperialism by all the other nationalities when they enjoyed so few fruits of empire. But Gorbachev saw clearly where Yeltsin's uncompromising defense of the Russian Federation would lead. "If, comrades," he told Russian deputies in 1990, "you very seriously subject to analysis what he [Yeltsin] is offering under the banner of restoring the sovereignty of Russia, this is a call for the disintegration of the union."

If Yeltsin had won most ordinary Russians over with his rejection of the Soviet empire, he could not be so sure of the attitude of Russians in the military, who had taken an oath to defend the Soviet Union. After the Vilnius killings, Yeltsin issued a special appeal to Russian servicemen, urging them to disobey orders to fire on Baltic demonstrators—which unleashed a fierce anti-Yeltsin propaganda campaign inside the army. But he refused to concede the military to Gorbachev and the unionist position. Five months after the Vilnius assault, on the eve of Russia's first presidential election, I watched Yeltsin campaign at an army installation outside the city of Tula. As paratroopers put on a spectacular show of war games in the fields before him, Yeltsin sat in the bleachers alongside his host, General Pavel Grachev, an Afghanistan War hero and the commander of Soviet paratroopers. Given the army's official propaganda against Yeltsin, the two men seemed to have a remarkable, backslapping camaraderie. Several young officers told me they were avid Yeltsin backers, agreeing strongly with him that Russian troops had no business intervening in other Soviet republics. The bloodshed in Vilnius had taught them that Russian officers would become scapegoats for unpopular interventions in other republics while politicians dodged responsibility.

The afternoon closed with Yeltsin, surrounded by earnest boys in miniature paratroopers' uniforms, promising 100,000 rubles from his deficit-plagued Russian Federation budget to support the "Young

Paratroopers" club. Some liberal Russian journalists on hand sneered at this crass political pandering to the army, whose top brass overwhelmingly supported Yeltsin's opponents in the presidential race—former Soviet Prime Minister Nikolai Ryzhkov, Gorbachev aide Vadim Bakatin, reactionary army general Albert Makashov, and populist Russian chauvinist Vladimir Zhirinovsky. But Grachev and the boys gave Yeltsin a big cheer. A few months later the scene would become more than just an interesting footnote to Yeltsin's successful presidential campaign.

9

After:
The Coup-Proof
Society

VLADIMIR KRYUCHKOV: As chairman of the KGB I don't see a real threat that someone will try to establish a dictatorship. If we found out about such a thing, we would immediately move against it. It seems to me that that is the task of the security organs.

Literaturnaya Gazeta: Really, if someone wanted to carry out a coup d'état, would he inform the chairman of the KGB about it ahead of time?

KRYUCHKOV: No one's going to inform us, of course, but as the saying goes, we do something for our pay. We wouldn't be worth much if we didn't have any idea what was happening in the country.

 —*Literaturnaya Gazeta,* January 23, 1991

I need someone at my side I can trust!
 —Mikhail Gorbachev, December 27, 1990, insisting that the Congress of People's Deputies confirm his vice-president, Gennady Yanayev

The possibility of a coup d'état had been hanging over Soviet politics like a paralyzed thunderhead ever since reform began, never

[245]

loosing the anticipated storm yet never dissipating. Perhaps a half-dozen times since 1989 edgy journalists or legislators had caught wind of suspicious troop movements around Moscow and set off brief panics. Some general or other would condescend to tell the press or parliament that no unusual maneuvers had occurred, or that they were part of a long-planned exercise, or, implausibly but truthfully, that the soldiers had been brought in to help harvest potatoes. Late one foggy night in the spring of 1991, driving back into Moscow from Domodyedyevo Airport, I was waved to a stop by a policeman—and saw a row of armored vehicles in the square ahead, lit by brilliant spotlights. A wave of horror came over me, and my mind raced: At last, the worst had happened. Was my family safe? Would I be able to file a story? Then the cop spoke through my open window. "They're making a film," he said. "Drive slowly, and keep to the right."

The fear of a coup was based in part on the impalpable nature of the information revolution that had taken place. In a remark of legendary cynicism, Stalin had once replied to criticism from the Vatican by asking, "How many divisions does the Pope have?" Well, how many divisions did the democrats have? True, people knew more. True, people saw the world differently. Intellectually the changes seemed momentous. But there had been no storming of the Winter Palace, no arrest of the former rulers, no trial of the old regime—except for such trial as had taken place on celluloid and newsprint. The changes that seemed so profound had not been institutionalized. The traditional triad on which the regime rested—Communist party, army, KGB—was battered, perhaps, but appeared essentially intact.

Yet if it was easy to imagine hard-line Communist ideologues or captains of the military-industrial complex wanting to seize power, it was hard to imagine what they would do once they got it. The conservatives' program amounted to hazy nostalgia for an earlier era. "Back to 1984" did not make a compelling slogan, even from the point of view of a military that would again face a high-tech threat from the United States. Besides, domestic military coups were not part of Russian or Soviet tradition.

On the other hand, neither was outspoken political dissent, a more-or-less free press, contested elections, entrepreneurial capitalism, republican independence movements, or a lot of other things that had been happening. Moreover, Soviet forces had engineered military coups in Budapest in 1956, Prague in 1968, and Kabul in 1979, and what happened in Vilnius in January 1991 looked very much like a trial run. Of the fourteen people killed in the assault on Lithuanian television, thirteen were identified as Lithuanian demonstrators, the fourteenth as a twenty-one-year-old Russian officer, Lieutenant Viktor Shatskikh. But the army insisted it had no soldier by that name. After a couple of days of confusion, the KGB issued a terse and ominous acknowledgment: Shatskikh had been one of theirs.

The KGB's role in Vilnius underscored an unsettling fact: the agency that had quietly supported the launch of perestroika in the mid-1980s had by 1990 grown noisily disenchanted with the turn it had taken. In March 1990 an anonymous group of KGB officers had circulated an appeal in the Soviet parliament, decrying attacks on "the holy name of Lenin" and expressing alarm about "the fate of the Socialist fatherland." In a December 1990 interview, Filipp Bobkov, Kryuchkov's No. 2, who had joined the secret police before Stalin's death, stressed the KGB's crucial backing of Gorbachev in 1985—on a platform of "October Revolution, Lenin, and socialism." In five years the situation had changed drastically, Bobkov warned: "Now is the very limit. We are standing at the threshold of the breakup of the state."

By the end of 1990 KGB chief Vladimir Kryuchkov himself had added his voice to the chorus of hysterical warnings. In a wild speech to parliament he charged that some Western shipments of grain and foodstuffs were contaminated with radiation and chemicals and called for a crackdown at home. "Fears are heard that if we today embark on decisive action to restore order, that we have to knowingly consent that blood will be shed," he said. "Respected people's deputies, is blood really not being shed already?" Just three weeks after Kryuchkov's speech, the KGB's Group Alpha, of which Shatskikh was a member, led the Vilnius assault. Then, at the end of March, fifty thousand police and troops were deployed in Moscow in an obvious move to intimidate Yeltsin and the Russian Federation parliament. One night in May a bomb destroyed the headquarters of the pro-Yeltsin Democratic Russia reform coalition, a few blocks from the Kremlin; most of the dozens of spectators who gathered to stare at the rubble smoking in the illumination of the firefighters' spotlights suspected the hand of the KGB.

The KGB had swallowed glasnost; the problem was that glasnost had consequences. The leadership let the press delve into Stalinism, and soon the press was attacking the KGB. Yeltsin was permitted to go on television, and soon Siberian miners were striking in support of his political program. They finally admitted the truth about the Molotov-Ribbentrop Pact, and suddenly Baltic leaders were using that piece of history to justify their declarations of independence.

All these developments, of course, had alarmed not just the KGB but Gorbachev himself, who had dramatically retreated from reform between the fall of 1990 and the spring of 1991. One reason for the retreat, his aides would say later, was the information he was getting from Kryuchkov's KGB, including exaggerated reports of the dangers of violence and disorder. During the dark winter of 1990–1991, Kryuchkov, with the cooperation of Gorbachev's chief of staff, Valery Boldin, kept Gorbachev in an "information aquarium," in the apt phrase a Soviet journalist would later apply. Indeed, at the end of 1990 Gorbachev fired Vadim Bakatin, the liberal head of the ministry of internal affairs, because the information he gave Gorbachev often conflicted with the far darker view of the KGB, Bakatin said later. Alexander Yakovlev would recall that Gorbachev had actually believed, in March 1991, a preposterous KGB report that Yeltsin supporters were planning to put ladders against the Kremlin walls and mount an assault.

But in April, following the coal miners' strike, Gorbachev's political realism took hold. He finally rejected the alarmist rhetoric he was hearing from Kryuchkov and publicly accepted the principles of a new Union Treaty. The treaty would drastically decentralize power, eliminating the massive economic bureaucracy in Moscow and turning the mighty Soviet Union into a loose confederation of independent states. Yeltsin was pleased; he liked to joke that his old rival, Gorbachev, would soon have as much real power as the queen of England.

But the Communist reformers, whose goal remained a modernized but still socialist Soviet state, considered Gorbachev's turnabout a betrayal. One day in June, Kryuchkov, Defense Minister Dmitry Yazov, and Internal Affairs Minister Boris Pugo—the hard-liner who had replaced Bakatin—went to the Supreme Soviet for a highly unusual closed session. One after another the three security chiefs warned in apocalyptic tones of the disintegration of the country; liberal deputies and leaks to the newspapers later revealed their messages. In a throwback to the worst of cold war paranoia, Kryuchkov read to the deputies from a 1977 KGB report outlining a supposed CIA plot to recruit Soviet "agents of influence" who would "create certain difficulties of a domestic political nature in the Soviet Union, slow the development of the economy, and divert scientific research into dead ends." In other words, perestroika was a CIA plot and Gorbachev either the Americans' agent or their dupe. With this outrageous charge ringing in their ears, the deputies heard Prime Minister Valentin Pavlov suddenly ask parliament to transfer some of Gorbachev's powers to him. Gorbachev then showed up in parliament and managed to sidetrack Pavlov's scheme. But he failed to discipline or remove any of the four men involved in the drama.

If Gorbachev failed to draw conclusions, the democratic press did not. The newspaper *Literaturnaya Gazeta* and the magazine *Novoye Vremya* (New Times) urged Gorbachev to fire Kryuchkov. Other papers spoke of an "attempted coup." The front page of *Demokraticheskaya Rossiya*, the newspaper of the Russian democratic movement, headlined: "The rebellion has been put down. . . . Still not a plot [*zagovor*], but already a shady deal [*sgovor*]." Displayed prominently above the word "plot" were the faces of Pavlov, Kryuchkov, Yazov, and Pugo. They would be back in the news before long.

The contretemps in parliament was alarming, but the very fact that the press wrote about it so scathingly seemed a good omen: as long as a newspaper could accuse the KGB chief of a plot, the plot had not succeeded. Change ran in so wide and deep a current that to reverse it seemed almost impossible.

My impression was strengthened by a trip, a few days after Gorbachev had deflected Pavlov's power grab, to Izhevsk, the town in the Urals where Andrei Mironov had been arrested. (The name change to Ustinov had lasted only from 1985 to 1987.) Though Andrei's parents and brother, Alexei, still lived in Izhevsk, he had avoided the city, partly because he feared old enemies in the KGB might frame him or arrange an "accident." Now he wanted to visit, and I wanted to assess political change in this provincial outpost of the military-industrial complex which had been opened to foreigners only in 1990. We were both curious to confront those responsible for locking Andrei up. Would they be repentant, or would they insist that they had been right to imprison an enemy of the state?

Our first morning in the city, the first sight we saw was a political demonstration. Andrei, who had told me of the legendary placidity of the population of Izhevsk, was visibly astonished. A score of women in white uniforms held hand-drawn posters in front of the government center in the middle of town. They turned out to be pest-control workers complaining about budget cuts and an incompetent boss. They looked almost like a parody of a Moscow rally: "Stop the Sabotage of Work in the Battle Against Rodents and Insects!" said one poster. "No Place on the State Committee for Sanitary Inspection for Conservative N. A. Zabrodin," the despised boss, said another. Even in Izhevsk, in the heartland of Russian conservatism, "conservative" had become a label of opprobrium.

The newspapers at city newsstands showed where the pest-control rebels were finding encouragement for their audacity. The standing motto of *Izhevskiye Novosti* (Izhevsk News) was a quotation from the landmark 1990 Soviet press law: "The press and other mass information media are free. Censorship of mass information is not permitted." Dominating the front page of a special issue published on the eve of the first Russian presidential election was a huge picture of a counterculture icon, folksinger Vladimir Vysotsky, along with a quotation from one of his songs: "Don't spare your voice," a pun on *golos*, which means both "voice" and "vote." Inside were photographs of a big pro-Yeltsin rally in Izhevsk, a sardonic lyric by Alexander Galich mocking big-shot officials, and a reply to conservative readers' complaints about the newspaper's publication of a photo of a smiling, slightly silly-looking Lenin. The editors' note was not apologetic: "The leader [*vozhd*, a reverential word for Lenin, here used sarcastically] only got to smile at the theory of socialism; it's our lot to have fun practicing it."

In the nooks and crevices of the rusting military machine that still dominated Izhevsk were sprouts both of grassroots politics and a private economy. Andrei's father, Nikolai Alexeyevich, was regularly attending meetings of the fledgling Izhevsk Democratic Club—though he complained that most of the participants were retirees. Andrei's younger brother, Alexei, was a partner in a brand-new private business, significantly in the burgeoning information industry—a computer-programming venture called Hacker. His earnings had allowed him to buy a beat-up Zhiguli sedan, not a bad prize in car-starved Russia.

Closed, backward Izhevsk seemed to be awakening from a long sleep. "It is such a strange feeling for me," Andrei told me as we were trudging down a back street, "to be walking around this city with an American, going in and out of official buildings. All of this was unimaginable before."

Yet if much had changed, nearly all the officials responsible for Andrei's imprisonment were still on the job. When Andrei walked into his office at my side, Viktor Pokhodin, chief prosecutor of the republic of Udmurtia, froze and blanched as if he had seen a ghost. In a long, rambling interview, Pokhodin, fifty-six, a nondescript man with receding grey hair, insisted that he personally had always opposed political prosecutions under Article 70. "Whether the prosecutor likes the law or not, he has to carry it out," he said. But at the same time he declared that both in Stalin's day and now there were real enemies of the state—implying that one of them might well be the man he kept addressing as "Mironov," the usual form of address for a convict. Pokhodin seemed an obedient functionary, prepared to carry out whatever orders came from above—glasnost or crackdown, even if he did have a little more personal sympathy for the latter. He brought to mind the policeman pilloried in Chekhov's story "Chameleon," whose opinion of a dog-bite incident depends completely on the social status of the dog's owner. Pokhodin sounded most sincere when he answered a question about the state's quick-change politics, according to which Andrei's treasonous slander had been transformed virtually overnight into normal newspaper material and "especially dangerous state criminals" into wronged citizens.

"I should answer you with the words of Lenin," Pokhodin replied, dipping into the veteran Soviet bureaucrat's ample store of such maxims for all occasions. " 'The law is a political measure. Politics *is* the law.' "

This equivocal interview was the closest we could come to the dramatic confrontation with officialdom we had imagined. The judge—promoted to a higher court since sentencing Andrei—was said to be on vacation; the defense attorney was ill; the jail warden too busy to meet. At the jail a blond, athletic-looking assistant to the warden named Petrov recognized Andrei instantly. "You have no quarrel with us," the man said. "Your quarrel is with Sovietskaya Street," the address of KGB headquarters.

We arrived unannounced at the KGB's big, columned building, with very tall ceilings and the chilly interior that Andrei remembered well. We asked to speak with any of several KGB officers involved in the case. Flustered, the young uniformed guard picked up the phone and explained in hushed tones this strange invasion by a dissident and a foreigner. For nearly an hour we sat in the entrance hall, and in that hour only twice did anyone enter the KGB headquarters. First it was three people dragging a gargantuan burlap sack of scallions. After a while another man in civilian clothes appeared, carrying two plucked chickens, one in each hand. The guard diffidently asked him where he was going. "Where the hell do you think I'm going?" the chicken man shot back. The guard let him pass. In a time of worsening shortages, the chief function of the KGB seemed to have become the scavenging of food for its own employees.

Finally the KGB bosses dispatched a young officer, Leonid Silantin, to meet with us in a little room near the door, presumably monitored for sound. Silantin's main qualification for meeting us was that he had joined the Izhevsk KGB office only in 1988, safely after Andrei's case, so that he could claim ignorance of the affair. We talked with him for quite a while anyway. A prematurely greying man in his thirties, dressed casually in a blue-and-red-striped sport shirt, Silantin shocked us by remarking that "No one is really in power in Moscow," that the political situation was unclear and the state of the Soviet Union "very dangerous." Kryuchkov's secret speech to the parliament, he acknowledged, had been distributed throughout the huge KGB apparatus.

But Silantin also groused about the pay and demands of KGB work, volunteering that many officers were quitting to get into the more lucrative private sector. Andrei asked him for whom he had voted in a recent presidential election—perhaps for Nikolai Ryzhkov, the former prime minister and candidate of Communist reform, or for Albert Makashov, the military man who promised a return to neo-Stalinist "order"?

No, the KGB man said, "I voted for Yeltsin." He appeared to be telling the truth.

The phone woke Andrei Mironov at 7 a.m. on August 19. It was Lyudmila Lobstein, a seventy-one-year-old woman who had arrived in Moscow for a planned congress of Russian emigrés. She awoke early and switched on the TV set in her room at the Hotel Rossiya. She heard the announcer say Gorbachev was ill and power was in the hands of the State Committee for the State of Emergency—the GKChP, Geh-Kah-Cheh-Peh, in its Russian initials. She was baffled and upset, and in all Moscow she knew only Andrei; at the request of mutual acquaintances he had met her plane the day before and helped her get settled in the hotel. She dialed his number and told him to turn on the television.

"My first reaction," Andrei recalled later, "was to think: 'Sons of bitches! How stupid you are! You'll last a few months, maybe two or three years.'" His next reaction, he said, was to look at the clock and wonder why he had not been arrested. "I didn't get it—7 a.m. and they hadn't come for me," he said. "I thought I'd be on the list of those to arrest, and arrests usually come before 7." He switched the radio on and tuned to Ekho Moskvy, a year-old independent radio station that squeezed uncensored news coverage between rock music.

"They were reading the orders of the committee and adding angry commentary. Then they played a rock song that kept repeating, '*povorot*'," which means turning point and is close to the word for coup, *perevorot*. "And then I thought, 'How can they still be broadcasting?'"

Six years before, in the same month of August, in Izhevsk-Ustinov, the KGB had come for Andrei. In those six years most of the views that had got him sent to Dubrovlag had been transformed from "anti-Soviet propaganda" to mainstream opinion or official Soviet policy. The Afghanistan invasion had been denounced as a mistake and the troops withdrawn. Stalinism was now openly compared with German fascism. The one-candidate election system had been admitted to be a fraud and replaced with contested races. The economy had been acknowledged to be in dire straits. The Italian magazines confiscated from his apartment and scrupulously recorded in the evidence against him were for sale on Moscow newsstands. The books he and his dissident colleagues had secretly photocopied had been serialized in official journals and were freely sold at sidewalk book tables.

And now, after everything that had happened, they—*oni*—were trying to turn the clock back. "I thought: It's starting all over again. I thought about what I had in the apartment that could get someone else in trouble," Andrei said. He put his tiny address book, each page crammed with names in his neat hand, in a plastic bag with a few other potentially compromising papers, and caught a trolley around the Garden Ring to the bureau of the *Baltimore Sun*. Figuring foreign press offices might escape KGB searches, he asked to hide the bag in the bureau.

In Izhevsk Andrei's parents rose and heard the news. Their first thought, too, was about evidence. They began gathering up incriminating papers: documents related to Andrei's case, papers from the new Izhevsk Democratic Club, whose meetings Nikolai Alexeyevich had been attending—who could tell now what might mean trouble? Some they destroyed, others they hid in places they thought safe from KGB inspectors. Then they settled down with the radio on, awaiting the ring at the door. "We weren't afraid for ourselves, but we were afraid for Andrei," Yevgeniya Semyonovna said later. For people of her generation, she said, the nerve of fear still lay just beneath the skin. Instantly the sense of liberation that had come in the last few years was snuffed out, an ephemeral flicker of light in a long continuum of darkness. The old instincts were still intact: when in danger, destroy or hide incriminating information.

Television, whose reach and persuasive power had put it at the heart of the information battles of the last few years, was the messenger that signaled the coup. The medium that had carried the hypercandid discussions and video exposés of Vzglyad and its offspring, that had broken the information monopoly with fierce parliamentary sessions and preelection candidates' debates, suddenly was broadcasting the same thing on all three major channels. (When a TV reporter would put a microphone to the mouth of a five-year-old Moscow kindergartner a few days later and ask what a coup was, the boy would answer without missing a beat: "That's when they show the same thing at the same time on all the channels.") Suddenly television language shifted back to the old fibs and veils, a language nearly devoid of facts but, to the veteran Soviet citizen, rich in hints and symbols. One such symbol was classical music; in 1982, 1983, and 1984 the interruption of regular programming with a somber concert had signaled the death of the party leader. Now the funereal music coming from millions of television sets watched by millions of anxious and puzzled citizens across the Soviet expanse seemed to speak of another death, the death of something more profound and powerful than one man. The music alternated with stone-faced announcers—under the gaze, it turned out, of soldiers with Kalashnikov submachine guns—reading the GKChP's turgid statements: "In connection with the inability for reasons of health for Gorbachev, Mikhail Sergeyevich, to carry out the duties of President of the USSR ... overcoming the deep and all-encompassing crisis ... chaos and anarchy ... sovereignty, territorial integrity, freedom, and independence of our Fatherland. ... sliding of society into national catastrophe ... State of Emergency in various locations in the USSR...."

For journalists, who were both agents and beneficiaries of the information revolution that had shaken the country for five years, word of the coup came like a punch in the gut. Like many privileged Muscovites, Yuri Sovtsov, an editor at the labor newspaper *Trud*, was still at his dacha outside the city on that Monday morning. He sleepily switched the TV on and saw a man playing a cello. "I thought immediately: 'Gorbachev's health has just taken a turn for the worse.' And ten minutes later the announcer came on and said just that." His first thought was about his work. "I had this feeling of horror, of revulsion. Were we really going to have to go back to trying to squeeze the truth in between the lines of what we wrote?"

Now would come the test for an epoch of change. Perhaps the sensational revelations of the press and television, the passionate election campaigns and daring parliamentary speeches, entrepreneurs' dreams of a privatized economy and republics' steps toward independence, riveting as they had been over the past five years, had been a mere distraction from the real power game. Freedom, such as it was, had been offered at first as a gift from above, switched on like a light; now perhaps the switch could be pulled again and the country plunged back into darkness.

Together, after all, the plotters seemed to represent not only the triad of party-army-KGB on which the Soviet government's enormous power traditionally rested, but the entire power structure, with no significant institution left out. On August 20 Gorbachev was scheduled to sign the Union Treaty that would drastically decentralize power, shifting the lion's share of economic and political authority from the central Soviet bureaucracy to the governments of the fifteen republics, Yeltsin's Russian Federation first of all. It was to forestall this catastrophe for the Soviet Union that the coup plotters chose to move on August 19.

On the GKChP were KGB Chairman Vladimir Kryuchkov, Defense Minister Dmitry Yazov, Internal Affairs Minister Boris Pugo, and Prime Minister Valentin Pavlov—the four men involved in the abortive power-grab in parliament in June. The committee was nominally headed by Gorbachev's second-in-command, Vice-President Gennady Yanayev, whose confirmation Gorbachev had furiously forced through a skeptical parliament less than a year earlier. Not on the GKChP but nonetheless in on the plot were a top representative of the Communist party hierarchy, Central Committee

Secretary Oleg Shenin; Gorbachev's old friend and chairman of the Soviet parliament, Anatoly Lukyanov; the KGB officer in charge of the presidential guard, Yuri Plekhanov; and even Gorbachev's chief of staff and right-hand man, Valery Boldin. Only had Gorbachev himself assented to join the crackdown, when it was presented to him as a fait accompli at his Black Sea villa the day before, could the lineup have been more complete.

Against this array of might, what chance could there be for a ragtag collection of democratic politicians and their followers, however numerous they might be? What could Yeltsin and his Russian Federation government do, who had popular backing and moral authority but no army and no security police of their own? How could a revolution of newsprint and videotape, deputies' mandates and private business deals, stand in the face of military hardware? In those first hours it seemed to many people likely that all the drama of reform would now be snuffed out instantaneously: the tanks would roll, and the leaders would lie, and the people would again grow silent.

The coup seemed to cleave the world in two that first day, posing point against counterpoint as if in recapitulation of the great political symphony that had unfolded over the previous five years. In their television images, in their use of language, in their economic principles, even in their attitudes to popular culture, the two sides seemed on the coup's first day to replay the themes of the information battles of the glasnost years.

Television beamed around the world—and to Soviet viewers, we shall see—the electrifying image of Yeltsin, with his flair for drama, climbing atop a tank to shake a defiant fist as nervous security men held up bulletproof briefcases to shield him from snipers. TV showed a diverse, growing crowd of coup resisters rallying to Yeltsin's headquarters at the Russian White House, the marble palace on the Moscow River which Brezhnev had built for the Russian Federation government. As they patched together barricades from furniture scavenged in the White House, construction materials dragged off from outside the nearby U.S. embassy, trolleybuses and telephone poles, the mood was determined but joyful. Notorious for their scowling, elbowing, cursing public persona, Muscovites had never been so nice to one another. "It was the happiest place in Moscow," Andrei Mironov said later of the atmosphere around the White House. "People had a feeling of something real taking place in their lives."

And on the other side television showed the nasty-sounding GKChP, its grey personalities lined up behind a table for a press conference, at their center the would-be president Gennady Yanayev, ashen, hands visibly trembling. Their appearance "would have made for a 'Saturday Night Live' skit if so much had not been at stake," Walter Goodman, appropriately a TV critic, later wrote in the *New York Times*. Rallying around them was no one at all, really, apart from security men with automatic weapons. After their one attempt to explain themselves, they withdrew into bickering, confusion, and alcohol, leaving no human faces to pose against those of Yeltsin and his backers.

The coup plotters' language was a throwback to the traditional Bolshevik word-magic, the "glorious destiny" to which Soviet propaganda since Stalin had referred. Over the channels of official television and radio, again and again, came their "Appeal to the Soviet People"—this people that nationalists in the republics lately said was a Communist myth, did not exist, and had never existed. "Fellow citizens!" the appeal began. "Citizens of the Soviet Union! In a grave hour, critical for the fate of the Fatherland and our peoples, we appeal to you! Above our great Native Land hangs a fatal danger!... The pride and honor of Soviet man must be restored in full measure." It hammered on the mantras of Soviet patriotism, repeating ten times the words *Rodina* (native land or motherland) and *Otechestvo* (fatherland), both capitalized when the appeal was printed in official newspapers the next day.

And in answer, Yeltsin, the leader of populist reform, fired back with a flurry of counterappeals. If the GKChP turned back to the old rhetoric of the Soviet illusion, Yeltsin tapped into the new, harsh history of Stalinism that made Russians wary of calls for the "iron fist" and the supposed peace and efficiency it would produce. "The 'order' promised to us by these newly appeared saviors of the Fatherland," Yeltsin said in his appeal to military servicemen, "will turn into concentration camps, the crushing of dissent, nighttime arrests. The 'better life' will turn out to be a propaganda trick. Clouds of terror and dictatorship are gathering above Russia."

Meanwhile, in the other republics the boldest answer to the coup came from Lithuanian President Vytautas Landsbergis, who urged other countries to seize precisely this moment to establish full diplomatic relations with independent Lithuania. Like Yeltsin, Landsbergis used the recovered history of the Stalin era to make his point, referring to the Molotov-Rippentrop Pact, the Balts' greatest victory in the propaganda war with Moscow. Foreign governments should state officially, "before it's too late," Landsbergis said in a written appeal, "that occupation of Lithuania by Soviet authorities will be a continuation of the Molotov-Ribbentrop Pact."

In economics the GKChP's specialists were Alexander Tizyakov, a powerful representative of the archipelago of secret factories and closed institutes that made up the military-industrial complex, and Vasily Starodubtsev, the loudest voice still defending collective farms, the top-down hierarchy into which Stalin had hammered agriculture. Together they stood for the two branches of the Stalinist economy, in which commands took the place of information. The GKChP's appeal promised to "raise the level of production" by restoring "labor discipline and order."

Speaking out vehemently against the coup were the leaders of the new *birzhi*, the private commodities exchanges that were multiplying around the country. The birzhi were putting information back into the economy, connecting buyers with sellers and bypassing the state bureaucracy of Gosplan, Goskomtsen, and Gossnab. "I call on all birzhi of the country to follow our example and begin a campaign of civil disobedience to the self-appointed junta. Without a free society there will be neither free trade nor private business," said Yuri Milyukov, head of the Moscow Commodities Exchange, in a statement of protest August 19. A crowd of *deeleri* and *brokeri* from the Russian Commodities Exchange, dressed in pinstripes and toting attaché cases, left the trade floor en masse, chanting anticoup slogans and carrying an enormous Russian flag on their way to defend the White House.

Even the skirmishes over the new popular culture found their reflection in the coup. The GKChP, in its long list of reasons for the state of emergency, declared, "Never in the history of the country has the propaganda of sex and violence reached such proportions, putting at risk the health and life of future generations." It was an assault on the detective novels, the video salons, the rock music lyrics, and the risqué publications that had boomed under glasnost.

Meanwhile, at the barricades outside the White House, several of the country's most famous rock groups showed up to perform gratis for the mostly young defenders. It was a gesture of self-interest as well as solidarity: rock musicians knew that the coup was not only about independence for Lithuania and multiparty elections, it was about the right of Russian youth to listen to whatever raunchy music they pleased. Along with the musicians, comedian Gennady Khazanov turned up for an impromptu performance outside the White House August 19. He felt awkward about using humor as tanks rolled around the city, but people were urging him to speak, to raise morale. Khazanov stepped out in front of the crowd, and the square was filled with the familiar voice of . . . Gorbachev. "Brothers and sisters!" Khazanov began, playing off against Gorbachev's invariable "Comrades." "I inform you that I'm feeling wonderful! And I will say as well: clean politics cannot be done with dirty, trembling hands!" The performance sent just the right message to this crowd, which was deeply distrustful of the man whose reinstatement they were demanding. We're not here to defend Gorbachev, Khazanov implied. We're here to defend our right to ridicule him or any other leader.

At 3:32 p.m. on August 19 the Russian Information Agency, an alternative to Tass sponsored by Yeltsin's Russian Federation government, carried a curious item, one that in its terse pragmatism might have said more about the nature of the coup and the resistance to it than all the contradictory reports of tank movements

and street protests that RIA carried that day. The item reads in its entirety as follows: "MOSCOW (RIA): RSFSR Secretary of State Gennady Burbulis [a top Yeltsin aide] has issued an appeal to keep all fax machines on the territory of Russia on automatic-receive mode."

The word *faks* had appeared in popular Russian only perhaps two years before; but the word, and the technology, had taken the country by storm. Now, as the coup plotters mobilized tanks, their opponents switched on their fax machines. Yeltsin faxed his appeals to newspapers, to other republics, to foreign embassies, to other cities. Landsbergis faxed his appeal to Western governments and to Lithuanian emigré groups. Milyukov, the commodities exchange man, faxed his protest to his fellow Russian capitalists; no self-respecting *beeznessman* was without a fax machine.

In the Bolsheviks' seizure of power in 1917, one of their first moves was to seize St. Petersburg's Central Telegraph Office and the Russian Telegraph Agency. Now the GKChP too seemed to keep in mind the importance of communications. They surrounded the main Moscow telephone exchange with tanks and dispatched a squad of soldiers to seize control of broadcast facilities at Ostankino. Their second resolution banned all but nine newspapers, sanctioning the more conservative publications. On a list of seventy people to be arrested first, approved by Kryuchkov at 7:20 a.m. August 19, were many key media figures, including Yegor Yakovlev, editor of *Moscow News*; Vitaly Korotich, editor of *Ogonyok*; Mikhail Poltoranin, the Yeltsin government's information minister; and Oleg Poptsov, chief of Russian TV and radio.

But in 1991, seizing control of communications was considerably more complex than it had been in 1917. The regime that had banned accurate maps until 1989, ignoring twenty years of satellite photography, did not plan well for a modern media crackdown. The information blockade imposed by the GKChP turned out to be more like a tennis net than an iron curtain.

It was a revolution driven by information that the coup was designed to halt: information that had undermined ideology, exposed the bureaucracy, and shattered the Soviet family of nations. But it was also the liberating power of information that doomed the coup to failure—both the information that over five years had changed people's views of the world, and the information that now fueled the resistance with minute-to-minute reports. People were better informed than ever before about the past consequences of totalitarianism, helping them to understand now what was at stake. Information from the thicket of new publications, by exposing the official lies of the past, produced powerful public skepticism toward the grand promises of the GKChP. Information flowed over the borders where customs agents and radio-jamming towers had so long attempted to halt it, in the form of millions of Bibles and Korans, sharp-tongued emigré newspapers, and especially the now-clear voices of Radio Liberty and other shortwave stations.

Inside Soviet borders the new information was reproduced, multiplied, amplified, and disseminated by the technology that had flooded the country. Fax machines and photocopiers, video recorders and personal computers outside the government were no longer exotica but a sprawling, living nervous system that linked the Russian political opposition, the republican independence movements, and the burgeoning private sector. Tied informally together, this equipment constituted a network of considerable scale.

At their heart the events of August had less to do than it seemed at the time with the physical trappings of battle that kept the world rapt: the snipers supposedly spotted on rooftops near the Russian White House; the handcuffs the GKChP had ordered up for its enemies; the tanks tearing up the capital's already potholed streets; the barricades built by Yeltsin's defenders, emblems of courage to be sure but likely to create no more than a few minutes' annoyance for those same tanks. Those were external symbols for an internal process. The real battle was a battle for public opinion, and it had already been lost and won—lost by the Soviet illusion, won by the dis-illusioning information that had poured out of the media. It was left to the coup simply to add up the score and reveal the outcome.

Vitaly Tretyakov, the brilliant *Moscow News* alumnus who was editor-in-chief of *Nezavisimaya Gazeta* (Independent Newspaper), wrote an "Appeal to Free Journalists of the World" the evening of August 19. "Freedom of information, the sole substantial achievement of perestroika in domestic policy, was liquidated first," he wrote. "That in itself is an answer to questions about the meaning and sense of the events taking place in the USSR. We, the journalists of *Nezavisimaya Gazeta*, banned starting today, are collecting information from the entire country but do not have the means to convey it to residents of the USSR. We compare our information with what is being broadcast by Soviet television and printed in official newspapers. Conclusion: the country has returned to the pre-1985 era."

The analysis was right, but it was soon clear that the conclusion was wrong. This was not pre-1985. Tretyakov himself disproved it by faxing not only his appeal but the entire banned edition of *Nezavisimaya Gazeta* on August 20 to Paris, where it was published in a 100,000-copy French edition. Thousands more copies of an "emergency issue" were run off on photocopiers at the State Library for Foreign Literature, an overnight revival of the dissidents' old practice.

Other banned newspapers responded with similar feisty creativity. *Demokraticheskaya Rossiya*, which had headlined its prescient "plot" warning the previous June, was printed at the Russian Ministry of Education. *Moskovsky Komsomolets* got out five photocopied issues. *Moscow News* was offered such an embarrassment of alternative printing facilities that it later ran an official thank-you note: "August 19–21 we expected at any hour that the KGB would burst into the *MN* editorial offices, lock up our photocopiers, cut off our fax machines and telephones.... That's why our friends and like-thinkers rushed to offer help." But the KGB never burst in, and *Moscow News* joined with ten other banned periodicals in the joint publication of *Obshchaya Gazeta* (Shared Newspaper) starting August 20.

In Leningrad, Mayor Anatoly Sobchak, after Yeltsin the most prominent democratic politician in the country, worked to ensure the publication of newspapers containing Yeltsin's appeals and decrees. "The illegal information blockade will be broken," he told a late-night news conference August 19, using a word with potent emotional associations in Leningrad since the nine-hundred-day German blockade. The Leningrad daily *Nevskoye Vremya* (Neva

Times) supplemented its own editions with eighteen one-page bulletins distributed free on the streets August 19 and 20.

The airwaves too were saturated with opposition viewpoints. Ekho Moskvy, the rock station, managed to return to the air five times despite several visits from the KGB. The Yeltsin government set up a low-powered AM station called Radio White House, recruiting such star announcers as the hosts of the hit TV shows Vzglyad and Fifth Wheel. Radio Liberty's young Soviet reporters set up shop on the eleventh floor of the White House, broadcasting around the clock.

Thousands of Muscovites got an accurate account of events because their television sets could pick up a slightly fuzzy picture of CNN from the microwave relay that served the Kremlin, the Foreign Ministry, and some hotels. "The morning of August 19, about 8 a.m., when they cut off Ekho Moskvy, the situation [of those trying to follow events] seemed almost hopeless," wrote Moscow media critic Lydia Polskaya. "You couldn't listen endlessly to the 'appeal' of Yanayev! But at about 10 a.m., without any hope, I pushed the button for the fourth channel, where I can get CNN, and I was stunned: there were the Americans working as if nothing had happened.... That's how I survived for three days, knowing for certain what was happening not far from my home."

Nowhere was information control complete, not even in the most staid party-loyal media. Sergei Medvedev, a boyish TV reporter who was scheduled to be the anchor on the main evening news show, Vremya, the night of August 19, arrived at work to discover that he had been replaced. Medvedev was no rebel, but TV boss Leonid Kravchenko wanted an even more reliable comrade for the first night's broadcast. Freed from his anchor duties, Medvedev teamed up with a cameraman and hit the streets, filming demonstrators on Manege Square beside the Kremlin, Yeltsin's denunciation of the coup, and the growing crowd of protesters at the Russian White House. "We didn't especially hurry back, frankly, because we were sure they wouldn't let our material on the air," Medvedev recalled later. But to his astonishment he was told to get the footage ready. Even as the Vremya announcer that evening spoke of broad support for the state of emergency, four minutes of Medvedev's video dramatized the opposition. Half the members of the GKChP called to complain, but the damage to their cause was done.

Trud's Yuri Sovtsov and his staff, many of whom were ashamed that their paper had not been banned, decided to write up the resistance to the coup and include it in the next day's edition. Believing they were defying the junta, the *Trud* editors were astonished when the issue passed uncensored to the printer, so that millions of readers the next day saw on the front page of *Trud* not only the GKChP's statements and appeals but also Yeltsin's denunciation of the "anticonstitutional" seizure of power, his call for a general strike, and a description of the barricades at the White House. Even in *Pravda*, of all places, the attentive reader could find (buried in a meandering article on page 2) word of Yeltsin's strike call.

In the early hours of August 21 Radio Liberty reported the coup's first and only casualties—three young men killed while trying to block tanks they believed were headed for the White House. Andrei Mironov was listening in his apartment. "I felt ashamed to be inside while people were dying," he said later. He left the building and began heading around the Garden Ring toward the American embassy, where the bloodshed was reported. To his surprise he found dozens of young people headed in the same direction, having heard the news the same way. He was moved, he said, that people were running toward the scene of the violence, not away from it. "People were angry," he said. "If more people had been killed, I think it's possible that all Moscow would have risen up against the junta."

As in the case of these Radio Liberty reports, the media were having an instantaneous impact on the actual situation on the ground in Moscow and other Soviet cities. A remarkable series of feedback loops were in operation. CNN cameras were broadcasting live pictures from outside the Russian White House via satellite to Atlanta studios; from there the pictures were broadcast back via satellite and were picked up in Moscow by the television center at Ostankino; from Ostankino the pictures went by microwave to the paying customers in Moscow hotels, the Kremlin, and so on; and on the way the signal was intercepted by Muscovites who had the right kind of antenna and TV set—and who in some cases were inspired by what they saw to join the crowd at the White House.

Likewise, a reporter for Radio Liberty would speak through a telephone inside the White House directly to the station's Munich studios. His voice would be beamed back to the Soviet Union, where it would crackle out of shortwave receivers all over the country— including some in the White House offices down the corridor from where the reporter was speaking.

Every cycle of the feedback loop amplified and encouraged the resistance to the coup. For instance: Yeltsin climbed on the tank August 19 to defy the junta. His image went to thousands of Muscovites via CNN, his words to more thousands via photocopied leaflets and the White House radio station, prompting thousands more to join the protest. News of Yeltsin's and the crowds' resistance and the peaceful response of the troops reached millions via short-wave radio, Sergei Medvedev's video on Vremya, and the newspapers; and by the second day the crowd at the White House ballooned to more than fifty thousand. Now shortwave and the newspapers were carrying the reports of large-scale resistance and of the continued failure of the troops to attack the demonstrators or the White House. Such news encouraged more demonstrations in other cities and may well have prompted certain key politicians who had responded cautiously at first to denounce the coup publicly. The combined effect of the media was to create a community of resistance from millions of isolated people who, in the absence of knowledge of the events in Moscow, might have been merely puzzled.

Leonid Ionin, writing a few weeks later in *Nezavisimaya Gazeta*, concluded that the importance of the media, especially shortwave, could not be overstated: "Radio Liberty and the BBC defeated the KGB and the CPSU [Communist party]. . . . If the high-level plotters had followed the tested recipe of General Yaruzelski [in declaring martial law in Poland]—seized the newspapers, radio stations, television, cut off the telephones and isolated the White House from Moscow, and Moscow from the rest of the Soviet Union and the world—they would likely have succeeded. Any other way, they were doomed."

It was telling that the country's top pollsters, at the All-Union Center for the Study of Public Opinion which had pioneered this neglected science since it opened in 1988, leaped upon the opportunity presented by the coup. Already on the evening of August 19 they were conducting a telephone poll on the day's events—and incidentally demonstrating to those they called that the crackdown had not stopped or deterred pollsters. By the end of the evening of August 20 the center's interviewers had talked to a representative sample of 4,567 people in ten cities and four republics. The next day their results were being faxed around the country. Like the journalists, the pollsters went about their work with defiant determination and were surprised to find that no one interfered. "We didn't know if we'd exist the next day or not," veteran pollster Yuri Levada told me afterward, "but we just kept working."

Their results offer an interesting snapshot of the public state of mind. About 1 in 5 respondents backed the coup, considering it legal and believing it would lead to economic improvement. About 3 in 5 strongly opposed it, declaring it illegal and likely to lead to economic disaster and mass repression. Even these numbers may understate the real opposition to the coup, for two reasons: especially on August 19, an ordinary resident of the provinces may have believed Gorbachev really was ill and the takeover legal; and some respondents, uncertain about the identity of the pollster, may have been afraid to criticize the coup.

Why were the pollsters able to make their calls? Why were reporters permitted to roam and film? Why were newspapers and television allowed to inform the public of Yeltsin's resistance? Why, indeed, was Yeltsin left free and unharmed? Why did the *putchisti* not secure the White House and other potential resistance headquarters at dawn on August 19? Why did they not seal the borders, halt the trains, and close the airports? Perhaps most important, why did they not mow down the first thousand protesters who dared appear in the streets?

Those questions remain at the heart of the mystery of this clumsy, amateurish affair. Surely one explanation is incompetence, compounded by haste, secrecy, and disunity among the GKChP, two of whose key members, Pavlov and Yanayev, seem to have been drunk by the second day. A regime that lost a third of each year's harvest on the way to market and made the queue a national institution would not necessarily prove more competent in carrying out a coup d'état.

There was another, more important reason: though the world adopted the journalistic shorthand of calling them hard-liners, the coup leaders were not all so ruthless as the name implies. They were Gorbachev's appointees, after all, and for the most part they remained loyal to the original goals of Communist reform. They had not moved to shut off glasnost or to stop the 1989 elections or to preserve the party's legal monopoly on power in 1990. Only the prospect of the dissolution of the union drove them to action. "Their maximum aim was to roll back the videotape three to four years," the political observer Leonid Radzikhovsky wrote later.

Of course the coup might well have taken its own, bloody course, and Kryuchkov and Pugo, the policemen, seemed especially cool about the possible necessity of taking lives. Nonetheless this junta led off not with a bloodbath but with a press conference. Their "Appeal to the Soviet People" promised not only "labor discipline" and "law and order" but "truly democratic processes," "consistent political reform," and even "private entrepreneurship." However disingenuous, the rhetoric reflected the Communist reformers' persistent belief in the possibility of partial reform: free elections in a one-party system; innovation and competition in a state-run economy; "sovereign" republics that obeyed Moscow; glasnost, in Gorbachev's phrase, in the interests of socialism. The GKChP lacked the will of true Stalinists: Stalin was willing to kill wholesale, and for nothing; the putchisti preferred not to.

Ultimately, however, what guaranteed the coup's almost bloodless collapse was insubordination in the military and the KGB. Had a poll on the coup been taken among those in uniform, it would have revealed a profound split, possibly one not so different from that in the public at large. Soldiers and secret policemen too had been reading Ogonyok and watching Vzglyad, listening to the comedians

Zadornov and Khazanov, and taking in such films as *Malenkaya Vera* and *Tak Zhit Nelzya*. They too had learned a great deal from the press, and undoubtedly it had influenced their views. The young Izhevsk KGB man who had told us he voted for Yeltsin was far from alone.

Orders, it turned out, had been issued for the arrest of Yeltsin and other democratic leaders and for the storming of the White House. But enough officers, at high enough levels, were so skeptical or hostile to the coup that they were prepared, at enormous personal risk, to delay carrying out orders, to disobey them, or even to join the resistance. The presence of tens of thousands of people around the White House obviously raised the stakes for these officers, making clear that the use of force to carry out the junta's orders would come at a very high price in civilian blood.

While still at his dacha outside Moscow on the morning of August 19, Yeltsin phoned General Pavel Grachev, commander of Soviet paratroopers—the Afghan War hero with whom just two months earlier he had watched the war games outside Tula. Grachev readily agreed to provide some troops to protect the Russian leadership. By Monday night the White House was surrounded by light tanks from Tula's 106th Airborne Division, commanded by another officer Yeltsin had met during his visit, Major General Alexander Lebed. Their guns were pointed outward. By Tuesday Grachev and General Yevgeny Shaposhnikov, commander of the Soviet air force, having revealed to one another their disgust at the coup, were already hatching wild plans to foil it. They considered dropping troops into the Kremlin by parachute to arrest the junta. They even discussed unleashing air strikes on the Kremlin in the event an attack on the White House was imminent. "Say there was an order to storm [the White House]," Shaposhnikov recounted later. "I go to them with an ultimatum: 'Cancel the order. If in ten minutes I don't show up at [the air force command post], or call there, bombers will fly here and nothing is going to be left of us. Hey, it's the air force!' "

Another crucial act of insubordination came on the part of the KGB's Group Alpha, the elite commandos who were instructed to prepare to seize the White House. They refused, according to

several authoritative accounts. After Viktor Shatskikh, the young
KGB lieutenant, was killed in Vilnius the previous January, no one
from the KGB leadership had bothered to meet the plane that
returned his body to Moscow or to attend his funeral. When the
press revealed Group Alpha's role, whoever had given them their
orders that night in Vilnius—whether Gorbachev, Kryuchkov, or
someone else—remained silent, leaving the young soldiers alone to
bear the brunt of public revulsion. For the soldiers the incident and
its aftermath "probably was the last straw," a *Komsomolskaya Pravda*
investigation concluded.

Others in the lower ranks of the KGB actively took the side of
Yeltsin. KGB officers opposed to the coup made available a special
communications network that permitted statements from the Russian White House to reach six hundred key addressees; prepared
printing facilities; provided access to weapons caches; and offered to
hide official Russian government documents. Former KGB officers
who had opened private businesses reportedly collected one million
rubles in cash and delivered the money to the White House.

The papers the morning of August 21 contained the
GKChP's detailed resolution on muzzling the media, halting cable
TV, singling out the Ekho Moskvy radio station, revoking broadcast
journalists' accreditations, and so on. But the papers were on the
street only a few hours when the Soviet radio channel called *Mayak*
(Lighthouse) suddenly reversed course. "From the very beginning of
the coup we were deprived of the chance to transmit honest and
objective information about the tragic events taking place in the
country," the announcement said. Now, it said, "we shall try to
inform you fully and accurately." It concluded with a barb for the
bosses: "We hope that our desire to remove the current discredited
heads of radio and television broadcasting acccords with yours." On
the Russian Television channel, also suddenly restored, a news
anchor reported with joyous sarcasm the likely dismissal of "that
man beloved by us and treasured by you TV viewers, Leonid
Petrovich Kravchenko."

By that night Gorbachev was back in the capital, regaling journalists with tales of his own exploitation of information technology. He had followed events from his Foros dacha on the foreign "radio voices" he had once scorned, BBC, Radio Liberty, and the Voice of America. He had filmed his denunciation of the coup on videotape, which was divided into four parts and smuggled out of the besieged vacation home. Yet, oblivious to the public state of mind, he bewildered and exasperated his liberators by using the occasion of his press conference the next day to swear his fealty to socialism and the October Revolution and to lecture the more outspoken newspapers for "rudeness and vulgarity." Gorbachev showed the same peculiar combination of vision and blindness that were responsible for both perestroika and the coup. A few days later, in *Moscow News*, reform journalist Pavel Gutiontov replied: Precisely the publications Gorbachev was scolding "had warned the president of the mistakes he now has been forced to confess himself. Precisely they defended the policies proclaimed by Gorbachev—even when it became necessary to defend them from Gorbachev himself."

The morning of August 19 Andrei Mironov and his parents had been hiding documents they feared might put people in danger. By the morning of August 22 the tide had reversed. In the headquarters of the general staff at the Ministry of Defense, in the Lubyanka, and at the Communist Party Central Committee, paper shredders were operating at full volume, destroying the documents that could reveal the cooperation of hundreds of officials in the coup.

Galina Starovoitova, a liberal member of parliament, told a story that seemed to capture why the coup collapsed. Starovoitova was in London on August 19, visiting a publisher for whom she was writing a book. On that Monday morning, she said, she got a message faxed to the publisher from a friendly KGB officer in the Lubyanka. It informed her that the coup had taken place and advised her not to return home for the time being, because she was No. 8 on the list of those to be arrested. She accordingly delayed her return—but went on BBC's Russian broadcast service to urge resistance to the coup.

The episode captures so much change: an anti-Communist politician, elected in a contested election, travels freely abroad to publish a book, receives a fax, from a dissident KGB agent, and speaks to her fellow citizens via an unjammed foreign shortwave station. Each of these elements alone stands for a Soviet galaxy of change; together they describe a transformed universe. Many insiders in Russia and experts abroad had suggested that a hard-line coup could succeed because of the absence of any democratic tradition, the fear of disorder, the yearning for strong-arm leadership, for *zheleznaya ruka*, the iron hand. Promise the people sausage and order, *poryadok*, these people thought, and they'll gladly part with their elections, their newspapers, the other frills of freedom. But they were wrong.

Unnoticed, the old Russian boundary between us and them, *my* and *oni*, had broken down. Even the army and KGB, confronted with this stark choice of pronouns, divided. It is an interesting irony that the members of the GKChP may have overestimated their chances for success precisely because they were more isolated from the changes bubbling away around the country than most of the population. Seeing the people through the windows of their speeding Zil limousines, they moved to stop the revolution, unaware that the revolution had already taken place. People at the top of the Soviet pyramid, for so long the information monopolists, were peculiarly blind to the transformation of minds that information had carried out.

In a postcoup interview with Yevgeny Shaposhnikov, soon to be defense chief of the Commonwealth of Independent States, *Nezavisimaya Gazeta* asked: What stopped the coup?

"Here's what I think," Shaposhnikov answered. "Everything came together. All told—excuse me for my banality—it was the times themselves that stopped it." It was the right answer.

It became a cliché to describe the days and weeks following the collapse of the coup with the quite appropriate metaphor of the videorecorder: history on fast-forward. The crowds around the Lubyanka, who in 1989 had encircled the building in a candlelight vigil and in 1990 had placed their memorial stone, now finally toppled the statue of Felix Dzerzhinsky. Andrei Mironov told me he watched the operation with mixed feelings—euphoria at the symbolic defeat for the KGB, but regret at the implied rejection of history. As a former museum restorationist, he said, he wanted to see all the trappings of communism preserved. As Bolshevik monuments fell across the country and the Communist party dissolved, it was a drama not of revolution but of resolution. Processes that had begun some years before were simply brought to a swift, decisive completion. Everything that was bound to happen happened faster because of the clarity created by the last spasm of the old order.

Within a couple of weeks of the coup's failure, the entire Soviet era in Russian history could be felt to be receding swiftly into the past. In a quiet, sunlit park beside the Central House of Artists opposite Gorky Park, the great iron and stone statues that had been removed from their pedestals were dumped in random disarray. The park became part museum, part playground. At the beginning of September I watched parents posing their children for snapshots on Sverdlov's ample lap or jumping from the head of the prone Dzerzhinsky. A radio reporter crawled into the base of the Dzerzhinsky statue for a unique, echoing interview. The atmosphere was contemplative and cheerful, not angry.

At the Museum of the (other) Revolution, canny employees hustled together an exhibition on the *August* Revolution, a rush job that undoubtedly owed something to the workers' hope to preserve their jobs. Nikita Petrov, an amateur historian of the KGB and friend of Andrei Mironov who in 1985 had been repeatedly interrogated, was appointed to a commission assigned to review the archives of the Moscow KGB. He was soon gloriously immersed in arcane documents, though he was uneasy about what his own file might reveal about unsuspected informants among his friends. T-shirts appeared with the slogan "I survived the coup." Lapel buttons, at 1 ruble, 58 kopecks, identified the purchaser (truthfully or otherwise) as a "Defender of the White House."

Andrei Mironov and I took a stroll around my neighborhood the day before I left, to say goodbye. We stopped in the headquarters of Memorial, the anti-Stalinist group, to read the bulletin board. There was an announcement of a newfangled veterans' organization: the

Union of Defenders of the Russian White House. There was a handwritten poem, lightly mocking Gorbachev:

TO THE PRISONER OF THE CASTLE OF FOROS

In August the Crimean landscape is stunning;
The waves froth at the cliffs.
If you name your friends as your deputies,
You can consider your vacation a total loss.

Andrei said he had no plans to change his line of work—part-time translator, part-time political activist. "I think I'll have lots to do," Andrei said. "If before there were lots of violations of human rights and little you could do about them, now there may be fewer violations, but there's more you can do." We speculated about the future—relations between the republics, prospects for economic change, the spectre of fascism. It was an uncertain but optimistic moment.

Outside, on Petrovskaya Street, the big glass display case inscribed "Leading Workers of the Sverdlovsk District" was empty, its marble base crumbling, the poster-sized photographs of unsmiling local heroes removed. It seemed an ironic comment, as if to say: There are no Leading Workers here; the old heroes are gone, the new heroes not yet arrived. Across the street, Petrovka 38, Moscow's once-infamous police headquarters, looked physically unchanged. But inside the new chief of police was Arkady Murashyov, the physicist and liberal parliamentarian whom I had watched three years earlier denouncing the one-party system in a televised candidate debate. Murashyov acknowledged cheerfully his complete ignorance of crime-fighting; it was as if Mr. Rogers had been appointed chief of the FBI. People-watching now was an inexhaustible entertainment. As we sat and chatted, a striking blonde-haired young woman walked by, wearing a sweatshirt with an inscription mocking the KGB; in the other direction passed a gentleman in the full, traditional dress of the Cossacks, presumably off to lobby for the newly discovered cause of Cossack rights.

The old identifying placards were gone from the Sverdlovsk *raikom*, the district Communist party committee building from which the district had been run until not long before. Next to the front door was a new sign identifying the building's new use: Committee for the Privatization of Municipal Property. Their mission was presumably to throw into reverse the old Bolshevik slogan: Expropriate the expropriators! But a piece of paper had been taped to the door, one whose scribbled message would console those who mourned the passing of the Soviet way of life.

"For technical reasons," the note said, "the committee is not working."

Epilogue

Information and Russia's Future

[Allied victory in World War II] will produce no lasting solution of the minority problems in the European jigsaw puzzle. It will provide no cure for the inherent disease of the capitalistic system. It will not mark a decisive step in the ascent of the human race. But it will bring enormous temporary relief to the people of the Continent, it will bring salvation to millions whose life seemed doomed, and a certain minimum of liberty, decency, security.... That means we are beginning to realize that this war is not the final cataclysm, not the ultimate showdown between the forces of darkness and light, but perhaps only the beginning of a new series of convulsions, spread over a much larger period of history than we originally thought, until the new world is born.

> —Arthur Koestler, "Knights in Rusty Armor," 1943

When we say we are rehabilitating somebody, graciously forgiving them for certain errors of past years, all this, it seems to me, smacks of hypocrisy. It is not them whom we are forgiving but ourselves.

> —Alexander Yakovlev, on the official rehabilitation of victims of Soviet oppression, August 1990

I don't want to repeat the old mistakes. I want to make new mistakes. I love making new mistakes.

> —Sviatoslav Fyodorov, eye surgeon, entrepreneur, and former Central Committee member, 1991

In the harrowing world imagined by George Orwell in *Nineteen Eighty-Four*, every home contains a two-way "telescreen" that bombards the citizens of Oceania with propaganda while keeping an eye on their every movement and an ear on their every word. Winston Smith, the novel's battered hero, skulks nervously about his own apartment, fearful that the telescreen may catch him in some impolitic action or subversive remark. "Day and night, the telescreens bruised your ears with statistics proving that people today had more food, more clothes, better houses, better recreations—that they lived longer, worked shorter hours, were bigger, healthier, stronger, happier, more intelligent, better educated, than the people of fifty years ago," Orwell wrote. "Not a word of it could ever be proved or disproved." Such antiinformation is produced by the Ministry of Truth, "whose primary job was not just to reconstruct the past but to supply the citizens of Oceania with newspapers, films, textbooks, telescreen programs, plays, novels—with every conceivable kind of information, instruction, or entertainment, from a statute to a slogan, from a lyric poem to a biological treatise, and from a child's spelling book to a Newspeak dictionary."

One day Winston Smith stumbles across an old newspaper clipping, accidentally preserved, about three political leaders who have long ago been purged from life and history. The news photograph and its caption instantly expose the official version of history as a monstrous distortion, a tapestry of lies: "This was concrete evidence; it was a fragment of the abolished past, like a fossil bone which turns up in the wrong stratum and destroys a geological theory. It was enough to blow the Party to atoms, if in some way it could have been published to the world and its significance made known." But far from hoping to publish the scrap of newsprint, Smith is terrified that the telescreen will observe him reading it. He manages discreetly to drop the clipping to be burned in the "memory hole" that has incinerated a people's collective memory. The totalitarian system triumphs.

Orwell's invented Oceania borrowed many features from the Bolshevik experiment in the Soviet Union as well as from what seemed to him the ominous political potential of the emerging technology of television. So it is a remarkable historical irony that he set the novel almost in the very year when the Soviet Union began to reverse its course, unraveling what might be called, in the Western cliché that grew from *Nineteen Eighty-Four*, the most Orwellian elements of propaganda and information control. Far from propping up the state, the "telescreen" and its electronic progeny played a central role in undermining official ideology and breaking up the Soviet empire. It was as if Winston Smith's long-censored newspaper scrap had been published after all and had indeed demonstrated the power to "blow the Party to atoms."

Had he lived to see it, the demise of the Soviet colossus might have been a satisfying vindication for Eric Blair, the British socialist who wrote under the pen name George Orwell. Blair came to believe that, as he once wrote, "the destruction of the Soviet myth was essential if we wanted a revival of the Socialist movement." So in 1945 in *Animal Farm* he produced a bitter allegory of the purges and betrayals of the first twenty-five years of Soviet history. Four years later, in *Nineteen Eighty-Four*, he extrapolated the Soviet system to a sinister imaginative conclusion. Though neither book mentions the Soviet Union, and *Nineteen Eighty-Four* is ostensibly set in a future Britain, Soviet censors didn't miss the point. In the mid-1980s *Animal Farm* and *Nineteen Eighty-Four* were among the forbidden books that Andrei Mironov and his friends secretly photocopied. By the end of the 1980s they had been published for the first time in Russia and were for sale on Moscow's book tables.

Was Orwell wrong, then, that electronic technology would inevitably enhance the power of the state over the citizen? It is a tantalizing conclusion. The last years of the Soviet Union demonstrated that information technology could be turned to unpredictable ends, and the course of events seemed to turn Orwell's thesis on its head. Such shows as Vzglyad demonstrated that television could undermine state ideology as efficiently as it could promote it. Mass-circulation newspapers could print the same contents in twenty million copies, but if the articles were accurate accounts of long-distorted historical events, the effect could be liberating. Meanwhile, the exploding arsenal of electronics—cellular telephones, fax machines, VCRs, satellite dishes, computers with modems—demonstrated a trend for technology to become more compact, portable, versatile, and inexpensive. As such, the new machines seemed to be weapons the citizen could wield against the state as readily as the state could use them on the citizen.

Evidence for the revolutionary political power of electronics was to be found far beyond the borders of the USSR. The shah of Iran was overthrown in 1979 partly as a result of Iranian magnitizdat, the circulation of audiocassettes of Ayatollah Khomeini. Underground videocassettes linking Filipino security forces to the murder of dissident Benigno Aquino in 1983 fueled resistance to the regime of Ferdinand Marcos, contributing to his ouster three years later. Amateur video footage of Los Angeles police officers beating Rodney King in 1991 set off a fierce controversy over police brutality, dramatizing the fact that citizens could use video to reverse Orwell's Big Brother and keep an eye on the wayward agents of government. The Thai middle class effectively defeated a military crackdown in 1992 by exploiting electronics in what was dubbed by the *New York Times* a "cellular telephone revolution."

From such events it is possible to build a case for a kind of future information utopia, a borderless world in which semiconductors empower the masses and check authoritarian power. Some writers have sketched such a possibility. In *The Twilight of Sovereignty* Walter B. Wriston argues not only that "the information age is rapidly giving the power to the people" but also that "modern information technology is...driving nation-states toward cooperation with each other so that the world's work can get done." Other writers argue that video technology naturally leads toward democracy or even that in the information era, war is becoming obsolete.

But there is plenty of evidence that humanity will resist the pull of electronic paradise. The real lessons of the role of information in the Soviet collapse are mixed and tentative. On the one hand, surely the kind of information control exercised by the Soviet state until about 1987, including severe restrictions on some of the most important new technologies of the century, has been shown to be incompatible with economic strength. Information and its technology proved their power to undermine totalitarian states of the Soviet type by sowing doubt, eroding faith, exposing falsehood, and uniting dissidents. Certainly fax and cable and videotape made it tougher to protect official news and history from the competition of facts from other sources. Once the highest authorities cracked the door to information from closed archives and the outside world, a highly educated and literate population was eager to take it in.

Yet the achievement, while momentous, was negative in character: a revolution that cleared the space for new developments but did not dictate what those developments might be. Outraged Communists who accused Vzglyad and *Moscow News* of being "destructive" were absolutely right. Information demonstrated an awesome capacity for destruction of the existing order—but no equivalent capacity for creation. "I know more, therefore I doubt more," Montaigne wrote; it is the nature of information to undermine authority, whether that authority is the state, or a religion, or an ideology, or a parent. The moral landscape and public mood in Russia were far bleaker two years after the Soviet demise than during the dynamic, hopeful two years that preceded it. The void that resulted from the shattering of Leninist faith and Stalinist control could, and did, accommodate not only productive markets but brazen crime, not only democratic politics but violent nationalism.

Indeed, the most troubling obstacle that stood between the information revolution's destruction of Communist rule and the vision of future democratic prosperity was primitive ethnic chauvinism. To the surprise of nearly every observer in West and East, ethnic conflict made a mockery of the promise of postcommunism, not only in former Yugoslavia but in a half-dozen former Soviet republics. The rubble of Bosnia and Georgia and Tajikistan, the thousands of refugees in the Balkans, Transcaucasia, and Central Asia, are a dispiriting dissent from epochal optimism about the consequences when faxes and television do away with the police state. Tribal warfare, unleashed in part by information's destruction of the old regime, has been shown capable of turning a modern city into a wasteland where faxes and television do not function and even the water supply and the medical system fall apart.

The Leninist dogma, as articulated by generations of Soviet ideologists, had been for many people a comforting faith. When it was dashed, some retreated to the old verities of territory and ethnicity. *Eto nasha zemlya!* It's our land! It was a phrase in Russian, *lingua franca* of the crumbling Communist empire, that I heard pronounced passionately with two dozen or more accents: Estonians talking about the Russian-dominated port city of Narva; Armenians waxing emotional about Nagorno-Karabakh, the mountainous patch of Azerbaijan over which war would rage for years; Abkhazians vowing to defend their stunning piece of the Black Sea coast against the claims of Georgians; Nenets natives of Siberia speaking of the taiga and tundra that Russian oilmen had despoiled—the list was endless. The furious absolutism of their territorial claims erupted in many places in bloodshed that pitted neighbor against neighbor and seemed sometimes to baffle even the combatants. Far from the "twilight of sovereignty," the phrase "parade of sovereignty" became part of the political lexicon in the early 1990s, as not only former Soviet republics but restive provinces, pockets of ethnic minorities, and even Moscow neighborhoods solemnly declared their "sovereignty." Rather than the borderless world promised by the futurists, new borders were appearing, complete with customs posts and armed guards and visa requirements, around every former Soviet socialist republic.

It was true, of course, that as the Soviet order crumbled, so did the walls, literal and figurative, that cut the USSR and its satellites off from the rest of the world. A person could watch CNN in St. Petersburg (the original name of Peter the Great's window to the West, restored by popular vote late in 1991); Ukraine could contribute troops to United Nations peacekeeping missions; Azerbaijan could entertain competing bids from multinational oil companies prospecting for crude. Yet what if what CNN showed was civil war between former Communists and Islamic insurgents in Tajikistan? What if the Ukrainian troops were dispatched by the UN to the cauldron of ethnic enmity in Bosnia? What if the oil companies were scared off from Azerbaijan by its interminable conflict with

Armenia? The tribal and the global, seemingly opposite trends, were running in tandem.

Despite our wishful thinking, technology remains a maddeningly neutral tool, as it has been since man discovered that fire could preserve life or destroy it. The Soviet television tower at Ostankino could broadcast with equal efficiency the numbing speeches of Brezhnev or the electrifying iconoclasm of Vzglyad. Once mocked as a hypodermic needle for ideological inoculations, the tower proved itself to be as impartial as a real hypodermic, which can produce either addiction or vaccination. The microchip is no panacea; utopia, it is worth remembering, literally means "no place."

The Soviet Union shaped the century's American politics, from the allied intervention in the Russian civil war, to the strange bedfellows of the anti-Hitler coalition, to the Red Scares, domino theories, basement bomb shelters, and budget-busting military spending of the cold war. When the Soviet state ceased to exist at the end of 1991, such backwardness and disgrace marked its passing that it was hard to remember that for most of its seven decades it was far from a forgone conclusion that Soviet communism would perish while American capitalism—and European capitalism, and Asian capitalism—survived, and not the other way around. But one system was equipped to ride the wave of economic and political change that information technology brought. The other used its elaborate system of dikes and dams to keep the information wave out. When it opened the dikes slightly in the late 1980s, it was swiftly overwhelmed.

American society is as saturated with information as Soviet society was starved of it. But certain common patterns of behavior can be detected even in these disparate countries. Not only in the Soviet Union but in every developed country, the United States included, government and people are engaged in a constant battle over information, one that waxes and wanes in intensity and prominence but never disappears. By tradition, law, and ideology, the Soviet government had an overwhelming advantage over Soviet citizens in the struggle over information, and the Russian government has inherited a modified version of that advantage. American law and tradition run the other way, and the American people often prevail in the battle for information over the American government.

The difference, however, albeit huge, is one of degree. American history includes not only the Bill of Rights but the Sedition Act of 1798, which could be used to imprison anyone who dared "write, print, utter or publish . . . any false, scandalous and malicious writing or writings against the government of the United States." American schools and scholars still struggle to do justice to the portrayal of the history of Native Americans and African Americans, since what was taught in the past was selective, tendentious, or untrue. This century includes not only Supreme Court decisions that strongly affirm the public's right to information but the disinformation and censorship that were guiding principles of McCarthyism and of J. Edgar Hoover's half-century reign at the FBI. Many of the major debacles in recent American history involved to one degree or another government's ability to keep information secret: Vietnam, FBI harassment of civil rights and antiwar activists, Watergate, the Iran-Contra affair, even the savings-and-loan collapse.

Conversely, information carried by television and other media has played a crucial role in watershed events in the century's American politics. In the early 1960s, television pictures of police attacking peaceful demonstrators in the South fed the groundswell of support in the North for the civil rights movement. A decade later, television images of combat in Vietnam were critical fuel for the antiwar movement. In both cases, as in the Soviet experience, television was an amplifier for a grassroots movement, empowering citizens in their struggle with state power. But the state learns from its battles, and the combat continues. Restrictions on the movements and actions of reporters during the Persian Gulf War were far greater than those in effect in Vietnam—in part, surely, because of lessons the Pentagon had learned from Vietnam. Among the consequences were that published information on the total number of Iraqi dead remained contradictory and incomplete while the U.S. media initially accepted exaggerated military claims for the performance of "smart bombs" and Patriot missiles. Despite press-friendly laws, aggressive and well-endowed media, and a culture that rewards journalists who question the government, the American public still is sometimes deprived of adequate information on important issues.

Americans were captivated by Soviet glasnost partly because it showed the raw power of information to change minds, spark debate, motivate people. Poverty, for instance, whose existence within Soviet borders had been denied for so long, suddenly was exposed for the first time. The papers and crusading television shows were filled with interviews with homeless people living in Moscow bus and train stations, exposés of infant mortality in rural Central Asia, and portraits of elderly Siberian villagers who survived almost exclusively on bread. People were scandalized by these reports, ashamed of the poverty, angry that their government had covered it up. To an American such a furor seemed both refreshing and naive. Citizens of the far richer United States are so used to information about poverty in their own country that it often seems to numb rather than shock. In the ocean of information that laps at Americans from the media—news, entertainment, and advertising from newspapers, magazines, and dozens of TV channels—even the most remarkable fact is at hazard of getting lost. Jonathan Kozol, documenting in his 1991 book *Savage Inequalities* the gap between rich and poor American public schools, acknowledged that he was far from the first to expose these disturbing inequities. "Even the most thorough exposition of the facts within the major organs of the press is neutralized too frequently by context and a predilection for the type of grayish language that denies the possibilities for indignation," Kozol wrote. "Facts are cited. Editorials are written. Five years later, the same facts are cited once again. There is no sense of moral urgency; and nothing changes." It is a useful reminder that information sometimes proves impotent against entrenched political and economic power. But is it just the "grayish language"? Is it not also the very volume of information Americans are exposed to, which can make all the competing problems seem overwhelming, permanent, and insoluble? Facts in the Soviet Union had political power because of their novelty, which by definition could not last.

The feisty and diverse press, radio, and television that developed between 1987 and 1991 were one of the most vital legacies of Soviet reform to the post-Soviet republics. A few republics swiftly squandered the gift, clamping down on local media. But in the reemerging Russian state the media remained a power to be reckoned with, greatly strengthening the hand of the public in its struggle with government for information. Given the long history of government control of media, occasional assaults on the independence of the press are to be expected, and the tendency to clamp down on the media at the first sign of political crisis lives on. Television in particular is susceptible by its very nature to government control and manipulation, since creating an independent TV network is far more difficult than opening an independent newspaper. But a generation of journalists has worked for years now largely un-fettered, and it will not relinquish its freedom without a fight. Plenty of politicians and citizens will defend their right to know what is happening at home and abroad. Short of a prolonged campaign of force and intimidation, the Russian media will not return to anything like their subservience of the pre-glasnost period.

Yet as the Soviet Union receded into history, popular interest in the media sharply declined. Already by 1992 the huge, rapt audiences for history and politics in the likes of periodicals such as *Ogonyok* and television shows such as Vzglyad, circa 1988–1991, had shrunk dramatically. The huge public appetite for information, of course, was bound to fade: the tenth or twentieth television show on the Gulag or street crime or corrupt politicians naturally was less sensational than the first. The feast that followed a long famine had to come to an end. Simultaneously the advent of free prices for paper, printing, and postage put the multiple subscriptions common in intellectual families beyond their economic grasp. Some anti-Communist papers that had thrived under Communist rule by promoting a market economy swiftly succumbed to the market forces they themselves had championed. In retrospect it was evident that the old regime had unwittingly subsidized its own destruction via cheap newspapers and government-financed television.

No surprise, either, was the fact that Russians didn't use their hard-won freedom of information exclusively for high moral and political purposes. About a year after the failed August coup, *Dosug v Moskve* (Leisure in Moscow), a weekly guide to entertainment in the Russian capital, listed sixty-four different films being shown around the city. Forty-nine of them were foreign, and thirty-two, exactly half, were American—including such titles as *In Bed with Madonna*, *Hostage Dallas*, *Ninja Terminator*, and *Sex Visit*. Of the fifteen Russian films, most appeared to be seeking to compete with these U.S. imports. A new Russian film called *Migrants*, for instance, was advertised as offering the discerning viewer "sex, bloody fights, unlimited humiliation and...love, all-powerful and victorious."

The economic basis for freedom of information in Russia steadily gained strength. Many of the new Russian millionaires who suddenly appeared on city streets in their Mercedeses and Fords—Russia is one of the last places on earth where an American car is a potent status symbol—made their fortunes by importing information technology. Russian business publications, upstarts themselves, overflowed with advertisements for computers, fax machines, and portable phones. A Russian programmer, representative of a corps of blazingly talented computer specialists, devised the handwriting-recognition software that made possible the latest electronic gadget, the personal digital assistant.

Boris Yeltsin moved swiftly in 1992 to free most prices, squarely facing the problem before which Mikhail Gorbachev had hesitated for so long. With stunning rapidity the classic problem of the Soviet economy—the queue—largely disappeared. But it was replaced by the classic Western economic problem: people too poor to afford the goods on sale. The old shortage of goods was supplanted overnight by a new shortage of money. Meanwhile, to manage the information flows of the new economy, new birzhi, or commodities exchanges, sprang up like mushrooms after a rain, as the Russians say. Late-night television in St. Petersburg had a remarkable show called *Telebirzha*. It was an on-the-air commodity exchange in which a sultry female announcer read an endless list of proffered goods (three thousand tons of cement, twenty-five Volga cars, fifteen thousand liters of apple juice...) while rock videos played in the background. However crudely or strangely, economic feedback was beginning to operate.

Yet side by side with the emerging new economy was the unreconstructed Stalinist economy of collective farms and industrial plants where most people still worked more than two years after the end of the USSR. The economic conflict between the new entrepreneurship and the old industrialism underlay the continuing political clashes. In a city like Magnitogorsk, the entire population of 430,000 depended on the making of steel that the world economy did not need. If the factory went bankrupt, what would people do? Yet to keep it afloat by printing rubles would be to turn the steel plant into an inefficient welfare system. The information revolution let people know of their predicament, but it didn't solve it.

The twin continuities of Russian history, both before and after 1917, have been imperial expansion abroad and despotic rule at home. The persistence of these traits through five centuries or so makes one hesitant to suggest that they now may give way before more powerful historical factors. But the information revolution that contributed to the collapse of Communist rule and the dissolution of the Soviet Union marked a distinct break with these Russian traditions. The new rules of global economics and the momentum of free media and democratic politics suggest the changes may last.

Despite the titanic transition that already has taken place, and the sense of closure that came when the Soviet flag over the Kremlin came down at the end of 1991, the struggle for Russia's future will go on for many years. The information revolution of 1987 to 1991 could yet prove a fleeting exception to the consistent values of Russian history if the new freedom erodes under the pressure of slipping living standards, ethnic conflict, and political reaction. Such a pattern of retrenchment can be found in Russian history. A striking parallel for the reforms of Gorbachev can be found in the

Great Reforms of Alexander II in the 1860s, which likewise touched the press and many institutions of government and in which the emancipation of the serfs was a centerpiece comparable to the demise of the Communist party. Alexander II, like Gorbachev, became deeply unpopular; in both cases the public reaction appeared to result from uncertainty, instability, and the tendency of reform to infuriate the privileged while failing to satisfy the underprivileged. In 1881 the twenty-six-year rule of Alexander II was ended by a terrorist's bomb. Alexander III, in a flurry of moves that came to be known as the "counterreforms," halted work on the constitution, revived autocracy, and decisively reimposed censorship.

Hence the logic of history and culture weigh in favor of a restoration of imperial reach and autocratic rule for Russia. The very different post-Soviet paths of Estonia (stable capitalism) and Georgia (secessionism and civil war) do suggest a strong role for culture in determining where a republic is headed. The news from Russia has offered plenty of reasons for pessimism. Yeltsin's showdown with the Russian parliament in October 1993 was the first serious political bloodshed in Moscow since the Bolsheviks consolidated power—and significantly, the first shots were fired during the opposition's reckless attempt to seize broadcasting facilities at Ostankino, placing television at the heart of another political battle. The short-lived rebellion was led by Alexander Rutskoi and Ruslan Khasbulatov, the vice-president and parliament chairman who had risen to prominence as Yeltsin's protégés and risked their lives standing beside him against the coup in 1991. The parliamentary election that followed in December 1993 gave terrifying evidence of popular despair and confusion in the unexpected strength of the misnamed Liberal Democratic party of Vladimir Zhirinovsky, a volatile and glib neofascist who spent the last years of Soviet rule as a KGB provocateur. The Russian military seemed nostalgic for empire in its posturing and interference in former Soviet states from Moldova to Tajikistan.

In other post-Communist states—Georgia may be the best example—the appearance of civil violence and extreme nationalism proved a threshold to continuing chaos and decline. Yet the evidence from Russia was contradictory. The Moscow violence did not spread. The 1993 election put in place a constitution that clarified the powers of president and parliament. Russian meddling in other republics could represent fading Soviet habits rather than a resurgence of imperialism. If some Russians experience nostalgia for empire, many others feel imperial fatigue and will not be eager to send their sons to die in other states' civil wars. The yearning for "a normal country" remains a powerful brake on any tendency to return to empire and autocracy. Moreover, in the global information economy, hostile relations with other countries and totalitarian control at home will be penalized severely. The traditional payoff for conquering neighboring lands—natural resources and unskilled labor—is much diminished in an economic world that values finished consumer goods and highly educated workers.

In making sense of post-Soviet Russia, Americans might do well to consider their own history. In the 1780s, following the victory over British rule, came such harbingers of breakup and anarchy as Shays's Rebellion, an armed rising of two thousand Massachusetts farmers. Political leaders who had been unified by revolution now fell to bickering and competition. Patrick Henry, remembered best for the revolutionary fervor of "Give me liberty or give me death," denounced the Constitution as "this fatal system" by which "instead of securing your rights you may lose them forever." Corruption of politicians was the rule, and far from all leaders displayed an appropriate republican modesty. As president, George Washington rode abroad on a white horse with a leopard-skin saddlecloth edged in gold; in his farewell address he warned of dire consequences if more than one political party were permitted. The crime of slavery would last for seven decades after the Constitution, cost 600,000 lives in its last stand, and have consequences that are still felt painfully today. Next to such crises of American nation-building, the chaos, division, corruption, and inconsistency of post-Soviet Russia seem nothing extraordinary.

If the transformation of 1987 to 1991 away from imperial totalitarianism proves permanent it will be a watershed in Russian history of greater significance even than the westernizing of Peter the Great in the 1700s, the Great Reforms of Alexander II, or the Communist coup of 1917 with its sweeping consequences. It will be persuasive evidence of the potent influence of information over politics.

But dismantling utopia is a formidable and hazardous undertaking. This behemoth of a country, poised by geography between Europe and Asia, West and East, now seems poised between two futures, one determined by Russian history, the other governed by technological and social change. On Russia's course will depend the fate of its neighbors and of the world it has now rejoined.

Acknowledgments

This book owes much to our closest friends in Moscow, Boris and Masha Ryzhak, and their children Yasha, Mariana, Nyusha, and Gleb. They corrected grammar, explained jokes, clipped articles, passed on TV tips, called about demonstrations; led us everywhere in Moscow and dispatched us to friends from Leningrad to Tbilisi; and introduced us to the pleasures of dacha life. During the long evenings around the dinner table that are such a consoling feature of Russian life, they struggled to help us understand a very different society from the inside. For their generosity I am very grateful.

Andrei Mironov's contribution will be evident to those who read this book. He was a reliable friend to all of us and for me a tireless guide to the shifting political drama. Lisa Steiger helped not only with Russian but with introductions and insight into the Moscow cultural scene. Among many others who aided my understanding of various places and phenomena were Artur Glechyan, Yakov Borokhovich, Alla and Sasha Nagovitsyn, Mishi Yukhma, Viktor Girshfeld, Boris and Lyusya Yarkov, Valery and Lisa Timofeyev, Anahit Bayandur, Vasily Dvornikov, Vasily Selyunin, Alexander Fedorovsky, Valery Avidzba, Elena Belskyte, Anton Gustaitis, Merzakhmed Alimov, Nikolai Engver, and Marju Lauristin. My colleagues in the foreign press corps were great companions through it all.

Steve Luxenberg's extensive comments on the first draft were invaluable. Antero Pietila, my predecessor in Moscow and a shrewd observer of Russia, and Professor Albert Resis saved me from mistakes of fact and judgment. Matt Watkins, Bill Driscoll, Francie Weeks, and Susie Shane also made useful suggestions.

I'm grateful to my editors at the *Baltimore Sun* for sending me to Moscow at the right moment in history and for their flexibility while I wrote and revised the book. My successors in the *Sun*'s Moscow bureau, Kathy Lally and Will Englund, sent newspapers and polling results and helped me stay abreast of post-Soviet developments. The bureau's staff, Nadya Mayevskaya, Viktor Karasyov, and Rimma Fotyanova, supported me during hectic times.

My greatest debt is to my wife, Francie Weeks, who interrupted her own life and friendships to go to Moscow and who then mastered Russian and threw herself into a sometimes trying experience with courage and curiosity. She was a sounding board for the ideas here, a stimulating companion on many journeys, and a source of steady encouragement as the book got written. She helped turn a job for me into an adventure for us and for our children, Martha, Laura, and Nathan. This book is for her.

S. S.

Baltimore
January 1994

Notes

Introduction

pages 3–4, ban on maps: *Izvestiya*, September 2, 1988; *Pravitelstvenny Vestnik*, March 1989.

pages 4–5, Paul Kennedy on "dynamic for change" and on Gorbachev's 1986 speech: Paul Kennedy, *The Rise and Fall of the Great Powers* (New York: Vintage Books, 1989), pp. 438, 489–490.

page 5, Leonid Batkin story on Gorbachev: I heard it on Moscow television in 1990, but it has joined the rich political folklore of Russia.

page 7, Roy Medvedev on V. I. Mezhlauk: *Let History Judge* (New York: Vintage Books, 1973), p. 402.

1: *Before: Information Criminal*

page 14, Solzhenitsyn on arrest: Alexander Solzhenitsyn, *The Gulag Archipelago* (New York: Harper & Row, 1974), chap. 1 ("Arrest"), especially pp. 4–5.

page 17, Gorbachev to *Washington Post* and *Newsweek* on Grigoryants: see Robert G. Kaiser, *Why Gorbachev Happened* (New York: Simon & Schuster, 1991), p. 220.

page 20, Soviet press began writing about 1957 Urals disaster in mid-1989: *Pravda*, August 25, 1989. Zhores Medvedev's book was *Nuclear Disaster in the Urals* (New York: W. W. Norton, 1979).

page 25, Anatoly Yakobson on Sinyavsky-Daniel: Joshua Rubenstein, *Soviet Dissidents: Their Struggle for Human Rights* (Boston: Beacon Press, 2nd ed., 1985), p. 62. Joshua Rubenstein on the human rights movement: Rubenstein, *Soviet Dissidents*, p. 310. Robert Kaiser on small number of dissidents: Robert G. Kaiser, *Russia: The People and the Power* (New York: Pocket Books, 1976), p. 437.

page 26, statistics on educational levels: Goskomstat SSSR, *Narodnoye Obrazovanye i Kultura v SSSR* (State Statistics Committee, *Education and Culture in the USSR*) (Moscow, 1989). Moshe Lewin on urbanization: Moshe Lewin,

The Gorbachev Phenomenon (Berkeley: University of California Press, 1988), p. 31.

page 27, Galich song on magnitizdat: "My ne khuzhe Goratsia" (We're Not Worse Than Horatio), translation from "Magnitizdat: Uncensored Songs of Dissent," by Gene Sosin, in Rudolf L. Tokes, ed., *Dissent in the USSR* (Baltimore: Johns Hopkins University Press, 1975), p. 286.

page 29, Joshua Rubenstein on 1982 crackdown on samizdat: Rubenstein, *Soviet Dissidents*, p. 329.

page 36, Andrei Sakharov on Dubrovlag: Andrei Sakharov, *Memoirs* (New York: Alfred A. Knopf, 1990), p. 478.

2: *Information Control and the Soviet Crisis*

page 44, Gorbachev speech on Andropov budget secrecy: *Pravda*, December 10, 1990.

page 46, Billington on "the dilemma of the reforming despot": James H. Billington, *The Icon and the Axe* (New York: Vintage Books, 1970), p. 219. Pushkin, Nicholas I, Count Beckendorff: Tatiana Wolff, ed., *Pushkin on Literature* (London: Methuen, 1971), especially pp. 108–109, 179–182, 206, 325–328.

page 47, banning of Radishchev book: Thomas Riha, ed., *Readings in Russian Civilization*, vol. 2 (Chicago: University of Chicago Press, 1970), pp. 261–279. Prince Mirsky's thirty references to censorship: *A History of Russian Literature* (New York: Vintage Books, 1958), index p. iii. Marquis de Custine: *Empire of the Czar* (New York: Doubleday, 1989), p. xvii.

page 48, resistance to railroad and U.S. rail aid: W. E. Mosse, *Alexander II and the Modernization of Russia* (New York: Collier Books, 1958), p. 11.

pages 48–49, Lenin's exile and the railroad: see Adam Ulam, *The Bolsheviks* (New York: Collier Books, 1965), pp. 127–133.

page 49, rail mileage doubled between 1895 and 1905: Nicholas V. Riasanovsky, *A History of Russia* (New York: Oxford University Press, 1969), p. 441. Vladimir Nabokov on tsars vs. Bolsheviks: *Lectures on Russian Literature* (New York: Harcourt Brace Jovanovich, 1981), pp. 2–3.

page 50, literacy figures: Riasanovsky, *A History of Russia*, p. 631. Lenin on the press: both quotes from George Seldes, *The Great Quotations* (Secaucus, N.J.: Citadel Press, 1983), entry on Lenin.

page 51, Solzhenitsyn on ideology: Solzhenitsyn, *The Gulag Archipelago*, pp. 173–174. Osip Mandelstam on Russia's respect for poetry: cited in Benedikt Sarnov, "Zalozhnik Vechnosti: Sluchai Mandelshtama" (Hostage to Eternity: The Case of Mandelstam) from *Ogonyok*, 1988.

pages 52–53, Gide telegram to Stalin and "glorious destiny": André Gide, *Return from the U.S.S.R.* (New York: McGraw-Hill, 1964), pp. 45–46, 74.

page 53, Havel on language under socialism: Vaclav Havel, "On Evasive Thinking," in *Open Letters: Selected Writings, 1965–1990* (New York: Alfred A. Knopf, 1991), especially pp. 11–12.

page 54, Soviet political dictionary: *Kratki slovar-spravochnik agitatora i polit-informatora* (Short Dictionary and Reference Book for the Agitator and *Polit-*

ical Information Specialist) (Moscow: Politizdat, 1988), pp. 208–209. Authoritative Soviet text on Marxism-Leninism: Clemens Dutt, ed., *Fundamentals of Marxism-Leninism* (Moscow: Foreign Languages Publishing House, 1961), p. 17.

page 55, Kaiser on the Soviet pretense: Kaiser, *Why Gorbachev Happened*, p. 133. The original essay was published in *Foreign Affairs* in October 1986.

page 56, Pasternak to Italian publisher: Ronald Hingley, *Russian Writers and Soviet Society, 1917–1978* (London: Methuen, 1979), pp. 249–250. Vladimir Semichastny calling Pasternak a pig: Michael Scammell, *Solzhenitsyn* (New York, W. W. Norton, 1984), p. 404 and note.

pages 56–57, Suslov remarks to Grossman: newspaper article in *Sovietskaya Kultura*, October 25, 1988, p. 6.

page 57, Solzhenitsyn on glasnost: Scammell, *Solzhenitsyn*, p. 676. Medvedev on Solzhenitsyn: author's notes of press conference.

page 58, Ministry of Fisheries and ban on items thrown overboard: article on Glavlit in *Izvestiya*, February 10, 1989. 1981 brochure listing banned books: "Spisok knig, ne podlezhashchikh pasrostraneniyu v knigotorgovoi seti" (List of Books Not to Be Distributed by the Book-trade Network) (Moscow, Kniga, 1981).

page 59, USSR leadership in production of steel, cement, lumber, oil, etc.: see, for example, *USSR in Statistics, 1989* (Moscow: Goskomstat, 1990).

page 60, Shevardnadze on Andropov: interview with Gary Hart reported in Hart, *Russia Shakes the World* (New York: HarperCollins, 1991), pp. 20–21. Marshall Goldman on Soviets winning the wrong race: Marshall I. Goldman, *U.S.S.R. in Crisis: The Failure of an Economic System* (New York: W. W. Norton, 1983), p. 33.

page 61, jamming apparatus in Byelorussia: Minsk paper *Zvyazda*, February 3, 1989, in *BBC Summary of World Broadcasts*, SU/0388, p. i.

page 62, 200,000 microcomputers: Don Oberdorfer, *The Turn* (New York: Poseidon Press, 1991), p. 215. Wiener and cybernetics: Norbert Wiener, *Cybernetics* (New York: John Wiley, 1948) and *The Human Use of Human Beings: Cybernetics and Society* (New York: Houghton Mifflin, 1950), especially chap. 7, "Communication, Secrecy and Social Policy."

page 63, Lyubarsky trial speech: *Moyo poslyednyenye slovo—My Final Word: Speeches of Defendants at their Trials, 1966–1974* (Frankfurt: Possev-Verlag, 1974).

page 64, Kennedy: Paul Kennedy, "What Gorbachev Is Up Against," *Atlantic Monthly*, June 1987. This article is based on part of Kennedy's book, *The Rise and Fall of the Great Powers*.

page 65, Gorbachev's March 11, 1985, speech to Central Committee: *Pravda*, March 12, 1985.

page 66, Gorbachev in village near Krasnoyarsk: Soviet television, September 12, 1988, reported in *BBC Summary of World Broadcasts*, SU/0256, p. C1/3. Gorbachev on window dressing and information: *Pravda*, January 10, 1989. Gorbachev on glasnost serving socialism: *BBC Summary of World Broadcasts*, SU/0256, p. C1/4. Gorbachev speaking in oxymorons: *Pravda*, September 25, 1988. Venclova: *Glasnost: How Open?*, colloquium with emigré intellectuals, March 7, 1987 (Washington, D.C.: Freedom House, 1987), p. 8.

page 67, Gorbachev's May 1985 Leningrad speech: Soviet television, May 21, 1985, in *BBC Summary of World Broadcasts*, SU/7959, May 23, 1985. Gorbachev to June 1985 conference on science and technology: *Pravda*, June 12, 1985. Gorbachev to 27th Party Congress: *Pravda*, February 26, 1986.

page 68, Fyodor Burlatsky on high-technology revolution: article in *Literaturnaya Gazeta*, October 31, 1984, p. 14. Alvin Toffler to Gorbachev: quoted in Walter C. Clemens, Jr., *Can Russia Change?* (Boston: Unwin Hyman, 1990), p. 186. Shultz lessons for Gorbachev: Oberdorfer, *The Turn*, pp. 223–224.

page 69, Gorbachev to student group: *BBC Summary of World Broadcasts*, SU/0616, November 17, 1989, p. B/8. Marshal Ogarkov on military technology: interview with *Krasnaya Zvezda*, May 9, 1984. General Odom on effect of U.S. military buildup: Daniel Abele, "Looking Back at Sovietology: An Interview with William Odom and Alexander Dallin," Kennan Institute for Advanced Russian Studies, *Occasional Paper No. 239*, p. 17.

page 71, Gorbachev's 1987 speech to Komsomol congress: "Molodyozh—Tvorcheskaya Sila Revolyutsionnogo Obnovleniya" (Youth—Creative Force of Revolutionary Renewal), brochure containing text of April 16, 1987, speech (Moscow: Politizdat, 1987), pp. 18–19.

page 72, Valentin Turchin on removing absurdities: quoted in *Glasnost: How Open?*, p. 7.

page 73, Gorbachev's November 1990 speech on grandfathers and walk with Shevardnadze: the uncensored version was shown on Soviet television, November 29, 1990, and is translated in *BBC Summary of World Broadcasts*, SU/0936, p. B/1–5.

3: *What Price Socialism? An Economy Without Information*

page 77, USSR No. 1 in shoes: *U.S.S.R. in Statistics, 1989* (Moscow: Goskomstat, 1990).

page 79, beef at 1.77 rubles per kilogram costing 4.75: Morris Bornstein, "Price Policies and Comment on Shmelyov," in Ed A. Hewitt and Victor H. Winston, eds., *Milestones in Glasnost and Perestroika: The Economy* (Washington, D.C.: Brookings Institution, 1991), p. 192.

page 80, Alexander Zaichenko on wages in U.S. and USSR: "On Our Daily Bread," *Moscow News* No. 34, August 21, 1988, p. 12.

page 81, Nikolai Shmelyov on distorted prices: "Rethinking Price Reform," in Hewitt and Winston, *Milestones in Glasnost and Perestroika*, p. 154. 19th Party Conference on price reform: from the official decrees of the conference, cited in *Short Dictionary and Reference Book for the Agitator and Political Information Specialist*, p. 155.

page 82, John Scott quotation: John Scott, *Behind the Urals* (Bloomington: Indiana University Press, 1989), p. 3. Scott's fascinating memoir was originally published in 1942.

page 83, 25 million items: Nikolai Shmelyov in *Moscow News*, December 11, 1988. Richard Ericson on ball-bearings: interview with the author, September 1987.

pages 83–84, washing machine ownership figures: Alan P. Pollard, ed., *USSR Facts & Figures Annual*, vol. 14, 1990 (Gulf Breeze, Fla.: Academic International Press, 1990).

page 84, milk production in U.S. and USSR: *Narodnoye Khozyaistvo v 1989* (Moscow: Goskomstat, 1990), pp. 692–693.

page 85, Boris Pugo and Party Control Commission: *Pravda*, September 1989.

page 86, statistics on steel, plastics, woolens, synthetics: *USSR Facts & Figures Annual*, vol. 14, p. 30. U.S. shift from steel to plastic: Tom Forester, "The Materials Revolution," in *The Futurist*, vol. 22, no. 4 (July–August 1988), 21–25.

page 90, Stephen Kotkin on Magnitogorsk: "The Soviet Rustbelt," in *Harriman Institute Forum*, vol. 4, no. 2 (February 1991). Kotkin's book on contemporary Magnitogorsk is *Steeltown, U.S.S.R.* (Los Angeles: University of California Press, 1991).

4: *The KGB, Father of Perestroika*

page 100, transcript of Moscow party meeting attacking Yeltsin: published in *Moskovskaya Pravda* and *Pravda*, November, 13, 1987.

page 104, Ernst Neizvestny on KGB and feedback: recorded in *Glasnost: How Open?*, pp. 3–4.

page 105, secret KGB department on the economy: Kaiser, *Why Gorbachev Happened*, p. 57.

page 106, Yevgeniya Albats on the KGB: these quotations are from the most comprehensive of Albats's many articles on the KGB, in *Moscow News*, no. 16, April 21, 1991, pp. 8–9.

page 107, Chebrikov's role in compromising Grishin: see, for example, Zhores A. Medvedev, *Gorbachev* (New York: W. W. Norton, 1987), pp. 172–173. November 6, 1985, Chebrikov speech: Christian Schmidt-Hauer, *Gorbachev: The Path to Power* (Topsfield, Mass.: Salem House, 1986), p. 198.

pages 107–108, Mark Zakharov on KGB role in choosing Gorbachev: Mark Zakharov, "Vlecheniye k KGB" (Attraction to the KGB) in *Ya* ("I"—the Russian personal pronoun and the name of a new Moscow magazine), January 1991, pp. 57–60.

page 108, Viktor Chebrikov's report to the party on reduction in anti-Soviet literature: document on display in "Revelations from the Russian Archives," exhibit at the Library of Congress, June–July 1992.

page 116, KGB phone-in TV show: *BBC Summary of World Broadcasts*, SU/0606, November 6, 1989, pp. C2/1–10.

page 117, Konstantin Kharchev on his ouster: *Ogonyok*, no. 44, 1989, pp. 17–21.

page 118, Oleg Kalugin on rouging the KGB's flabby face: quoted in Amy W. Knight, "The Future of the KGB," *Problems of Communism*, November–December 1990, p. 27.

page 120, Kryuchkov on KGB's serving the president: Kryuchkov interview to Tass, April 29, 1990.

5: *The Press and the Restoration of History*

page 121, Alexander Milchakov's articles: of Milchakov's numerous publications, some of the most interesting are in *Semya*, no. 36 and no. 40 for 1988, no. 5 for 1989, and no. 13 for 1990; and in *Vechernyaya Moskva*, April 14, August 10, and November 27, 1990.

page 123, *Izvestiya* on cancellation of history exams: June 10, 1988.

page 124, Gorbachev seventieth anniversary of the Revolution speech on Stalinism: Mikhail Gorbachev, "October and Perestroika: The Revolution Continues" (pamphlet published by the Novosti Press Agency, 1987).

page 125, Mikhail Solomentsev interview with *Pravda* on rehabilitation commission: *Pravda*, August 19, 1988.

page 126, Zinaida Filippova: her recollections were recorded by Milchakov in *Semya*, no. 40, October 5, 1988, p. 9.

pages 127–128, Gorbachev's Stalin reference met by applause: see Schmidt-Hauer, *Gorbachev: The Path to Power*, pp. 129–130.

page 128, Gorbachev on Stalinism being invented: *L'Humanité*, February 8, 1986. Gorbachev on the arrests of his grandfathers: speech to cultural figures, November 28, 1990, transcribed in *BBC Summary of World Broadcasts*, SU/0936 (December 1, 1990), p. B/1. Gorbachev on Stalinism in *Perestroika: Perestroika i Novoye Myshleniye Dlya Nashei Strani i Dlya Vsyego Mira* (Perestroika and New Thinking for Our Country and the Whole World) (Moscow: Politizdat, 1987), p. 37.

page 129, board of Memorial: the membership of Memorial's public council were listed by Natalya Filippova in *Moscow News*, September 4, 1988. The publication set off a stir by listing "A. Solzhenitsyn" among the members; Solzhenitsyn later telegrammed his good wishes but declined to join the board, saying his "memorial" to the victims of terror was his massive *Gulag Archipelago*.

page 132, *Moscow News* with Chernenko voting on the cover: no. 10, March 11, 1984.

page 133, Ligachev and fire-hosing of skeletons: the incident was reported in a Siberian paper and widely repeated in the Soviet press. For an account by an American journalist, see Adam Hochschild, "The Secret of a Siberian River Bank," *New York Times Magazine*, March 28, 1993, p. 28.

page 134, poll on repressed relatives: poll results are reported in a pamphlet: "Chelovek i legenda: Obraz A. D. Sahkarova b obshchestvennom mnenii" (The Man and the Legend: The Image of A. D. Sakharov in Public Opinion) (Moscow: All-Union Center for the Study of Public Opinion, 1991), p. 20. Galina Klokova on Soviet history-writing: *Pravda*, January 13, 1989. Bukharin's widow's memoirs in *Znamya*, no. 10, 1988. Anna Larina's memoirs were later published in English as *This I Cannot Forget* (New York: W. W. Norton, 1993). Yevgeniya Albats in *Moscow News* on Vavilov's interrogator: May 8, 1988. *Ogonyok* on Mandelstam: Benedikt Sarnov, "Zalozhnik Vechnosti" (Hostage to Eternity), in *Ogonyok: Lushchiye Publikatsii 88 Goda* (Ogonyok: Best Publications of 1988) (Moscow: Ogonyok, 1989), p. 222.

page 135, Dombrovsky's *Faculty of Unnecessary Things: Novy Mir*, no. 8, 1988, p. 6. *Life and Fate* published in Switzerland: Grossman, *Zhizn i Sudba* (Moscow: Knizhnaya Palata, 1988), p. 815. Brodsky collection published in 1990: *Osennii Krik Yastreba* (Autumn Call of the Hawk) (Leningrad: MXM, 1990), p. 3. Roy Medvedev on number of Stalin's victims: Medvedev article in *Moscow News*, no. 48, November 27, 1988, pp. 8–9. List of army commanders purged under Stalin: the list is reprinted in Alec Nove, *Glasnost in Action* (Winchester, Mass.: Unwin Hyman, 1989), p. 87.

page 139, Valentin Falin at Novosti's August 16, 1988, press conference: *BBC Summary of World Broadcasts*, SU/0240, August 26, 1988, pp. B/5–6. General background on Molotov-Ribbentrop Pact and its protocols: a recent, thrilling account of the pact is Anthony Read and David Fisher, *The Deadly Embrace: Hitler, Stalin and the Nazi-Soviet Pact, 1939–1941* (New York: W. W. Norton, 1988), especially chaps. 23 and 42. *Rahva Haal* first publication to print the secret protocols: *BBC Summary of World Broadcasts*, SU/0245, September 1, 1988, p. B/1. *Sirp ja Vasar* article: *BBC Summary of World Broadcasts*, SU/0245, September 1, 1988, p. B/2.

page 140, Yakovlev speech on Molotov-Ribbentrop commission findings: *BBC Summary of World Broadcasts*, SU/0650, December 30, 1989, pp. C/1–7.

page 141, mass graves in Kuropaty, Minsk, Byelorussia: the photographs of skeletons were in *Ogonyok*, no. 39, September 1988, pp. 28–29.

page 142, Milchakov's "duel" with the KGB: *Vechernyaya Moskva*, April 14, 1990.

page 143, lists of those executed found in KGB archives: *Vechernyaya Moskva*, November 17, 1990.

6: *Television and the Revival of Politics*

page 146, Yuri Vlasov chat with Gorbachev at Congress before speech: interview with Andrei Karaulov in *Vokrug Kremlya* (Around the Kremlin) (Moscow: Novosti, 1990), p. 282. Vlasov speech to Congress: *BBC Summary of World Broadcasts*, SU/0477, pp. C/16–19.

page 148, poll on percentage of people watching the congress: the poll was reported in *Izvestiya* and reprinted in a collection of *Izvestiya* articles, *Proryv v Demokratiyu* (Breakthrough to Democracy) (Moscow: Izvestiya, 1990), pp. 150–151.

page 152, first radio report after Revolution, Lenin letter to Stalin, other facts on early radio: *Radio Liberty Research Reports*, RL 299/73, September 24, 1973.

page 153, ten thousand television sets in 1950, 4.8 million in 1960: Ellen Mickiewicz, *Split Signals: Television and Politics in the Soviet Union* (New York: Oxford University Press, 1988), p. 3. 1960 Central Committee resolution on television: "Ob uluchenii sovetskogo radioveshaniya" (On the Improvement of Soviet Broadcasting), resolution of the Central Committee of January 29, 1960, reprinted in *KPSS o sredstvakh massovoi informatsii i propagandy* (CPSU on Mass Information and Propaganda Media) (Moscow: Politizdat, 1987), pp. 535–545. 8,828 TV broadcasting stations and 90 million

TV sets: *Narodnoye obrazovaniye i kultura v SSSR* (Popular Education and Culture in the USSR) (Moscow: Finansi i Statistika, 1989), p. 367. Television reaching territory with 96 percent of population: *Molodyozh SSSR* (Youth of the USSR) (Moscow: Finansi i Statistika, 1990), pp. 222–223.

page 154, Ellen Mickiewicz on Soviet and U.S. television news: Mickiewicz, *Split Signals*, p. 8. Mickiewicz's 1988 book, while obviously overtaken by events, is prescient in underscoring the reach and power of television in Soviet politics. Drunk scene cut from Gogol's *Inspector General*: Elizabeth Pond, *From the Yaroslavsky Station* (New York: Universe Books, 1981), p. 65. Alexander Yakovlev on television: quoted by Harrison Salisbury, "Gorbachev's Dilemma," *New York Times Magazine*, July 27, 1986, p. 33. Dmitry Likhachev on television: quoted by Tatyana Zemskova, ed., *15 Vstretch v Ostankinye* (15 Meetings at Ostankino) (Moscow: Politizdat, 1989), p. 5.

page 155, Eduard Sagalayev on TV as the greatest dissident: this and other quotations from Sagalayev are from the author's interview on July 16, 1991.

pages 155–156, Alexander Tikhomirov on Gorbachev in Krasnoyarsk: interview with *Vechernyaya Moskva,* June 25, 1991.

page 157, man who watched Vzglyad standing up: *Small Fires: Letters from the Soviet People to Ogonyok Magazine* (New York: Summit Books, 1990), p. 73. Tatyana Khloplyankina on the interest in television: *Moscow News*, no. 14, April 2, 1989, p. 11.

pages 162–164, controversy over Mark Zakharov's comment on burying Lenin: Zakharov's comment was on Vzglyad April 21, 1989; the comments of Zhukov, Aksyonov, and others were at the Central Committee plenum on April 25, 1989.

page 164, Mikhail Nenashev on the destructiveness of Vzglyad: Andrei Karaulov, *Vokrug Kremlya* (Moscow: Novosti, 1990), pp. 331–332.

page 169, Gorbachev on glasnost in 1987: Russian-language edition of *Perestroika*, p. 72.

page 171, Leonid Kravchenko on discussion with Lapin and on job of TV chief: interview with Kravchenko in *Sobesednik*, no. 21, 1991, p. 10.

page 173, KGB film "The Face of Extremism": shown on Soviet TV's First Program on January 4, 1991. KGB officials later acknowledged to me that their agency had produced that film as well as a later film attacking Radio Liberty.

page 174, Gorbachev calling for suspension of the press law: he made the remarks in the Supreme Soviet on January 16, 1991.

page 175, TSN anchors' battle over Baltic coverage: a detailed account of these events is Julia Wishnevsky, "The Purge of 'TSN': A Ban on Information," Radio Liberty's *Report on the USSR*, April 5, 1991, pp. 4–9.

7: *A Normal Country: The Pop Culture Explosion*

page 184, best-seller lists: *Knizhnoye Obozreniye*, no. 33, August 17, 1990, pp. 8–9; and no. 23, 1991, pp. 8–9.

page 188, five million Krishna books sold: reported by the *Chicago Tribune*, March 8, 1992, p. 3.

page 189, Vasily Aksyonov on the lure of American culture: Vasily Aksyonov, *In Search of Melancholy Baby* (New York: Random House, 1987), pp. 12–13.

page 190, Andrei Voznesensky and Artemy Troitsky: Voznesensky's comments are in his preface to *Rok muzyka v SSSR* (Rock Music in the USSR) (Moscow: Kniga, 1990), p. 5. Troitsky's comments are in his introduction, pp. 8–9.

pages 190–191, Mikhail Borzykin lyrics and Artemy Troitsky on rock vs. the press: these are from a separate history of rock by Troitsky with a similar title: *Rok v SSSR* (Rock in the USSR) (Moscow: RIO, 1991), pp. 98–99, 108.

page 193, Mikhail Zhvanetsky on beer: he used the joke in late 1989, and it was reprinted in *Izvestiya* in approximately October 1989. Gennady Khazanov: his Makashov routine was transcribed in the magazine *Stolitsa*, no. 22, June, 1991, p. 1. Mikhail Zadornov on Communist bureaucrats: he used this item often and included it in his collection *Ne Ponimayu!* (I Don't Get It!) (Vilnius: Polina, 1991).

page 198, Eduard Radzinsky book on Nicholas II: *The Last Tsar* (New York: Doubleday, 1992).

page 199, *Sobesednik* on popular idols: *Sobesednik*, no. 13, March, 1990, back page.

page 200, fifty million viewers for "Malenkaya Vera": Nancy Traver, *Kife: The Lives and Dreams of Soviet Youth* (New York: St. Martin's Press, 1989), p. 242. Traver's book is a lively portrait of Soviet youth in the early Gorbachev years with much interesting reporting on popular culture.

8: *Letting Go of the Leninist Faith*

page 215, poll results: compiled for me by the Data Information Agency of the All-Union Center for the Study of Public Opinion. Nearly all these figures were published in the Soviet press at various times.

page 216, Sidney Hook on disillusioned foreign Communists: Sidney Hook, "The Literature of Disillusionment," in Julien Steinberg, ed., *Verdict of Three Decades* (New York: Duell, Sloan & Pearce, 1950), especially p. 606. Sakharov on his belief: Sakharov, *Memoirs*, p. 164

pages 217–218, *Trud* article responding to veteran's letter: *Trud*, April 30, 1988.

pages 234–235, Yeltsin at 26th and 27th Party Congresses: excerpts from both speeches are in an attack on Yeltsin in *Pravda*, March 5, 1991.

pages 236–237, Yeltsin to parliament on the KGB: *BBC Summary of World Broadcasts*, SU/0513, July 20, 1989, p. C/5.

page 238, *Glasnost* on Yeltsin and Chechen mafia: *Glasnost*, February 14, 1991.

page 239, Yeltsin on Italian account of drinking: Yeltsin, autobiography, *Ispoved na zadannuyu temu* (Confession on an Assigned Topic) (Sverdlovsk: Sredne-Uralskoye Knizhnoye Izdatelstvo), p. 227.

pages 239–240, Tass on Yeltsin's trip to America: this and other material is collected and translated in *BBC Summary of World Broadcasts*, SU/0565, September 19, 1989, pp. A1/1–4.

page 240, Yeltsin autobiography on Houston supermarket: Russian edition, pp. 226–227.

page 241, Yeltsin's speech to Congress referring to the "Russian Republic":
BBC Summary of World Broadcasts, SU/0772, May 24, 1990, p. B/11.

pages 241–242, Gorbachev criticism of Yeltsin speech for not using the word
"socialism": *BBC Summary of World Broadcasts*, SU/0773, May 24, 1990, p.
B/5.

page 242, Yeltsin's reply to Gorbachev on "Pol Pot socialism": *BBC Summary
of World Broadcasts*, SU/0776, May 29, 1990, p. B/7.

9: *After: The Coup-Proof Society*

page 247, identification of Viktor Shatskikh: "V spiskakh vsyo-taki znachilsya"
(He Was on the Rolls After All), *Moskovsky Komsomolets*, January 18, 1991.
KGB's role in Vilnius: Yuri Shchekochikhin, "Litovskaya Karta" (Lithuanian
Card), *Literaturnaya Gazeta*, July 10, 1991, p. 3. March 1990 appeal from
anonymous KGB officers: the text handed out at parliament was published
in the emigré newspaper *Russkaya Mysl* (Paris) in March 1990. See also
Alexander Rahr, "KGB Attack on Gorbachev and His Reforms," *Report on
the USSR*, Radio Liberty, Munich, April 13, 1990, pp. 4–6. Filipp Bobkov
interview: with Andrei Karaulov in *Nezavisimaya Gazeta*, December 28,
1990, p. 5. Kryuchkov speech to Congress of People's Deputies: one of many
accounts of the December 22 speech is Jonathan Lyons, "KGB Chief Says
Subversion, Sabotage Threaten Soviet Union," Reuters, December 22, 1990.

page 248, KGB involvement in Democratic Russia headquarters bombing: see,
for instance, "K voprosy o geografii vzryva" (On the Question of the
Geography of the Explosion), *Moskovsky Komsomolets*, May 23, 1991, p. 1.
Gorbachev put in an "information aquarium": the phrase was used by
Viktor Loshak in *Moscow News*, no. 37, September 15–22, 1991, p. 6.
Yakovlev on Gorbachev's belief democrats would assault Kremlin with
ladders: David Remnick, *Washington Post*, August 23, 1991, p. A24.

page 249, Kryuchkov speech to closed session of parliament: excerpts from the
June 17 speech were printed in *Sovietskaya Rossiya*, June 27, 1991, p. 3.
Demokraticheskaya Rossiya on "shady deal" of Pavlov, Kryuchkov, Yazov,
Pugo: no. 14, June 28, 1991, p. 1.

page 250, *Izhevskiye Novosti* with Vysotsky on cover: June 10, 1991.

page 255, five-year-old on what is a coup: Lydia Polskaya, "Televideniye i
putch: eksperiment zakonchen, vsyem spasibo" (Television and the Putsch:
The Experiment Is Over, Thanks to Everyone), in *Demokraticheskaya
Rossiya*, September 13–19, 1991.

page 258, Walter Goodman on GKChP as "Saturday Night Live": *New York
Times*, August 22, 1991, p. A18. GKChP's "Appeal to the Soviet People":
published August 20, 1991, in *Pravda* and other newspapers that were not
banned.

pages 258–259, Yeltsin's appeal to servicemen: Rossiskogo Informatsionnogo
Agentstvo, "Khronika Putcha" (Russian Information Agency, "Chronicle of
the Putsch"), pp. 18–19. This pamphlet, sold at Moscow newsstands in the
weeks after the coup, contains verbatim the dispatches of RIA between
August 19 and August 22.

page 259, Vytautas Landsbergis statement during coup: "Khronika Putcha," p. 8. Yuri Milyukov's appeal to brokers: *Nezavisimaya Gazeta*, August 22, 1991, p. 4.

page 260, GKChP on "propaganda of sex and violence": "Appeal to the Soviet People." Gennady Khazanov's Gorbachev imitation: see *Nedelya*, no. 35, August 26–September 1, 1991, p. 18.

page 261, Gennady Burbulis's order to turn on all fax machines: "Khronika Putcha," p. 12. List of seventy to be arrested: *Argumenti i Fakti*, no. 38, September 1991.

pages 262–263, Vitaly Tretyakov's "Appeal to Free Journalists of the World": *Nezavisimaya Gazeta*, August 22, 1991, p. 1.

page 263, *Moscow News* thank-you note: *Moscow News*, no. 35, September 1, 1991, p. 6. Anatoly Sobchak on "information blockade": *Nevskoye Vremya*, August 22, 1991, p. 3.

page 264, Lydia Polskaya on media, CNN, and the coup: *Demokraticheskaya Rossiya*, September 13–19, 1991. Sergei Medvedev on Vremya for August 19: *Sem Dnyei* (Seven Days, the official radio and television program guide), no. 36, September 2–8, 1991, pp. 1–2.

page 266, Leonid Ionin on media's role in defeating the coup: *Nezavisimaya Gazeta*, September 12, 1991, p. 8.

page 267, All-Union Center for the Study of Public Opinion polls on attitudes to coup: *Data-express* (bulletin of the center), August 21, 1991.

page 268, Leonid Radzikhovsky on goals of coup: *Ogonyok*, no. 41, 1991.

page 269, Pavel Grachev on conversation with Yeltsin, activities during coup: interview with *Soyuz*, no. 36, September 4–11, 1991, p. 12. Yevgeny Shaposhnikov on coup: interview with *Nezavisimaya Gazeta*, September 12, 1991, pp. 1 and 4.

page 270, *Komsomolskaya Pravda* investigation of Group Alpha: *Komsomolskaya Pravda*, August 28, 1991, p. 4. Mayak radio announcement indicating end of coup; Russian TV anchor comment: *New York Times*, August 22, 1991, p. 22.

page 271, Gorbachev tales from Foros, comments on press: *New York Times*, August 23, 1991, pp. A10–12. Pavel Gutiontov's reply to Gorbachev: *Moskovskiye Novosti*, no. 35, September 1, 1991, p. 6.

page 272, Shaposhnikov on why coup failed: *Nezavisimaya Gazeta*, September 12, 1991, p. 4.

Epilogue

page 279, video on the murder of Benito Aquino: Walter B. Wriston, *The Twilight of Sovereignty* (New York: Scribners, 1992), p. 50. Thailand's cellular phone revolution: *New York Times*, May 20, 1992, p. A10. Wriston on the information age: *Twilight of Sovereignty*, pp. 170, 174. Argument that video leads toward democracy: Michael J. O'Neill, *The Roar of the Crowd: How Television and People Power Are Changing the World* (New York: Times Books, 1993). Argument that war is becoming obsolete: see Carl

Kaysen, "Is War Obsolete? A Review Essay," *International Security*, vol. 14, no. 4, pp. 42–64.

page 284, Jonathan Kozol on failure of facts to change policies: Kozol, *Savage Inequalities: Children in America's Schools* (New York: Crown, 1991), p. 119.

Index